At the End of the Day

At the End of the Day

Lessons Learned in Inclusive Education

edited by

Marquita Grenot-Scheyer, Ph.D.
California State University
Long Beach, California

Mary Fisher, Ph.D.
Purdue University
West Lafayette, Indiana

Debbie Staub, Ph.D.
Casey Family Programs
Seattle, Washington

·P A U L·H·
BROOKES
PUBLISHING C9

Baltimore • London • Toronto • Sydney

·P A U L·H·
BROOKES
PUBLISHING Cº

Paul H. Brookes Publishing Co.
Post Office Box 10624
Baltimore, Maryland 21285-0624

www.brookespublishing.com

Typeset by Integrated Publishing Solutions, LLC, Grand Rapids, Michigan.
Manufactured in the United States of America by Versa Press, East Peoria, Illinois.

The case studies described in this book represent actual people and actual circumstances. Most names have been changed to protect individuals' identities. In case studies in which identities have not been disguised, written consent has been given.

Chapters 1, 2, 3, 5, 6, 7, 8, and 9 of this book were supported in part by the Consortium for Collaborative Research on Social Relationships of Children and Youth with Diverse Abilities, Cooperative Agreement No. H086A20003 awarded to Syracuse University by the U.S. Department of Education. The opinions expressed herein, however, are not necessarily those of the U.S. Department of Education, and no official endorsement should be inferred.

Library of Congress Cataloging-in-Publication Data

At the end of the day : lessons learned in inclusive education / edited by Marquita Grenot-Scheyer, Mary Fisher, and Debbie Staub.
    p. cm.
    Includes bibliographical references and index.
    ISBN 1-55766-480-3
    1. Inclusive education—United States—Case studies. 2. Handicapped students—Education—United States—Case studies. 3. School improvement programs—United States—Case studies. I. Title: Lessons learned in inclusive education. II. Grenot-Scheyer, Marquita. III. Fisher, Mary, Ph.D. IV. Staub, Debbie.
LC1201. A8 2001
371.9′046—dc21   00-056454

British Library Cataloguing in Publication data are available from the British Library.

Contents

10 At the End of the Day: What Do We Know? What's for Tomorrow?
Marquita Grenot-Scheyer, Debbie Staub, and Mary Fisher 163

Child Repertoire
Peer Skills, Expectations, and Support
Alyssa and Jimmy
Adult Mediation
  Facilitated
  Blocked
  Missed
Social-Ecology
  Systemic Change and Sustainability of Recommended Practices
  Policy Implications
  What's for Tomorrow?
  Inclusion and School Renewal Are Linked
  Inclusion Presents a Strong Moral Imperative
  Learning and Belonging Happen Together
  Equity, Access, and Support Are Critical
  Students Learn in Different Ways
  Inclusive Education Has Benefits for All Involved
  Collaboration Is Essential
What's for the Next Year and Beyond: The Next Decade,
    the Next Generation?
  Ideas for Procedures to Teach Society
  Identify Essential Components
  Clarify Multiple Outcomes with Participants
  Develop a Critical Mass
  Procedures to Teach Society
  What We're Looking for at the End of the Day: Moving
    on Toward Tomorrow
Care About the Whole Kid
  Know the Content Well
  Teach Well
  Collaborate with Others
  Be a Lifelong Learner
Conclusions

About the Editors

Marquita Grenot-Scheyer, Ph.D., Professor of Special Education, Department of Educational Psychology, Administration, and Counseling, College of Education, California State University, Long Beach, 1250 Bellflower Boulevard, Long Beach, California 90840; mgrenot@csulb.edu

In addition to her work as a professor and associate dean in the College of Education, Dr. Grenot-Scheyer coordinates the education specialist credential and the master's degree program in special education at California State University, Long Beach. She earned her doctoral degree in special education from the University of California, Los Angeles, and California State University, Los Angeles, in 1990. Previously, she was a co-director of the Consortium for Collaborative Research on Social Relationships of Children and Youth with Diverse Abilities (1992–1997). Her teaching, research, scholarly activities, and community action efforts focus on the social relationships of children and youth with and without severe disabilities, the improvement of inclusive education options for students with and without disabilities and their families, and the closer alignment of teacher education and special education.

Mary Fisher, Ph.D., Assistant Professor, Department of Educational Studies, Purdue University, 1446 Liberal Arts and Education Building, West Lafayette, Indiana 47907; mfisher@purdue.edu

Dr. Fisher's work involves the preparation of general and special education preservice teachers to meet the needs of all children. Since 1974, she has been involved in advocating for and creating first integrated and then inclusive school settings in various roles. These roles have included institutional aide, paraprofessional, special education teacher, general education teacher, central office administrator, researcher, and teacher trainer. She is young at heart and remains optimistic about the process of change in education. Her research interests include social relationships and friendships, naturalistic interventions, and personnel preparation for teachers of elementary school–age children.

Debbie Staub, Ph.D., Youth Services Coordinator, Casey Family Programs, 1300 Dexter Avenue North, Seattle, Washington 98109; dstaub@casey.org

Dr. Staub was formerly Project Coordinator for the federally funded research project, Consortium of Collaborative Research on Social Relationships of Individuals with Severe Disabilities, at the University of Washington site in Seattle. Since 1988, she has been studying the relationships of children with and without disabilities in inclusive environments. She has published several articles and book chapters on the subject for both professionals and practitioners, and she is the author of *Delicate Threads: Friendships Between Children with and without Special Needs in Inclusive Settings* (Woodbine House, 1998). As a lecturer in the special education program at the University of Washington, Dr. Staub has taught courses in the areas of educating students with autism, inclusion, curriculum design and instruction for students with severe disabilities, and collaboration and consultation among general and special educators. She is an active advocate for children with disabilities and is a member of national disability organizations. She lives in Redmond, Washington, with her husband and their three children.

Contributors

Barbara J. Ayres, Ph.D.
Associate Professor
Department of Special Education
  and Reading
Montana State University
1500 North 30th Street
Billings, Montana 59101

Ruth B. Coates, M.B.P.A.
Chief Operating Officer
National College of Complimen-
  tary Medicine and Sciences
1025 Connecticut Avenue, SW
Suite 1012
Washington, D.C. 20036

Jean Gonsier-Gerdin, M.S.
Assistant Professor and Doctoral
  Candidate
Gladys L. Benerd School of
  Education
University of the Pacific
3601 Pacific Avenue
Stockton, California 95211

Beth Harry, Ph.D.
Professor of Special Education
School of Education
University of Miami
Merrick Building, Room 312
Post Office Box 248065
Coral Gables, Florida 33124

Deborah L. Hedeen, Ph.D.
Assistant Professor
Department of Special Education
College of Education
Idaho State University
Box 8059
Pocatello, Idaho 83209

Stacey A. Hoffman, M.A.
Special Education Teacher
  and parent of a child with severe
  developmental disabilities
Sacramento City Unified School
  District
3066 Freeport Boulevard
Sacramento, California 95818

Susan Leonard-Giesen, M.S.
Lecturer and Fieldwork Supervisor
Education Specialist Credential
  Program
Department of Educational
  Psychology, Administration,
  and Counseling
California State University
1250 Bellflower Boulevard
Long Beach, California 90840

Hyun-Sook Park, Ph.D.
Associate Professor
Department of Special Education
California State University
6000 J Street
Sacramento, California 95819

Ilene S. Schwartz, Ph.D.
Associate Professor
College of Education
University of Washington
Co-Director, Experimental
  Education Unit
Office of Special Education
103 Miller Hall, DQ-12
Box 357925
Seattle, Washington 98195

Angie Tate
Parent of a child with autism
2811 East Migratory Drive
Boise, Idaho 83706

Joseph C. Vargo
Parent Consultant
JOENRO, Inc.
111 Schuler Street
Syracuse, New York 13230

Rosalind M. Vargo
Parent Consultant
JOENRO, Inc.
111 Schuler Street
Syracuse, New York 13230

Susan Whaley, M.A.
Special Education Teacher
Sacramento City Unified School
    District
520 Capitol Mall
Sacramento, California 95814

Foreword

This is a book that challenges its readers with more than how things ought to be. Marquita Grenot-Scheyer, Mary Fisher, and Debbie Staub have given us something different from most books—something very honest and very helpful. *At the End of the Day: Lessons Learned in Inclusive Education* tells us how things really are and what really happens in typical schools and communities when educators and families work together to achieve inclusive practices for young people with significant disabilities.

Until recently, written history seldom recorded the chronology of the experiences of the community of ordinary people. History typically told us about heroes, leaders, pronouncements, law, policy, and funding decisions. The milestones and maps provided by this top-down chronology can be enduring and inspirational—witness the U.S. Bill of Rights. But they also can sting and cause endless disappointment as we acknowledge that universal human rights are not yet a reality for most people—even in the United States of America, where the Constitution says it must be so. *At the end of the day*, the real history must be about what happens to typical people in ordinary circumstances, not what is possible with extraordinary resources and exceptional advocates, however important these may be.

Inclusive education is a vision of what schools and communities promise for all children. Since the 1980s when the word *inclusion* became preeminent to describe this goal, much has been said and written about what inclusion should look like and do for students, families, and the social good. Most books about inclusive education are published because what they have to say is "cutting edge," providing pictures of excellence to help educators be better at what they do in practice. Such books tell us about ideals, theoretical models, and recommended practices in classrooms and communities. With eager eyes and minds, readers search through the pages for bits that relate to their own individual experiences—new knowledge must build on existing knowledge for learning to occur—and thus put the book down armed with a personal map for new directions toward excellence. If the book has done its job, each reader is transformed in some way and helped to understand what to do in order to put good ideas into everyday practice.

Bookstores would categorize such books as nonfiction. They clearly are not fiction, in which we expect to find make-believe and dreams as well as harsher realities than most of us could ever imagine. The professional education literature is not fiction, and what we read is supposed to be true or, if not yet reality, the future as it could and should be if we were to take advantage of new information and research findings. The message of our books on inclusive education is consistent: Share this vision, take these maps, and do what needs to be done. *Your corner of the world can look like the one painted in this book if you are guided by the sound principles and practices presented here.* What must most teachers, parents, administrators, therapists, and people with disabilities think when their own particular corner of the world may not, in fact, look like the one in the picture? Is it their failure? Or is there something about our books that presents only one version of recommended practices—the exceptional one?

In the film *Galaxy Quest* (Parisot, 1999), those who inhabit another galaxy intercept videotape transmissions of a fictional television series about space leaders who travel throughout the universe to fight for truth and justice. Evil outsiders threaten to destroy their world, which is a good and kind place. Believing the electronic images to be documentaries, the inhabitants from far away beam up the television actors to save them, just as they've witnessed in documentary after documentary. Imagine someone who has read the many books on quality inclusive schooling and then ventures out to visit randomly selected, typical schools somewhere in the United States to see inclusive classrooms in practice. Searching for students with significant disabilities in those classrooms, our reader might also make initial contact with a family who has a child with autism and set out to visit some of the programs for such children in any member country of the Organization for Economic Cooperation and Development (OECD) anywhere in the world. They've studied the documentaries: What would they actually see? If our answer were an honest one, we would have to say, regretfully, that the educational recommended practices achieved in some circumstances for some children is not yet reality for most children in most schools and communities.

As the authors ask us in the introductory chapter: "Have we learned only to create small exceptions to the rule? That is, do our inclusive innovations stand and fall depending on super teachers, administrators, resources, and funding? Is inclusion simply a list of democratic ideals that are too impractical to implement?"

Disappointments about the slowness of the adoption of educational innovations often lead to talk of a pendulum that, when pushed too far to one extreme, must then inevitably return to its opposite—as if the world were full of binary decisions rather than complex ones. The pendulum metaphor is most unhelpful, as one never returns to exactly the position one occupied in the past—there is always change, growth, and movement forward. We should not be encouraged to return to segregated models of schooling, because the challenges of quality inclusive schooling have not yet been achieved for many children or because many professionals do not yet appear to be ready to pursue those challenges or able to put them into practice even when they are psychologically ready to do so. Quality inclusive schooling is a huge new direction: "Inclusion is really about school renewal and change to improve the educational system for *all* students." Why are we surprised that it is not as easy to do as many books make it sound? But most important, what should the next step be?

Grenot-Scheyer, Fisher, and Staub have edited a collection of case studies designed to do more than tell us about success stories and exceptional inclusive achievements. Their collection includes such success stories, but, in addition, the reader will find mixed stories in which success is intermingled with disappointment—sort of like real life. There are even stories that, at first glance, might appear to be failures because inclusion did not really seem to happen for the child in the picture, regardless of what the professionals said they were doing. Our educational literature about inclusion is all about success, isn't it? Our publishers and our journal editors have helped us by providing a chronology of the bright side of inclusion, but most educators and most parents are not part of those exceptional teams of leaders, super teachers, and outstanding advocates who are able to guarantee recommended educational practices at all times of the school day and in all corners of a child's life. Most educators and most parents confront real circumstances, limited budgets, inadequate training, and limited social support that challenge their ability to achieve the kinds of milestones and maps needed for quality inclusive schooling. Will more success stories help those real people? Or is it time to provide rich descriptions of the ups and downs of educational change along with honest portrayals of what has gone wrong? Perhaps we can learn as much if not more from these stories as we have tried to learn from the success stories.

In Chapter 6, Mary Fisher provides a picture of Andre, who appeared to be participating in quality inclusive schooling in an innovative school district with considerable financial and professional resource support. In a research study of friendship, classmates even selected Andre as a friend. Closer examination, however, revealed that Andre's interactions with schoolmates were not those of friendship. Although he enjoyed the kinds of participation that came along with being "just another student" in classroom activities, his day also included being ignored and being labeled as "the inclusion student." Fisher provides the reader with rich information about Andre's experiences—the positives and the negatives—to allow for analysis of what may have gone wrong. Perhaps some readers have been in the middle of circumstances involving students like Andre and had a nagging suspicion that things could and should be better but were unsure about what to do. We'll never know, will we, unless we look closely and carefully at our limitations as well as our successes.

Equally important is what we do when efforts to establish quality inclusive schooling do fail and everyone acknowledges that something is not working. We are not resilient enough in such circumstances. These situations arise when we start talking about pendulums and "better meeting the child's needs in a special . . . ." Perhaps our books and our professional educational literature have contributed indirectly to our lack of resilience and resolve because everything we read *worked brilliantly*. No wonder someone concludes that this child is different or these circumstances are different, and inclusion is thus immediately abandoned as the pendulum does indeed swing back to what feels, for a short time, comfortable. Of course, the comfort will be brief as the inevitable shift jolts us in another new direction, and we are dragged along with only the vision of how it is supposed to look to guide us.

What Andre's story and the other stories in this book tell us is what really happens in children's experiences in real schools. What these stories also can do is provide a more detailed map of our journey toward quality inclusive schooling—the distractions, the side roads, the barriers, and the poor conditions we'll have to confront if we are truly committed and willing to work hard. It's *not* as easy as they said, and we should not be discouraged if the first effort does not result in the Olympic gold medal equivalent of inclusion. As Schorr concluded in her eight strategies for promising initiatives, "Forget about getting your results overnight and be prepared to build for a future your generation may not see. Take a longer view" (1997, p. 382). Every case study, every attempt teaches us something—and we need more books that tell us about the real journey. That is what this book does for us.

Remember, we are seeing only a portion of Andre's life in Chapter 6, recorded here for the reader: *At the end of the day*, what matters is the cumulative experiences of Andre's life and the lives of his peers. *At the end of the day*, what matters is that we hold true to our values, tell the truth about what worked and what did not work, and learn from our mistakes so that we can do better next time.

We should be most grateful for a book that reassures us, as this one does, that each experience—good and not so good—can help us to build quality inclusive schools and communities. We cannot be afraid to look closely, or we'll repeat the same mistakes over and over and be no closer to our goal another 10 years down the road than we are now.

Luanna H. Meyer, Ph.D.
Massey University College of Education
Palmerston North, New Zealand

REFERENCES

Parisot, D. [Director]. (1999). *Galaxy quest* [Film]. Los Angeles: DreamWorks.

Schorr, L.B. (1997). *Common purpose: Strengthening families and neighborhoods to rebuild America.* New York: Anchor/Doubleday.

For the Reader

A primary goal of this book is to provide a forum for the many constituencies that education attempts to serve. For too long, professionals have developed and implemented education programs according to recommended practices and their own individual interpretations of what should be, what is in students' best interests, and what research and practice have shown to be effective for students. Such efforts have resulted in tremendous differences in program quality across individuals, education environments, and regions, despite the best efforts of dedicated teachers, administrators, specialists, and others. The focus of this book is on children and youth with and without disabilities in inclusive education environments.

In Chapter 1 we present a framework for understanding inclusive education, and Chapter 10 concludes with our hope for what is possible for tomorrow.

Chapters 2–9 each contain a case study of a young person with disabilities, and supporting research and practice information are woven into each chapter. These chapters also contain discussion questions to guide the reader. In addition, references related to the particular themes presented are listed in a separate section following Chapter 10.

Chapters 2 and 9 differ from the others in the book. The shift in format and tone in these chapters is intentional. Chapter 2 provides a glimpse into the struggles of a preschool-age child on the verge of entering the elementary school years and thus serves as an introduction to children's experiences during that transition period. Chapter 9 tells the story of a young man who is on his way out of public school and illustrates the bridge from the school years to work and life in the community.

Most important, this book provides a window through which the reader may come to see and understand students with and without disabilities, their parents, and their teachers in inclusive schools and communities. The authors' hope is that, *at the end of the day*, these stories, which describe all facets of inclusion, are useful to others on the journey toward providing a meaningful and appropriate education for all students.

Acknowledgments

We would like to thank the project co-directors of the Consortium for Collaborative Research on Social Relationships of Children and Youth with Diverse Abilities (1992–1997) for their support and encouragement, which led to the genesis of this book on a late afternoon in New York City. The co-directors of the Consortium, Luanna H. Meyer, Hyun-Sook Park, Marquita Grenot-Scheyer, Ilene S. Schwartz, and Beth Harry, always engaged in lively discussions regarding emerging research findings and provided the emotional and intellectual support to persist with this project. We are especially grateful to Luanna H. Meyer, whose efforts and accomplishments on behalf of children and youth with and without disabilities continue to inspire our work.

We would like to give special thanks to Anne Smith, Project Officer for the Consortium, Office of Special Education Programs (OSEP), U.S. Department of Education. We share her vision of school reform that embraces all students and truly admire her persistence and focus on improving the lives of individuals with disabilities.

We are grateful to Lisa Benson, our acquisitions editor, and Paul Klemt and Lisa Rapisarda, our production editors, at Paul H. Brookes Publishing Co. for their support and encouragement throughout the process.

We sincerely appreciate all of the efforts of the following colleagues who assisted us in our research efforts and greatly enhanced our work. We thank Peggy Abernathy, Joe Bernazzani, Lorayn DeLillo, Katie Deno-Vos, Sharon Dunmore, Chrysan Gallucci, Vivien Garza, Mark Larson, Susan Leonard-Giesen, Bonnie McBride, Stacey Minondo, Cap Peck, Nancy Provost, Gina Stankivitz, Deb Taub, Stella Whitehead, and Debbie Williamson.

Finally, we extend our gratitude to the children and their parents, teachers, and principals who allowed us a view of their social lives in schools. We have learned much from them, and, as always, we have many more questions as a result of our work.

To our children:
Alyssa & Kathryn
Thomas Carroll & Marguerite
Ben, Willie, & Carly

At the End of the Day

1

A Framework for Understanding Inclusive Education

Marquita Grenot-Scheyer,
Mary Fisher, and Debbie Staub

For many students, attending school with their peers in their neighborhood schools, learning the core curriculum that their school community deems essential, participating in all facets of school life, and having relationships with people of their own choosing are a reality. Such cultural markers of the American dream in schools are easy to attain and are taken for granted by these students. For children and youth with disabilities and their families, however, these cultural markers are often elusive and in some cases unattainable altogether. Contemporary education systems may either facilitate or impede the development and delivery of a free appropriate public education (FAPE) in the least restrictive environment (LRE) for students with disabilities. Many families face seemingly insurmountable hurdles in their attempts to obtain an appropriate education for their sons and daughters with disabilities. As one mother expressed eloquently, "My child is not a salmon. She can't swim upstream. . . . She can't get up your cascade. . . . If she tries, she'll drown" (Lusthaus & Forest, 1987, p. 5).

Some students with disabilities attend their neighborhood schools and receive an individualized education in an inclusive environment. Those

1

students are the lucky ones who have achieved the American educational dream of being included in general education classrooms with their peers. Tremendous variability exists, however, based on students' ages and types of disabilities as well as individual states' practices (Lipsky & Gartner, 1997). Although no legal definition of *inclusion* exists, inclusive models of education have long been guaranteed by federal mandates and state policies, and many educators and families have worked together to develop successful inclusive education programs for students with and without disabilities. The National Center on Educational Restructuring and Inclusion (NCERI) developed the following definition of *inclusion*, which is comprehensive and also is illustrative of the many published definitions of the term:

> Providing to all students, including those with significant disabilities, equitable opportunities to receive effective educational services, with the needed supplementary aids and support services, in age-appropriate classrooms in their neighborhood schools, in order to prepare students for productive lives as full members of society. (1995, p. 99)

This definition is useful in understanding the rationale for and all of the critical components of inclusive education.

Although some may question the necessity, feasibility, or ethics of inclusive education (Kauffman & Hallahan, 1995), the rationale and imperative for it seem clear to the authors of this book: If educators want students with disabilities to become full, contributing members of the community, then they must ensure that these students are part of the community from the beginning by allowing them access to the core curriculum and opportunities to develop relationships with their peers without disabilities. This outcome can be realized only if students are afforded an effective, high-quality education with necessary supports and services provided by educators and families who work collaboratively. Finally, students with disabilities must have access to the core curriculum in age-appropriate general education classrooms in which social learning and academic learning are clearly linked and scaffolded.

A critical component of the successful inclusion of students with disabilities is the provision of appropriate supports and services (Grenot-Scheyer, Jubala, Bishop, & Coots, 1996). Inclusive education is far more complex than just the provision of supports and services, however. Inclusion is really about school renewal and change to improve the education system for *all* students. Effective inclusion practices require changes in the curriculum, in how teachers teach, in how students learn, and in how students with and without disabilities as well as their teachers interact with one another. Inclusive education practices should not be viewed simply as an add-on program. Inclusive education practices are "intrinsic to the mission, philosophy, values, practices, and activities of the school" (Levin, 1997,

p. 390). Effective schooling practices and inclusive models of education are synonymous and interdependent.

SECOND-GENERATION INCLUSIVE PRACTICES

The educational reform initiative regarding inclusive education (sometimes referred to as *next-level inclusion* or *second-generation inclusion*) under way at the turn of the 21st century differs from past reform efforts in its redefinition of inclusion within the context of the broader school restructuring movement (Nisbet, 1996). Past reform initiatives were limited attempts to change special education techniques and strategies, to change how, where, and by whom services were delivered, or to add to approaches already being used in general education. Contemporary inclusion, however, is about a new vision of what is best for all students. Pugach described second-generation inclusion as a generative model rather than as an additive model:

> [Such] a generative model of inclusion would require complex change and is meant to be a catalyst for transforming the educational enterprise, forcing the production of new knowledge on the part of special and general educators alike from entirely new vantage points. The curriculum is not simply modified but instead is redesigned. (1995, pp. 216–217)

Inclusive education is about changing the structure of the parallel systems of special education and general education. It is about altogether transforming educators' thinking regarding how supports can be delivered to all students—those in need of supports and services as well as their peers who are developing typically. Ferguson articulated quite clearly this kind of reinvention of educational models from dual systems of education to a unified system:

> Inclusion isn't about eliminating the continuum of placements or even just about eliminating some locations on the continuum, though that will be one result. Nor is it about discontinuing the services that used to be attached to the various points on the continuum. Instead a more systemic inclusion—one that merges the reform and restructuring efforts of general education with special education inclusion—will disassociate the delivery of supports from places and make the full continuum of supports available to the full range of students. Every child should have the opportunity to learn in lots of different places. A more systemic inclusion will replace old practices (which presumed a relationship between ability, service, and place of delivery) with new kinds of practice (in which groups of teachers work together to provide learning supports for all students). (1995, p. 285)

Despite the descriptors or phrases some administrators (e.g., "our inclusion program"), teachers (e.g., regarding class enrollment, "I have 22 students plus 2 inclusion students"), or classmates (e.g., to a visitor, "You're looking for Mary Jo, the inclusion kid?") use to describe inclusion, inclusion is neither a new special education program nor a new category of special education services. It is not a place. It does not exist separately from the rest of the school community. Inclusion is not about relocating services. It is a philosophy that embraces fostering a sense of belonging among and the full membership of students with disabilities in schoolwide communities that extend from the preschool through the university. The translation of this philosophy into practice can be described as *engaging in a process of unification*.

A number of national, state, and local groups have begun to identify the principles and practices that characterize second-generation inclusive schools. Table 1 presents a list of qualities and beliefs of one such group, a statewide task force sponsored by a federal restructuring and inclusion grant. The task force was convened to address two difficult issues: high academic standards and full equity for all students, given students' diverse learning styles and abilities. Although resolution of those two issues was not achieved during the first year of meetings, task force members were

Table 1.   Qualities and beliefs of restructured, inclusive schools

1.   All students are valued members of society and of their school communities. *All students* means *every single student.*
2.   Schools help students to think clearly, develop their intellectual and creative potential, and in general learn to use their minds well.
3.   Schools respect each student's gifts and talents by recognizing and honoring demonstrations of effort and achievement.
4.   Schools see themselves as communities of learners in which a spirit of inquiry, reflection, and risk taking prevails.
5.   All students benefit from learning together with others who represent a spectrum of diversity including race, culture, gender, age, talent, temperament, and experience.
6.   Knowledge is as varied and interwoven as human experiences. This principle is reflected in the interdisciplinary nature of the curriculum.
7.   Teachers view themselves first as educators of students and second as specialists in a subject area. They are excited about learning and enthusiastic in their work with students.
8.   Class sizes are small enough so that teachers can personalize instruction. At the high school level, this means that no teacher must work with more than a total of 80 students per semester.
9.   Schools are democratic societies in which students share in decisions regarding governance, curriculum, and goal setting.
10.   All students benefit from opportunities to receive as well as to provide assistance and service to others and to their community.

From Fried, R.L., & Jorgensen, C.M. (1998). Equity and excellence: Finding common ground between inclusive education and school reform. In C.M. Jorgensen, *Restructuring high schools for all students: Taking inclusion to the next level* (p. 21). Baltimore: Paul H. Brookes Publishing Co.; reprinted by permission.

able to identify many values that they shared. Generally, inclusive schools are student-centered, democratic, reflective communities that view diversity as a strength and an opportunity. In the following section, the values necessary to ensure the optimal development of second-generation inclusive schools are presented.

CRITICAL VALUES UNDERLYING INCLUSIVE EDUCATION

Seven values are fundamental to inclusive education:

1. Inclusion and school renewal are linked.
2. Inclusion presents a clear and strong moral imperative.
3. Learning and belonging happen together.
4. Equity, access, and support are critical.
5. Students learn in different ways.
6. Inclusive education is beneficial for all involved.
7. Collaboration is essential.

These values are identified and described briefly in the subsections that follow and are unifying themes throughout this book.

Inclusion and School Renewal Are Linked

Although inclusive models of education have been available for decades, research (Meyer, Park, Grenot-Scheyer, Schwartz, & Harry, 1998a) has given the authors of this chapter cause for concern regarding the sustainability of inclusive education as it typically is structured. In light of contemporary social and political pressures, competing financial needs that affect schools, increased professional demands on teachers and other educators, and the growing complexity of learners in diverse, urban schools, renewal and change clearly must be coordinated, comprehensive, and efficient. In addition, research and practice support the contention that school personnel must respond to the increasing complexity of service delivery with a shared commitment to benefit all students. Special education and general education reforms have a history of occurring on parallel tracks (Roach, 1998), but an intersection of education reforms has emerged as a result of federal legislation (e.g., Goals 2000: Educate America Act of 1994, Title I of the Improving America's Schools Act of 1994 [PL 103-227], the Individuals with Disabilities Education Act [IDEA] Amendments of 1997 [PL 105-17]).

Inclusion Presents a Clear and Strong Moral Imperative

Inclusion presents education professionals with a clear, strong moral imperative to "do the right thing"—that is, to assist students with disabilities and their families to be part of their education communities. Far too many families are presented with an untenable choice for educating their children with disabilities: an appropriate education (i.e., special education services in a special education setting) or an inclusive education (i.e., in a general education environment). School personnel continue to offer placement choices in this diametrical manner, being either unaware of or unwilling to implement the legal requirement to provide all students with disabilities a FAPE in the LRE as agreed by the individualized education program (IEP) team.

Learning and Belonging Happen Together

It is has long been known that there is an inextricable relationship among learning, caring, and belonging (see, e.g., Schaps & Solomon, 1990). Noddings (1992) argued that the first job of schools is to care for students; children should be educated not only for competence but also for caring. The purpose of schooling should go beyond producing good learners and should embrace the responsibility to produce good people (Kohn, 1991).

Equity, Access, and Support Are Critical

From an equity perspective, *all* students, including students with disabilities, should have access to the core curriculum, which represents a culturally approved set of knowledge and skills. Regardless of their academic or developmental ability levels, all learners are entitled to an academic curriculum that is rich and stimulating (Coots, Bishop, Grenot-Scheyer, & Falvey, 1995). The concept of *all* is used often but rarely is meant to include all students with disabilities; far too few school districts realize that this phrase truly means *each and every learner.*

Students Learn in Different Ways

Interaction and learning require differentiated instruction, which allows students to gain access to the core curriculum through various doors. It is clear from both research and practice that each student learns in different ways and each teacher teaches in different ways. The key is to respect and value individual differences among learners and to teach in ways that respect the many ways that students demonstrate their intelligence (Armstrong, 1994).

Inclusive Education Is Beneficial for All Involved

Numerous positive outcomes for all students and their families, teachers, and members of the community can be identified. A growing body of research (e.g., Hunt & Goetz, 1997; McGregor & Vogelsberg, 1999) has described such outcomes, and numerous stories from families, students, and teachers illustrate the impact of inclusive education. As one father expressed it, "[Inclusive education] has opened the door, allowing our family to be a true part of the community through involvement at our neighborhood school. . . . It has given us hope that Blair can make a difference for the good and be a contributor to her community" (P. Brown, personal communication, June 1995).

Collaboration Is Essential

As the diversity of contemporary classrooms has continued to increase, a greater need for collaboration has developed among all teachers as well as all other education personnel in general and special education classrooms. Inclusive models of education require the development of a collaborative ethic and shared ownership of all students (Grenot-Scheyer et al., 1996). Such collaboration is important for *all* students, including those who have not received disability labels, who also can benefit from the vast experience of specialists. The values described throughout this section provide the foundation for successful inclusive education. In the following section, recommended practices in inclusive education are described.

PROMISING PRACTICES IN INCLUSIVE EDUCATION

Some mornings we seem to know a great deal about what makes inclusive education work. By afternoon, we may feel encouraged and enthused. By the end of the day, we may feel discouraged and alone. The slightest criticism, dissent, or question can deplete whatever reservoir of energy remained to argue for what we believe to be true. Have teachers learned only how to create small exceptions to the rule? That is, do inclusive innovations stand or fall depending on the presence or absence of super teachers, administrators, parents, resources, and funding? Are inclusive schools simply a list of democratic ideals that are too impractical to implement?

Disagreement still exists in the field regarding the philosophy as well as the practical implications of inclusion (e.g., the amount of time that a student spends in grade-level large-group settings when that student is eligible for special education support under the categorical label *severe disability* or *significant learning disability*). Some (Fuchs & Fuchs, 1994; Gresham & MacMillan, 1997; Hallahan, 1998) have argued that little if anything is known empirically and that what is known addresses a narrow group of students, is subjective, and is constrained by ideology. Others (cf. McGregor & Vogelsberg, 1999; Pugach, 1995) have reported that a significant body of data that can and does inform inclusive school practices already exists.

As Brantlinger (1997) articulated, these conflicted perspectives represent important ideological differences between professionals who support a traditional cascade-of-services approach and those who support inclusive schools. To achieve equity and respond to persistent problems in special education (e.g., overrepresentation of children who are members of minority cultural groups and whose families are of low socioeconomic status, lack of positive results associated with pull-out programs, lack of participation in the solution by children and their families), Brantlinger urged scholars and other education professionals to "think seriously about the impact of their educational preferences on the least powerful members of society" (1997, p. 425). In addition, this difference of opinion may reflect in part that we do not yet have all of the answers. In their synthesis of the theoretical and empirical underpinnings of inclusion, McGregor and Vogelsberg suggested that inclusive practice

> Is much like a still photograph of something in motion. The feeling of movement is present within a stationary object, creating a picture that is simultaneously clear and fuzzy, depending upon where one's attention is directed. Collectively, these component parts form a picture that communicates progress toward an outcome that is defined differently for each person who sees the picture, based on their particular experiences and interests. (1999, p. 70)

Thus, some focus on the image of all students as members of general education classes. For others, the predominant image is a lack of clarity in defining new roles for teachers or a lack of consensus among parents who are left wondering what is best for their child.

This book cannot resolve and is not meant to address the difference of opinion in the field of special education. As special educators, however, we do acknowledge this disagreement and our own chosen viewpoint, values, understanding, and work perspective are reflected at the beginning of this chapter. In this book, the authors join with those who are optimistic about education reform (McGregor & Vogelsberg, 1999; NCERI, 1994; Roach, 1998; Sapon-Shevin, 1999; Schorr, 1997). This book provides examples of how the contributing authors of this book are learning from previous mistakes through examination of and reflection on thought-provoking cases. Fixing schools for some children must mean fixing schools for all children. Students with disabilities do not represent the only source of diversity in the general education classroom.

> Even if there were no students with disabilities, the culturing of inclusive schools would still be important because the entrance of students with disabilities into general education classes does not signify the presence of diversity in the school; it recognizes and affirms the diversity that has always existed. (Shapiro-Barnard, 1998, p. 12)

We know that reforms are working in some schools, and we want to find ways to replicate those successes so that reform happens in all schools.

State of the Practice

We have learned that, as has been the case in other major educational reforms, inclusive classes and schools cannot be sustained in isolation. Inclusion must go hand-in-hand with other general education reforms. In her
call to action analysis for strengthening families and neighborhoods in the
United States, Schorr (1997) revisited the attributes of successful inclusive
programs (see Table 2) that she reported in her previous work (Schorr,
1989). She also examined in detail the strategies that have served to sustain
and expand some of these successful programs so that the system did not
ultimately defeat them (see Table 3). She posed the following questions:
What makes the difference in whether your wonderful demonstration can
thrive outside the hothouse? Is it money? One leader's charisma? Luck?
Among her compelling findings, particularly in the case of schooling, was,
"No reform in isolation will bring improved outcomes—many changes must
be aligned with one another" (Schorr, 1997, p. xiii).

Several promising efforts (cf. Slavin's [Slavin, Dolan, & Madden, 1994]
Success for All and Roots and Wings, Comer's [1996] school development
program, Zigler's [Finn-Stevenson & Zigler, 1999] schools of the 21st century, Levin's [1997] accelerated schools, and Sizer's [1992] coalition of essential schools) have shown that "simply improving parts of schools or implementing one or two elements of reform is not enough; schooling needs
to be comprehensively redesigned. Many changes must be made simulta-

Table 2.   Seven attributes of highly effective inclusive education programs

1. Successful programs are comprehensive, flexible, responsive, and
   persevering.
2. Successful programs see children in the context of their families.
3. Successful programs deal with families as parts of neighborhoods
   and communities.
4. Successful programs have a long-term, preventive orientation and a
   clear mission, and they continue to evolve over time.
5. Successful programs are well managed by competent, committed
   individuals with clearly identifiable skills.
6. Staff of successful programs are trained and supported to provide
   high-quality, responsive services.
7. Successful programs operate in settings that encourage practitioners to build strong relationships based on mutual trust and respect.

From WITHIN OUR REACH by Lisbeth B. Schorr with Daniel Schorr, copyright ©
1988 by Lisbeth Bamberger Schorr. Used by permission of Doubleday, a division of
Random House, Inc.

Table 3.   Eight strategies that have sustained and expanded success-ful inclusive education programs

1. Recognize the seven attributes of highly effective inclusive educa-tion programs and the environments that support them.
2. Distinguish between essentials that can be replicated and the com-ponents that must be adapted locally.
3. Tame bureaucracies by finding new ways to balance bureaucratic protections with the imperative of accomplishing the public purpose of education.
4. Make sure that funders, managers, front-line staff, and program par-ticipants agree on valued outcomes. Make sure that all stakeholders understand how the initiative's activities and investments are related to outcomes so that they will be able to use results to judge whether success has been achieved.
5. Give up searching for a single intervention that will be the one-time fix.
6. Forget about getting results overnight, and be prepared to build for a future that the current generation may not see. Take a longer view.
7. Recognize that maintaining intensity and a program's attaining criti-cal mass may be crucial. Operate at a high-enough level.
8. Forget about choosing between bottom-up and top-down ap-proaches. Depleted inner-city neighborhoods cannot be turned around without substantial help from outside the neighborhood, but neither can outsiders impose solutions.

neously and made to fit together" (Schorr, 1997, p. 276). In order to move beyond a single exception or only a few exceptions to the rule, educators must consider multiple outcomes, design interventions that are multifac-eted, interactive, and broad, work together with families and the commu-nity, and take a long and broad view. Success does not happen overnight. It may be only future generations that benefit from actions taken today.

In addition to the successes that Schorr (1997) reviewed, there are a number of examples of classes and schools in which an inclusive commu-nity thrives and the qualities outlined in Table 1 thrive (Fisher, Sax, & Pum-pian, 1999; Jorgensen, 1998; Thompson, Wickham, Wegner, & Ault, 1996). These environments are characterized by teachers and administrators who take risks as well as by involved parents and engaged students who work collaboratively (Janney, Snell, Beers, & Raynes, 1995; Olson, Chalmers, & Hoover, 1997). Although material, human, and financial resources are criti-cal, in these settings participants have built on what exists "naturally" within their communities and generally follow the direct dive-in approach cap-tured in the widely known sportswear advertisement dictate, "Just do it!"

Responsive Instruction Practices
and Differentiated Instruction Methods

With regard to the explicit general education curriculum, general reforms such as integrated thematic units, cooperative group structures, multilevel instruction, alternative assessment, and service learning do encompass many identified needs that are critical for appropriate access by students with disabilities. When these general redesign approaches appear insufficient to meet particular students' needs, teachers have several options by which they can identify a next level of curricular intervention in which individualized supports and accommodations can be implemented for these students (cf. Downing, 1996; Grenot-Scheyer, 1999; Grenot-Scheyer et al., 1996; Jorgensen, 1998; Richardson & Schwartz, 1998; Udvari-Solner, 1995).

New initiatives with regard to the implicit curriculum of schools also address the needs of students with disabilities. Although physical integration provides access and can result in an increase in interactions simply by virtue of proximity, meaningful social integration requires thoughtful facilitation by teachers and peers (Brinker & Thorpe, 1984; Kennedy & Itkonen, 1994; Meyer, Park, Grenot-Scheyer, Schwartz, & Harry, 1998b). Educators no longer take the position that social interaction is someone else's responsibility. Longitudinal involvement is critical for membership and belonging (Schnorr, 1990, 1997). Student-centered initiatives such as peer mediation, conflict resolution training, democratic class structures, and self-determination training create community processes that are receptive to facilitating membership and a sense of belonging for those who have been excluded in the past (Jorgensen, 1998; Sapon-Shevin, 1999).

Establishing Collaborative Culture, Structures, and Supports

Most critical to the practices of inclusive schools—and their underlying feature and basis—is the existence of a collaborative culture and the use of collaborative structures and supports (Friend & Cook, 1999; Pugach & Johnson, 1995b; Salend et al., 1997; Salisbury, Evans, & Palombaro, 1997). These include top-down administration that also nurtures bottom-up initiatives, co-teaching opportunities, regularly scheduled planning times, collaborative skills training for all staff and students, transition planning, parent and/or family participation, and community networking. This need for collaboration and shared expertise between what historically have been parallel fields of education is readily apparent in surveys of teachers, in IDEA, and in various standards documents promulgated by professional organizations (e.g., Interstate New Teacher Assessment and Support Consortium [INTASC], National Council for Accreditation of Teacher Education [NCATE]).

Outcomes for Children and Youth
Who Are Members of Inclusive Schools and Communities

Academic Outcomes   Despite disagreement in the field regarding the academic or subject matter skills acquisition success of students with disabilities who are served in inclusive classes and schools, a number of positive outcomes have been identified. For some students, this seemingly simple step created opportunities for learning new content. Hunt and her colleagues (Hunt & Farron-Davis, 1992; Hunt, Farron-Davis, Beckstead, Curtis, & Goetz, 1994; Hunt, Goetz, & Anderson, 1986) conducted a series of studies comparing outcomes of students with severe disabilities who were placed in inclusive classrooms with those of students with severe disabilities who were placed in segregated settings. Their findings indicated that the students placed in integrated settings had not only higher-quality IEP objectives but also a higher likelihood of meeting their IEP objectives (Hunt & Farron-Davis, 1992; Hunt et al., 1986). Students in inclusive settings had higher levels of engagement, affective demeanor, social interaction, and involvement in integrated activities (Hunt, Staub, Alwell, & Goetz, 1994). As noted previously regarding social interaction, placement in inclusive environments gives students with disabilities access to the general education curriculum and therefore an opportunity to benefit from an expanded curriculum (Ferguson, 1995; Fisher et al., 1999; Jorgensen, 1998). As yet, for students with severe disabilities, no group studies have been conducted regarding their subject matter content skills, although their levels of engagement in general education environments are reported to be comparable to those of their peers without disabilities in general education classrooms (Logan, Bakeman, & Keefe, 1997; McDonnell, Thorson, McQuivey, & Kiefer-O'Donnell, 1997).

Studies that have addressed content acquisition for students with mild disabilities have produced mixed results. In some large-scale studies (e.g., Wang & Birch, 1984), significant gains were demonstrated for all students. In other studies (e.g., Affleck, Madge, Adams, & Lowenbraun, 1988; O'Connor & Jenkins, 1996; Zigmond & Baker, 1990), gains were made in some curricular areas but not in others, for some students but not for others, and in classrooms of some teachers but not others. The problem, which Zigmond (1995) identified, is that despite the call for individualization, most instruction in general education classrooms is presented in a large-group instruction format. The individualization that does occur is limited to decreasing demands for particular students. Pugach (1995) suggested that the limitations of general education that are evident in studies are symptomatic of a failure of imagination with respect to new expectations that have yet to be identified for second-generation inclusive classrooms.

Social Outcomes   With respect to social outcomes, researchers (Brinker & Thorpe, 1984; Kennedy & Itkonen, 1994) have reported that simply offering access to general education environments can result in an increased number of social interactions for students with severe disabilities. Placement alone, however, cannot guarantee positive social outcomes or friendships for these students. Schnorr (1997), in her descriptive study, documented the struggles and barriers that students face in moving from acceptance to belonging and membership. Gains in communication, social competence, and social networks have been documented in situations in which students were provided with support through adult or peer mediation (e.g., Cole & Meyer, 1991; Fisher, 1996; Fryxell & Kennedy, 1995; Grenot-Scheyer & Leonard-Giesen, 1997; Staub & Hunt, 1993; Staub, Spaulding, Peck, Gallucci, & Schwartz, 1996). Although they are not the predominant outcomes, making best friends and maintaining friendships over time have been an important outcome of attending inclusive schools for some children with developmental disabilities (Grenot-Scheyer, Staub, Peck, & Schwartz, 1998; Meyer et al., 1998b; Staub, 1998).

The authors of this chapter have found that when children with and without disabilities have repeated opportunities to interact with and are in close physical proximity to each other for the majority of the school day, the likelihood of their developing sustainable relationships over time is increased greatly. For many children, these relationships are of a helper–helpee nature. For some pairs of children with and without disabilities, however, true friendships develop and last for a period of months or even years. Furthermore, positive outcomes can be identified for children with and without disabilities as a result of these relationships. Both children in these friendships derived equivalent, identifiable benefits from the relationship.

Attitudes, Preferences, and Willingness to Interact   When students without disabilities are surveyed, their responses are generally favorable regarding having increased opportunities to interact with students who have low-incidence disabilities. For example, Helmstetter, Peck, and Giangreco (1994) identified seven types of positive outcomes that high school students self-reported after participating in planned interaction opportunities. These included increased self-esteem, increased tolerance for individual differences, and growth in social cognition. Kishi and Meyer (1994), in a longitudinal follow-up study, found that high school students who had been involved with their peers with severe disabilities as young children reported more current contact with people with disabilities, although they characterized few students with disabilities as their friends. Evans, Goldberg-Arnold, and Dickson (1998) determined that young children without disabilities who were members of inclusive classrooms demonstrated a sophisticated understanding of fairness and equity regarding the participation of their peers with disabilities in the classroom. Grenot-Scheyer, Staub, and colleagues (1998) summarized three outcomes of friendships for children with and without disabilities, including warm and caring companions, growth in social cognition and self-concept, and development of personal principles.

Interestingly, perhaps it is the case that peers of students with high-incidence disabilities have not been asked directly to indicate their attitudes regarding their peers with mild disabilities, although sociometric and self-report studies have indicated that students with low-incidence disabilities are less accepted and have lower measures of self-esteem than their classmates who have not been identified as having disabilities or their classmates with low academic achievement (e.g., Fulk, Brigham, & Lohman, 1998; Stanovich, Jordan, & Perot, 1998). Students with high-incidence disabilities have been asked to indicate their preferences regarding educational placement, however. In their review of eight studies examining the perceptions of students identified as having learning disabilities in inclusive and resource room education environments, Vaughn and Klingner (1998) reported that the identified students liked the general education classroom, especially with regard to making friends. They reported that these students did prefer receiving help in a classroom other than the general classroom for part of the school day. In one of the reviewed studies (Pugach & Wesson, 1995) that also included interviews with children without disabilities who were classmates of students with disabilities, the peers without disabilities also reported a preference for receiving help in a room other than a large classroom.

Teachers of students with low- and high-incidence disabilities differ in their reported enthusiasm and support for inclusive schools. Responses appear to be correlated with both experience (i.e., those who have experienced inclusion favor inclusion) and the level of support that is either anticipated or actually provided. Parents' responses follow a similar pattern. Those whose children have participated in inclusive, well-supported classrooms, teams, or schools are strong proponents of inclusive school communities (e.g., Bennet, DeLuca, & Bruns, 1997; Grenot-Scheyer, Staub, et al., 1998; Larson, Minondo, & Vargo, 1995; Staub, 1998). Support for inclusion also has been documented among parents of students without identified disabilities (e.g., Diamond & LeFurgy, 1994).

This review suggests both optimism and support for inclusive school placement in light of already documented positive academic and social outcomes for students with and without identified disabilities. It also makes apparent the importance of continued examination of the inclusive school reform process. This continued reflection with regard to educational practices must be ongoing, multidimensional, and inclusive of the multiple voices of the people whom the practices affect. Inclusion is not an ephemeral reform idea whose time will soon pass. Inclusion is a result of shared beliefs regarding successful academic and social outcomes for all students as well as the willingness of education personnel, parents, and others to effect such change. This topic is discussed next. The authors in this book have chosen the case study method to explore and understand the many dimensions of inclusive practices and the resulting impact on students with and without disabilities and their families and teachers. In the following section, case study methodology is described.

USE OF CASE STUDIES TO HELP IDENTIFY FACTORS THAT FACILITATE OR INHIBIT SUCCESSFUL INCLUSION

The case study has a long history of use in clinical research. Perhaps Sigmund Freud is best known for the use of case studies to describe the outcomes of his clinical research. Educators began to see the value of case studies in the 1960s and 1970s. In 1983, Lawrence-Lightfoot published *The Good School High School: Portraits of Character and Culture*, in which she presented case studies of six different high schools. Her book recognized the importance of being able to place these high schools in context so that the reader could visualize the setting: the community and the people about whom she wrote. Through vivid descriptions and detailed narratives, Lawrence-Lightfoot revealed how case studies can be employed to describe the less tangible, more elusive qualities of an institution such as a high school.

A *case study* is defined as "reconstruction and interpretation based on the best evidence available, of part of the story of a person's life" (Bromley, 1977, p. 163). According to this definition, the case study is not a particular method of collecting information but rather a format for organizing and presenting information about a person and his or her circumstances that may draw on a variety of specific techniques of data collection. The contributing authors of this book used many different data collection techniques to construct and organize the case studies presented herein, ranging from interviews with stakeholders to sustained periods of observation.

According to Yin (1984), the case study has four different applications, the most important of which is to explain the causal links in interventions that are too complex to be uncovered through surveys or experimental strategies. Inclusion is a difficult phenomenon to understand. All of the different definitions, perspectives, and meanings of what inclusion is and is not make it nearly impossible for inclusive practices to be implemented. Case study methodology offers researchers an approach to understanding the possible causal links of inclusion to individual outcomes.

A second application of the case study is to describe the real-life context in which an intervention occurs. By using case study methodology, researchers are able to look for and describe the nuances specific to individual situations and participants. There is no exact recipe for creating the ideal inclusive education environment because the ingredients are never the same from classroom to classroom. An important aspect of each of the case studies presented in this book is the contextual descriptions—the "who, what, where, when, and why." By understanding the uniqueness of the contexts and participants in the case studies, readers will be better able to discern more clearly and more quickly which type of practice, strategy, or curriculum works best in particular circumstances.

Third, in using a descriptive mode, an evaluation can benefit from an illustrative case study of the intervention itself. By comparing their knowledge of effective inclusive practices with what they observed and measured in the case studies, the contributing authors were able to evaluate to what extent these practices were being implemented and with what kinds of outcomes they were associated. The authors were able to point to practices not identified previously in the literature as having a positive impact on outcomes for youth with disabilities in inclusive school environments.

Fourth, the case study strategy can be used to explore those situations in which the intervention being evaluated has no clear single set of outcomes. In some of the case studies, certain outcomes were expected a priori. For the majority of the case studies, however, the outcomes emerged over time as part of the case study process itself.

The case study methodology possesses several general attributes (Lancy, 1993). First, the case study uses many qualitative data tools often associated with the qualitative method. Case studies do not adhere to the qualitative paradigm, however. Questions or issues are at least partly predetermined. The authors of this book carefully delimited in advance what was selected for study. Second, as Lancy stated, "One's audience for the case study may include some subset of the academic community but it must include some well defined 'client group'" (1993, p. 143). One of the main purposes of writing this book, in fact, had to do with our audience. We wanted to make sure that we provided real stories about real children in an effort to give the reader an opportunity to understand his or her beliefs and practices about inclusive education. Although the case study is not always construed as an evaluation, the researcher assumes an evaluative stance. She or he compares explicitly or implicitly what is observed with some standard. For example, the qualities and beliefs of restructured, inclusive schools displayed in Table 1 of this chapter (see also Fried & Jorgensen, 1998, p. 21) served as evaluative markers and comparison points with regard to whether an inclusive environment and the associated education practices were of high quality and value.

The case study method involves the presentation and interpretation of detailed information about one individual in order to develop courses of action and to make decisions appropriate for an individual situation. In this book, the individuals who are described are eight children and youth who are participating in inclusive education environments. The contributing authors chose to use case studies not only for the reasons described previously but also for other purposes. First, they wanted to present holistic reports of experiences within a series of classrooms across a wide range of students. Second, the very diversity present in the classrooms that the authors came to know intimately was examined. Third, the authors used the case study method to address the wide range of issues and variables that were associated with the inclusive education environments and the individual children and youth who were studied.

We hope that these stories of students with and without disabilities and their families and teachers in diverse settings will enable others to translate these ideas into their settings to inform their own work. The struggle to renew schools and to meet the needs of all children and families, to see each child and his or her family as unique, and to invite families' participation as members of an inclusive school community are best viewed as a shared endeavor. We envision a world in which collaborative approaches are both the substance and the support by which we build and enact inclusive school communities. These stories are but one contribution to that work in progress.

IMPORTANCE OF LISTENING TO CHILDREN AND YOUTH

Researchers are at a disadvantage in understanding a child's educational experiences because they use their own definitions of what those experiences are and should be. Beginning with their own school histories and ending with their particular individual beliefs about what encompasses a quality educational experience, researchers have difficulties with preventing their perspectives from influencing what they observe and hear during the course of their studies. Furthermore, as providers of instruction to preservice teacher-training programs, researchers' ideas about education environments surely are influenced heavily by the professional teaching strategies that they espouse. Education researchers have become accustomed to evaluating programs in terms of whether what they consider to be recommended practices are present. As indicated previously, a growing body of research documents practices that are believed to be necessary to support successful outcomes of inclusion for youth both with and without disabilities.

The exciting level of diversity present in schools may in fact hinder a researcher's understanding of young people's experiences in schools if the researcher's own culture and gender are not congruent with those of the children and families that he or she attempts to understand. Indeed, many of the case studies in this book involve stories about children from cultures that are different from those of the authors. Even among the contributing authors to this book, cultural differences influenced our perspectives with regard to our thinking and how we felt about the children and youth whom we observed and studied. Listening to the voices of the children and their families and trying to understand how their own cultural experiences affected their perspectives was a difficult yet necessary and critical role that we needed to fulfill.

A longstanding cultural gap also exists between institutions of higher education and schools. Teachers (and consequently their students) view education researchers, who are sometimes armed with much theory and little practice, as being out of touch with the challenging realities of teaching students in a large, complex society. Crowded classrooms, students with a diverse range of learning styles, and lack of administrative and structural support are only a few of the challenges that teachers face in U.S. schools. Each of the case studies presented in this book has its share of unique barriers to including students with disabilities in general education settings successfully. The challenge that the authors of this book faced was trying to understand the culture (i.e., the culture of the school being studied) as outsiders. We needed to look past prejudices about what contributes to a high-quality education environment. As not only researchers but also outsiders, the authors' task was to interpret children's experiences and the meanings the children derived from those experiences. It was imperative that we ask a lot of questions about the meaning of what we observed. Even more important was that we listen carefully and critically to those who were supplying the answers.

The case studies presented in this book underscore the value of collaborative research that respects and honors the participation of students, their teachers, and their families. The general assumption is that researchers are objective observers and do not allow their perspective to color their interpretation of what they observe. Although it was not possible for the authors to leave their own perceptions at the classroom door, the children and youth themselves were in an excellent position to help us understand what we think we learned about their inclusive education experiences.

2

Carissa's Story

Looking Ahead and Standing Firm

Ruth B. Coates and Beth Harry

The Longitudinal Family Study was one of several studies conducted under the umbrella of the Consortium for Collaborative Research on Social Relationships of Children and Youth with Diverse Abilities. Over the course of 4 years, we conducted ethnographic interviews and observations with 10 families from a wide variety of cultural backgrounds. We began with seven families of children in elementary and secondary school programs whom we studied in participatory action research designed to assist the families in developing culturally appropriate social activities and relationships for their children who had disabilities. All of these children had started school in special centers and had been transferred between ages 10 and 15 to special education classrooms within general education buildings. In the third year of the study, we decided to recruit three families whose children were in inclusive early education classrooms because we wanted to study the role of parental advocacy in the transition process from Part C (entitled Part H at the time the study was conducted) to Part B services under the Individuals with Disabilities Education Act (IDEA) of 1990 (PL 101-476). All three families were African American and were referred to us by service coordinators at the local county chapter of The Arc of the United States. We did not attempt any interventions with this cohort of participants; our research was entirely descriptive and based on extensive interviews with families and observations of parent–service provider conferences and with the children in their home and school environments.

We began the Longitudinal Family Study with one clear goal in mind: to capture families' views of the social lives of their children with disabilities. By our third interview, we already had developed one of the views that was to become a central theme of the study: The parents' wish is that their children have *una vida normal*, or a typical life. The Spanish phrase is a quote from the family of a young man with Down syndrome who is from the Dominican Republic, but we heard it over and over again from all 10 families that participated in the research project. One of the discoveries we made as we proceeded, however, was that we could not assume that we knew what parents meant when they used this phrase. We were struck by the cultural and individual variations reflected in the families' definitions of *typical* for their children with disabilities.

All of the families' expectations for their children's social lives were for all of the children to be included fully within whatever was normative for each family, regardless of whether the families' structures were more extended or more nuclear and more outgoing or more home-based. Similarly, families' visions of the future for these children reflected whatever was normative for the families. For example, on the issue of planning for adulthood, we noted a range of parental attitudes. The two Hispanic families and the two African American families envisioned their children's adulthood as being within the supportive and flexible parameters of the biological family. Within a Palestinian family and a Trinidadian family, the spouses expressed differing views, which reflected the spouses' different levels of acculturation to American ways. For a family of mixed Chinese and Caucasian heritage, financial plans had already been made for the support of their two sons with disabilities, and the parents were confident that there were many residential programs from which they eventually would be able to choose when the time came that their sons would no longer live with them. With the families of the second cohort, parents' visions of their children's social and adult lives were less clear, because the children were still very young and were still encircled by the family, as is typical for preschoolers.

It was on the issue of inclusive schooling that we saw the greatest difference between the two cohorts of participants. The families of the younger children were quite definitely in favor of inclusive schooling opportunities, although the extents of their visions varied. For a variety of reasons, the families of the older children were accepting of separate programs for their children. For the two Spanish-speaking families, schooling a child with a disability was seen as a privilege rather than a right because neither family had been able to obtain access to schooling for their children in their respective native countries, the Dominican Republic and El Salvador. For the family from Trinidad, separate schooling in their native country had been available and was accepted as normative. For the family from the Palestine region and the two African American families, separate schooling seemed safer than the rough-and-tumble atmosphere of the general education environment. For the Chinese-Caucasian family, separate schooling was described as much more appropriate than an inclusive classroom, which the parents described as a one-size-fits-all solution. The views and experiences of eight of these families were detailed in a collection of case studies (Harry, Kalyanpur, & Day, 1999).

This chapter focuses on the Coates family, which was the first to join our preschool cohort and whose daughter, Carissa, was age 2 1/2 years when we met her. Our research team had the privilege of watching in awe as Carissa's family, led by her intrepid mother, Ruth Coates, negotiated—indeed, *created*—a path of inclusive schooling for Carissa over the course of the next 2 years of the study. Our study provided only a miniscule window into the beginnings of Carissa's education. The real researcher is her mother, whose personal narrative follows in this chapter.

CARISSA

Reflecting on the early years with Carissa, one can see that inclusion was a concept that naturally flowed from our family's belief system. It was a core value so deeply rooted within the family's personal framework of love and our view of life that we did not realize that it needed a name. After all, hadn't all of the civil rights issues—race, gender, and people with disabilities—been addressed through legislation?

Carissa was born into our Christian, middle-class family in the suburbs of a major metropolitan U.S. city on the East Coast. She received an early diagnosis of Down syndrome—*trisomy 21* in clinical medical terminology. There is a lot of burden for a child to bear embedded in each of those descriptors, yet Carissa has handled it with grace and style. She was a charmer in the special way that only babies can be. From the moment that our eyes first met, I sensed an inner strength and peace flowing from her sweet spirit. With help and guidance from God, we would make it. It would not be easy, but our vision of a full and productive life for Carissa was priceless and without compromise. We'd never planned to be advocates for the rights of people with disabilities or inclusive education; it just became a fact of life for us. The vision required it. This meant that decisions about her educational placement had to support our vision.

Carissa's Early Years

The early months were filled with doctors' appointments and cautious prognoses about Carissa's health and development. She spent her first week of life in a neonatal intensive care unit. We were thrilled though apprehensive about her health when she was able to come home. She thrived. She had a congenital heart defect, which was surgically repaired when she was 6 months old. We almost lost her shortly after the surgery, but she survived and thrived. Relatively minor medical issues occurred from time to time, but the truly distressing aspect of Carissa's having Down syndrome was the negative and/or condescending attitudes of far too many health care professionals. She's just another "Down's kid." "You're in denial." "Get over it." "Accept it." "Don't get your hopes up." "She'll never graduate from a regular high school." "Just take her home and love her." Our beautiful daughter deserved so much more. Why couldn't they appreciate her for her personality, her abilities, her tenacity, her smile, her value as a precious human being created in the image of God? Yet these and other, similar comments primed me for what was to come. Sadly, we encountered the same attitudes among providers of educational and related services. The weight of Carissa's medical diagnosis overshadowed her innate promise. I found out that the word *potential* could not be used in writing individualized family service plan (IFSP) or individualized education program (IEP) goals. The contrast in attitudes and expectations between service providers in the education system and community service providers was stark and increasingly evident over the years that we participated in the system.

For initial child care, we were blessed to find a family child care provider who was willing to care for Carissa despite her use of an apnea monitor. Carissa remained in that child care setting from ages 3 months to 2½ years. During that time, there were other children her age with whom she played. The children learned from each other naturally and formed healthy relationships. Carissa's disability and characteristics such as her speech-language delays did not define her in their eyes. She was just "Carissa." The children were not educated about people with Down syndrome, so they treated her as a friend and a playmate. The itinerant special education and related services providers blended nicely into the home environment, and the children and the service providers were able to participate in the "fun" physical therapy exercises and educational games. Carissa was happy, confident, and independent and was blossoming in her abilities.

Thoroughly appreciating the value of this arrangement, I became even more sure in my resolve that Carissa would not attend an early childhood special education center for toddlers—the typical, customary placement for children about to attain school age and make the transition to Part B services. No longer would itinerant service delivery be an option for us. Services could be delivered only at an early childhood center—so we were told. It was important to us that Carissa's life experience, even at such a young age, be indicative of our expectation for her adult life—living and working in the community with a diverse population, not on the fringes or in the shadows. She had to learn to live and function side-by-side with her peers without disabilities in the real world, not under a bell jar. As much as my maternal instincts wanted to keep her in a sheltered (i.e., safe) environment, I believed that that would prove to be a mistake down the road. The safest place for Carissa was "in the mix"! I believed that the law agreed with me, as evidenced by concepts such as natural environments and least restrictive environments (LREs).

So, armed with my values and my copies of the relevant federal and state regulations, I proceeded to enroll Carissa in a community child care center when she reached the age of 2½. Surely, if this placement proved to be as successful as family child care had been for Carissa, the school system would recognize the benefits of continuing community-based itinerant services for Carissa in the following school year during her transition to Part B services. Or would they? Simply put, Part H (since retitled Part C under the 1997 IDEA Amendments [PL 105-17]) services were delivered in natural environments, and Part B services were delivered in early childhood special education centers. That's just the way it was done. The education system was responsible for service delivery, and general education services (except for Head Start) were not provided for children between the ages of 3 and 5. Clearly, the same education system was sending contradictory messages about inclusion, natural environments, and LREs; but such issues often take a back seat when there are so many children to serve with so few resources.

Nevertheless, prior to transition, Carissa was enrolled in a community child care program from the age of 2½ until age 5. We denied every attempt of the school system to place her in a segregated early childhood education center. In the inclusive child care program, we saw the benefits to all of the children—sharing, learning, fighting, consoling, imitating, singing, climbing—of just being children. This experience—Carissa's inclusion with her peers—was priceless. She was not labeled, isolated, or expected to generalize skills acquired in a sheltered learning environment to the "real world." She was able to learn developmentally appropriate skills in a context that supported her development in all areas. She thrived. Some service providers agreed with and shared our vision and cheered us on; others, however, expressed disdain at our audacity to refuse the customary, template Part B placement. Children are not templates, so why should we have embraced such a program? The most encouragement and support came from the "regular" child care providers, who knew very little other than to love children and give them what they need—love, care, discipline, challenges, and encouragement. In the Biblical dictum, "the greatest of these is love," but love is an element that is missing from our school systems.

So successful was Carissa's experience in the 2-year-olds' class that in subsequent years we persisted in our determination to obtain from public service providers itinerant services delivered on site in classes for 3- and 4-year-olds. What is meant here by the term *successful*? Were Carissa's receptive and expressive language skills at a chronological age–appropriate level? What about her social skills? Her cognitive functioning? Her fine and gross motor skills? Was she performing at the same level as her peers without disabilities in all domains? The answer, clearly and emphatically, was *no*. (Do any of us? Or is it the power that we cede to the label that makes the difference? Why do we consign our children to a life of continual testing and labeling? Only for noble purposes, I would hope.) Academically, she knew the alphabet, could read and spell her name, could count to 10, and could identify many colors. Yet, our definition of *successful* in Carissa's case was *healthy, happy, growing, auspicious, laughing, sharing, learning, respected, understanding of differences,* and yes, even *typical.* This was our vision, and we were winning the right to see it unfold.

Carissa's preschool years passed by quickly, and soon it was time for Carissa to attend kindergarten. *Let's give the public system a chance to show its dedication to fulfilling its legal and moral obligations,* we thought. Never did they want to comply, but finally they consented to allow Carissa to attend her neighborhood school—a magnet school for academic and communication skills. *How appropriate,* I thought. *This is the perfect placement.* So why weren't academic goals developed for Carissa? Why wasn't in-service training provided for the general classroom teacher? Why did an administrator say that Carissa was expected to perform at the same level as her peers without disabilities? Simply stated, why were recommended practices for inclusion totally ignored despite my interventions? Yet, even with minimal supports, Carissa continued to grow and learn and charm.

The public school kindergarten was a half-day program, but because Carissa was then 5 years old, she was able to attend a school for half-days in the afternoons at our church. There, she was loved, taught, and nurtured. For example, teachers and service providers handled Carissa's behavior problems as they would have dealt with those of any child with her level of functioning and understanding, and these issues were not excused by virtue of her disability label. Carissa began to learn to read in a phonics-based curriculum. This method was so appropriate for Carissa, who is a visual learner. It supported her speech-language developmental needs. Her academic potential was obvious to those who had corresponding expectations for Carissa and the will to help her to learn. Too many public school service providers refused to acknowledge the individual child (so much for the "I" in IEP) by setting appropriate goals and providing the resources to support their achievement within the LRE. The weight that the public school system had ascribed to Carissa's label was a threat to our vision. An economies-of-scale issue on the school system's side of the table was a life-span quality indicator for us on the other side. We had an alternative, so we did not allow Carissa to return to public school the following year for first grade.

Carissa Today

Carissa continues to attend school at our church, along with her brother and several other children, just as she would have if she had not received a disability label. In fact, none of the children at our church's school have received labels, not even Carissa. She is a child who has to be taught. She is expected to learn and grow across all domains, and so she does. Our time is spent sharing her delight and pride in her receiving an "A" on her spelling test rather than debating the appropriateness of an academic goal in her IEP. Carissa's achievement of her potential is a viable option. Inclusion in this environment is automatic and natural, not a social or legislative mandate.

How do I reconcile Carissa's private school placement with our history of proinclusion activism? To understand the answer to that question, one has to see inclusion as multidimensional. Inclusion cannot be fit into a one-size-fits-all paradigm any more easily than a segregated special education system can. The models must be fluid enough to be molded to fit individual children and their families along as many dimensions as possible. Carissa is fully included in her school at our church. Her label has no bearing on her placement. This is also her brother's school, and he has received no diagnosis. This situation is "normal" for us. It's our *choice*, as it should be for all families—a choice that is based on a family's unique characteristics—values, cultures, ideologies, wants, likes, dislikes, and preferences. Public systems cannot be so accommodating—or can they? Is a template method of school administration the only cost-effective means of service delivery, or do what we see as good quality-of-life results for the family matter more? Our family had to make a choice, and we chose a full and productive life for Carissa that is based on our vision and the size that fits us as a family. There was no compromise.

At the time this chapter was written, Carissa was attending school for full days at our church school. Carissa continued to rise to meet the expectations of the teachers at the school and exceeded all of their goals regarding academic success. In the past, the public school staff had appeared to work from a deficit perspective and saw only Carissa's disability. The staff at the church school saw a little girl who needed to be educated and developed the supports and accommodations to teach her. Her label no longer seemed to be of such importance. Our family has come to realize what many families of children with disabilities know: As parents, we do have options, and we can create inclusive solutions for our sons and daughters with disabilities.

At the end of the day, Carissa's dad, her brothers James and John, her sister Carla, her Aunt Yvonne, and our church family talk about Carissa's latest antics and achievements. She is quite a young lady. One moment she is bossing and bullying the older children; the next moment she wants to cuddle. In either event, that telltale twinkle is in her eyes! Charming, flirtatious, manipulative, impersonator extraordinaire, loving, empathetic, determined, adventurous, insightful, caring, faithful, sheer joy—at the end of the day, we realize how much God is teaching us through Carissa, and we thank God for giving her, a precious gift, to us.

3

Jamal's Story

Troubles, Transitions, and Triumphs

Debbie Staub and Ilene S. Schwartz

As part of our research with the Consortium for Collaborative Research on Social Relationships of Children and Youth with Diverse Abilities (Meyer, Grenot-Scheyer, Harry, Park, & Schwartz, 1997), we came to know many children with disabilities and their families. One of those children is Jamal, an African American boy who has Down syndrome and associated medical issues, including heart trouble. We observed and got to know Jamal over the course of 4 years, from the time he was 4 years old. When Jamal was 6 years old and just about ready to finish his first year of kindergarten, we interviewed his teacher about his experiences in her class. We asked her to start by telling us Jamal's story:

> Well, I think it has been as one might expect. A good news, bad news type of story. In many respects, we've seen a lot of growth in Jamal, and I think all of the staff would agree, and his mom feels that way, too. In other respects, Jamal is hard to have in the classroom, and at times I feel that our expectations of him are unnecessarily ambitious.

Jamal's teacher accurately captured the essence of Jamal's educational history. His journey so far in his short life has included some bumps, ruts, and curves but also smooth periods. In this chapter, we share Jamal's story from both the good news and the bad news angles, and we highlight the unique aspects of including children with moderate and severe developmental delays in inclusive preschool settings. Given the importance placed on social context and outcomes in inclusive preschools, we also take a close look at the range of relationships that Jamal experienced during our observations of him.

JAMAL: A REWARDING CHALLENGE

Jamal is the youngest child and only son of Serena, a single mother who has a professional career. Jamal lives with his mother, a sister (9 years older), and a younger female cousin who was taken into Serena's home through the foster care system. Jamal's family lives in a large, urban area in the Northwest.

Jamal is described as "liking to be the center of attention." He is quite skilled at getting people's attention by using both appropriate and inappropriate behaviors. He uses a picture exchange system as his primary mode of communication but also uses understandable gestures and some vocal approximations and babbling in a communicative manner. In preschool and kindergarten, he loved the dramatic play areas and often could be found playing with dolls, gently giving them baths or combing their hair.

Because his disability was identified at birth, Jamal received special education services as early as 4 weeks of age at a local university medical center. Staff at the medical center recommended that Jamal attend an infants and toddlers program at the university. The program is administered by the university's Department of Education faculty and staff. Jamal attended the infants and toddlers program from approximately age 6 months until age 3 years. Until he was 18 months old, Jamal received services in a self-contained setting. At age 18 months, he entered the toddler classroom, an integrated program for youngsters with moderate and severe developmental delays and toddlers who were developing typically. The program is staffed by at least one certified teacher and several assistants, creating a high teacher-to-student ratio. In addition, related services are provided through the program. These services include occupational therapy, physical therapy, speech-language therapy, and family resource services. During the time that Jamal attended the infants and toddlers program, which is offered for only 2 hours per day, four times per week, he also attended private child care in a neighbor's home.

During his participation in the infants and toddlers program, Jamal experienced sporadic success in his development. His mother described Jamal's behaviors at ages 2–3 years as follows: "Jamal has not always been there. His first few years were difficult for him because of his speech-language delay. And then the biting." At about age 2½ years, Jamal began to engage in biting behavior directed at adults and his peers in the infants and toddlers program. His biting was frequently the result of his frustration with not being able to communicate his needs and wants clearly. Jamal's mother said, "When Jamal was younger, . . . the biting, it was a lot. I'd keep an eye on him everywhere we went. It is not very comfortable sitting in a place if you're constantly worried that he is about to bite somebody."

At age 3 years, Jamal made the transition to an inclusive preschool class at the same university program. He attended the daily 3-hour morning program from ages 3 years to 5½ years. The preschool program that Jamal attended at the center has more than 25 years of experience in serving young children with moderate and severe developmental delays. Originally a self-contained center serving only children with disabilities, the center opened its doors in the mid-1980s to preschoolers who are developing typically. The high teacher-to-student ratio (about 1:4 in the preschool classrooms), experienced certified teachers, and no tuition costs at the center resulted in an increased enrollment of children who were typically developing. Consequently, the preschool classrooms have become more integrated over time, reflecting a blended program with about 50% of the students attending having disabilities and about 50% not having disabilities.

Jamal's first year in the program was rough because the incidence of his biting behavior had increased significantly. Whereas a year before he had been biting on average only once per week, his preschool teacher reported that he was now biting at least once a day and as often as five or six times a day. Increasingly, his physically aggressive behavior was being directed at his peers. Furthermore, the function of his behaviors seemed to generalize beyond that of expressing frustration. Jamal was biting for several reasons, including attention, curiosity (to check the reactions of those whom he bit), escape, and frustration when his teachers and peers did not understand his communicative requests. Jamal's mother reported that though Jamal did bite at home and in his child care program, the majority of the biting incidents occurred at school. She believed that this discrepancy was because Jamal's child care provider and family members had a better understanding of his communicative requests and because "he knew that his sister and I weren't about to put up with that type of behavior." Serena reported that one day, when Jamal bit her, she bit him back. Since that incident, he has not tried to bite her again.

The preschool staff were not only committed to ensuring the safety of staff and children alike but also greatly concerned about Jamal's biting behavior and the barriers it was creating to his social development. Not long into his first year in preschool, Jamal's teachers conducted a functional analysis of his behavior and created a positive behavioral support plan for him. Although it took some time to implement the plan and see positive changes, eventually Jamal's behavior improved. His preschool teacher described the changes in Jamal's behavior and development after his first year in preschool:

His biting has decreased, and his language has increased. His ability to go through classroom routines has also increased. He does [use] some words that you can understand now, which is something he didn't have even a year ago. He has gone from mostly signing to using a communication board with symbols. The verbal language is emerging, although we are a little skeptical about how his language is going to work for him, because he is very difficult to understand.

By the end of his first year in preschool, Jamal's biting behavior had decreased significantly to a zero level of occurrence over a 3-month period. However, Jamal's behavior had returned to a point where he was biting about once a week after he returned to school following an extended summer break. His teacher reported that unlike the previous year, his biting behavior this school year was directed at three specific children:

It's interesting, because the three kids in the classroom whom he bites are all kids who are typically developing. And they are all kids who aren't real nice to him, either. So he discriminates. They ignore him when he tries to show them things. They are obviously afraid of him, so whenever he comes near them, they back up and look frightened. They have a reason to be frightened, but they also take it to the extreme.

In spite of Jamal's behaviors and the difficulties that they presented for his preschool teachers, Jamal's teachers were committed to decreasing his biting behavior. Eventually, his biting behavior did decrease, although his biting continued sporadically throughout his preschool experience. Jamal's mother attributes the decrease in Jamal's aggressive behavior to his learning outcomes at school:

Jamal is at a point where I think he is really enjoying himself. He seems to have learned some academic skills. We've definitely learned that structure works well for him. He's learned how to behave in a class-

room. All those social skills — how to get along with other children, play-
ing, how to share. He's increased his mobility skills, such as playing on
the playground, going down slides, and all that. Most important, he is
learning how to say a lot more words, and it makes his communication
with his peers and with other people better, so it makes him feel better
about it, too.

Jamal's mother also attributes the positive increases in Jamal's behavior to his participation in their church choir. She noted that the other children in the choir have always been accepting of Jamal and have included him quite naturally into their group: "They know Jamal, and we've been in church a long time, so they know him and treat him like everyone else." Serena believed strongly that Jamal's participation in the choir gave him a sense of belonging and comfort that he had not experienced anywhere else. She also noted that he had never bitten a child or an adult while at church and again attributed this to the fact that his peers at church treat him with respect and as a valued member of the church.

Understandably, while Jamal attended the preschool program, his mother began to plan and worry about his transition to kindergarten. She was anxious that Jamal attend an inclusive program but was concerned that his difficulties with transitions and his biting behaviors would be challenging for his teachers and classmates. Furthermore, Jamal's neighborhood school district historically had not included children with moderate and severe developmental delays in general education classes. The school district still maintains several self-contained school sites that serve homogeneous groups of children with disabilities, and it usually has been the rule that children with developmental delays in this district attend either segregated schools or self-contained programs with few opportunities for inclusion.

Jamal's mother has always considered herself to be involved actively in finding and maintaining inclusive education opportunities for Jamal. She stated,

I've been pretty heavily involved. I mean, my involvement is talking to
the teacher [at the preschool] at least once a week, visiting the class-
room at least one time a week. I haven't been involved in any commit-
tees or support groups, just because of my time. But as far as reading,
talking to educators, I have been very involved. I try to be responsive
because I am really interested in [inclusion].

When Jamal was halfway through his last year at the preschool program, Serena identified a child care center located at an elementary school campus near their neighborhood. Furthermore, the elementary school had on its faculty a kindergarten teacher who had dual certification in special and general education and who taught in a blended classroom. Serena's intent was to give Jamal sufficient transition time to kindergarten by having him attend the child care center:

I've given myself a little time before I start him up in a new child care to take a look at the kindergarten program and to make sure it's what I want, because I'm not going to switch him twice. I try to keep all transitions as small as possible.

Midway into his last year in the university preschool program, Jamal attended the inclusive child care center in the afternoons, following his time in the preschool. Serena believed that staff at the child care program welcomed Jamal's participation:

The teacher, I think, and the assistant have both taken sign language, and they are really interested and excited about having Jamal in their classroom. I've talked with them at length, as I do with everybody about Jamal, and they seem truly excited. They really do believe that they can work with him and his shortcomings or his needs, which are of course language development and then the biting off and on.

In addition to the child care staff's being interested and motivated in creating a successful experience for Jamal, Jamal's teacher from the preschool program worked closely with the child care staff. Jamal's mother reported:

They are willing to work together and collaborate on Jamal's progress and work. Jamal also goes to a speech therapist through a local health maintenance organization, and she is familiar with the child care program as well. All this collaboration really helped things go smoother.

Although Jamal's participation in the child care program included some bumps along the way, including some biting incidents and tantrums, Jamal's mother and teachers were pleased with the progress he had made during his time there. Furthermore, when asked whether she thought that Jamal's participation in the child care program and preschool had influenced his relationships with other children, Serena was positive:

He is being exposed to other children, and it helps him to learn to accept them and for them to accept him. Plus, he just really likes other kids. His social skills have really increased since he's been in preschool. I mean, he's always been pretty sociable. But I think this has increased, since he is now with children every day.

Several months before Jamal was to attend kindergarten, we asked Serena, "What kinds of things are you looking for in a kindergarten classroom?" She replied,

What I think would be good for Jamal is a class that doesn't have all [children who have received disability labels] in it but a smaller ratio of teacher to kids than a general kindergarten. What it sounds like at Jefferson [Jamal's neighborhood elementary school] is that there is a blended classroom where there is a certain percentage of children with special needs and children who are developing typically. A smaller classroom — maybe 20 kids with 2 assistants or something like that, which I like better because then there is a chance for Jamal to get help with his special needs, and then there will be other children for him to learn from. Plus, it is an all-day kindergarten program, and I think that would also be better for Jamal.

Serena's request to have Jamal placed in the Jefferson kindergarten classroom was granted, and Jamal began attending the program just before his sixth birthday. However, there were many planning meetings and informal discussions between the kindergarten teacher and Jamal's preschool teacher on how best to include Jamal in this classroom. The meetings took place long before Jamal entered the class. Furthermore, both the kindergarten teacher and Jamal's preschool teacher observed Jamal in the child care program on a couple of occasions, which gave them a common point of discussion about how best to meet Jamal's needs.

Well into Jamal's kindergarten year, we had the opportunity to meet with his teacher and ask her about how Jamal's kindergarten experience was going. As also noted at the beginning of this chapter, Ms. B, the kindergarten teacher, had mixed feelings regarding Jamal's participation in her class:

I can see the importance of Jamal's learning social behaviors that are commensurate with [those of] the other kids his age. And sizewise and in his chronological age, it is appropriate that he be with his peers. Because their day is quite highly structured, I have had thoughts about whether Jamal's developmental level — whether we are being fair in asking him to sit, stand in line, and follow those types of routines. If you set up a stringent rule, that is just an opening for some children to feel like it is oppositional. So, when we get in line and ask that the kids keep their bodies to themselves, Jamal pretty routinely nudges with his chest or hits with his hands, just for a reaction. On the other hand, when it is his turn to be the leader, he doesn't hesitate to try and boss the other kids around about their behavior.

On the one hand, Ms. B was concerned about Jamal's developmental ability to participate in appropriate ways with his peers without disabilities. On the other hand, she often believed that Jamal knew exactly what he was doing and that Jamal's behavior reflected a choice on his part, not a lack of knowing what to do. Ms. B also felt conflicted about the way other children perceived Jamal as a member of their class:

He is a part of our class. Nobody has ever said, "Why is he in here?" But he has come out of the bathroom a couple of times with his pants down around his knees and we just go, "Jamal, you know." Nobody gets real excited, but they also recognize that another kid might not do that. And again this week, he urinated out on the playground. My response to the kids was to tell them to come tell me individually, and I've tried not to let it become this big dramatic event.

In addition to his acceptance as a member of his kindergarten class, Jamal had experienced other positive outcomes during his kindergarten year, including a significant reduction in his biting. Ms. B attributes that to the fact that they provided adult support early in the school year to prevent Jamal from hurting others. Jamal had also increased his ability to communicate with others more effectively, and although his expressive verbal skills still tended toward vocal approximations, his teacher believed that he was more often than not using the right inflection and body language to express himself. Toward the end of our interview with Ms. B, we asked her to tell us her thoughts about where Jamal might go to school for his first-grade year:

Well, I have the same feeling of ambivalence about his staying with his age peers and our asking of him things that are not age-appropriate for him. My advice to his mom, knowing that it is important to her that he be with his peers, is that she consider at least placing Jamal for some part of his day in a more protected and slower-moving classroom so that he has a chance to learn the basics.

As it turned out, Serena was not satisfied with the options offered to Jamal at Jefferson for his first-grade year and beyond. Unlike the kindergarten program at Jefferson, which was a blended program, the other special education placement options were in self-contained settings. That was not a satisfactory option for Serena, who believed strongly that Jamal needed the opportunity to be with his age peers without disabilities for the majority of his school day. Consequently, Jamal attended a different elementary school during his first-grade year. In that school, he was included in a general education, multiage, first- and second-grade classroom for about 70% of his day with support from a teacher's aide.

As might be expected, Jamal's first-grade experience included triumphs but also trouble related to his physically aggressive behavior. Our most recent observation of Jamal in his new school (during his second-grade year), however, revealed that Jamal was clearly a member of his class and his school community and that he had made lasting relationships with his peers. Although Jamal's experiences in early childhood special education were uneven, many positive aspects of his school experience are cause for celebration. First, Jamal had the support and perseverance of his mother, who clearly desired to provide Jamal with the best education opportunities available, including certified teachers, a developmental age–appropriate curriculum, and age peers without disabilities. Serena worked closely with the preschool and elementary school staff to find the best approaches to meeting Jamal's needs. Second, the preschool teacher who worked with Jamal was diligent about providing him with positive behavioral supports to address his severe biting behavior. Finally, Jamal's preschool teacher, child care provider, and kindergarten teacher, as well as his mother, collaborated in a meaningful manner to provide a smooth transition for Jamal as he left preschool and entered kindergarten. Jamal's early childhood education history provided us with an opportunity to better understand the unique issues involved in educating young children with disabilities in inclusive environments and their peer relationships in particular.

PEER RELATIONSHIPS

Practice in special education in the 1990s, particularly in early childhood special education, placed continuing emphasis on the development of peer relationships. The recognition of the importance of a variety of experiences with peers has been one of the driving forces behind the practice of inclusive education. The view of the child's social environment also has broadened, and educators realize that it includes much more than one-to-one relationships with parents, teachers, and peers (Schwartz, Staub, Gallucci, & Peck, 1995). We also know that it includes being an active and valued member of a group in settings that are inclusive and culturally relevant (Billingsley, Gallucci, Peck, Schwartz, & Staub, 1996; Harry et al., 1995).

Humans are the most profoundly social of all creatures. Our development, well-being, and happiness are dependent on the quality of our relationships with others. From individuals' earliest social exchanges as infants with caregivers (Kaye, 1982) to the uniquely human construction of webs of significance and meaning as adults (Geertz, 1973), social relationships form the crucible within which people come to know the world—each other and themselves (Bruner, 1990). With this viewpoint in mind, we next describe the range of peer social relationships that we identified for the children in our study. We then highlight the role that these social relationships played in Jamal's development and share some of the strategies that teachers and other caregivers can use to support this process.

RANGE OF RELATIONSHIPS

The notion of a range of relationships supporting the social skills development of children with disabilities emerged from analysis of qualitative data about children with moderate and severe disabilities in inclusive educational placements. During a 4-year period, as part of the Consortium for Collaborative Research on Social Relationships of Children and Youth with Diverse Abilities (Meyer et al., 1992), 35 children were observed in their school placements. In addition to conducting in-depth observations, the children's parents, teachers, and instruction assistants were interviewed. The participating students ranged in age from 3 to 12 years when the study began, and all were attending inclusive or integrated preschool, child care, or elementary school programs. We implemented inductive category formation techniques as described by Lincoln and Guba (1985) and cross-case analysis techniques as explained by Miles and Huberman (1994) to develop a conceptual framework that describes the types of outcomes we observed for children with severe disabilities who attend inclusive schools.

In coding the data that described the relationships that children with disabilities had at school and in their communities with their peers with and without disabilities, we used a theory of social competence that Gaylord-Ross and Peck (1985) proposed. This theory is based on the idea of range of reaction, which suggests that students may demonstrate different types of behaviors in different environments and that students' strengths and abilities cannot be understood without observing them in all of the different environments in which they spend time. We drew a similar conclusion when we examined the data on the relationships of the students whom we observed. We noted that it was misrepresentative to make a general statement about a student's social relationships without examining the range of relationships in which the student participated. We identified four types of relationships across the sample:

1. Play/companionship

2. Helpee

3. Helper

4. Conflictual

Each of these types of relationships offers somewhat different developmental opportunities. In the following subsections, we present examples of each of the four types of relationships for Jamal and describe some strategies that we observed teachers and caregivers use to support students' learning within each.

Play/Companionship

The *play/companionship* theme refers to relationships that revolve around the mutual enjoyment of an activity or a type of interaction. The importance of play/companionship relationships and friendships as a dimension of a satisfying quality of life is widely acknowledged (Forest, 1991; Haring, 1991; Strully & Strully, 1985). We also believe that these kinds of relationships are extremely important for children as contexts for the development of social and communication skills and as avenues for achieving membership in large social groups. This was especially the case for Jamal.

We observed over time many instances of Jamal's engaging in playful/companionable interactions with his peers at school. Jamal had good play skills and demonstrated them across many areas in the preschool classroom. He had a strong preference for dramatic play, and most of his sustained social interactions occurred in that part of the preschool classroom. The majority of his interactions were nonverbal and included babbling, which he used in a socially appropriate manner. Many of his interactions with peers at school were mediated by an adult because of his aggressive behavior, most notably his tendency to bite his peers. Jamal's mother also reported that Jamal had many of these types of playful interactions at home, while participating in the church choir, and in other church activities. It was easy to enjoy our observations of Jamal in playful/companionable interactions, as the following example reveals:

> Jamal heads to the dramatic play area that is set up like a post office. He looks through the classroom's Yellow Pages and then picks up the play telephone and starts to talk (i.e., babble) in a very dramatic way. During this time, he is looking at Becky, a classmate without disabilities. Jamal picks up some play money while he is still holding the play telephone and waves it around. He puts down the telephone and walks over to Becky and hands her the money, and Becky hands him something in return. The teacher who is observing them says, "Jamal is buying stamps." Jamal is playing in the pizza parlor (in the dramatic play area). He takes a pizza out of the oven and puts it in a pizza box. Michael, a peer who is developing typically, walks up to the counter and asks for a piece of pizza. Jamal puts a piece on a plate and hands

it to Michael. Michael touches it and says, "Ow, it's hot." Jamal walks
over to the table and takes Kerry's pizza order. He walks back to the
kitchen and starts to cook.

Jamal appeared to be developing many appropriate relationships with his
peers, at least in activities that supported his nonverbal interactions. He
was more likely to initiate interactions than to respond to his peers' interaction initiations. Although his teachers attempted to facilitate rather than
interrupt interactions, the amount of adult support that Jamal received did
appear to interfere with some of his social interactions and potential friendships. In an interview, his preschool teacher identified the need to supervise him closely because of his aggression toward peers. The desire not to
interfere with Jamal's peer relationships and the simultaneous need to create a safe environment posed a great dilemma for the teachers who worked
with Jamal in both his preschool and kindergarten classrooms.

In order to facilitate playful/companionable interactions, children with
moderate and severe disabilities and their classmates need varied, frequent,
and regular opportunities to interact with each other. In both his preschool
and kindergarten classrooms, activities and schedules were arranged throughout the day to capitalize on opportunities for interactions. The dramatic
play area was a favorite location of Jamal's, and it provided a rich opportunity for him to have interactions with his classmates.

The impact of the general emotional tone or climate of a classroom
environment on children's feelings and performance has been well documented (Moos, 1979). In climates in which children believe they are vul-
nerable to judgment, rejection, and exclusion, they are not likely to take social risks inherent in affiliating with peers who appear to be different from
themselves. In order to make the classroom a safe and supportive place for
children who are developing typically to build positive personal relationships with their peers with disabilities, it must be made a safe place for *all*
children. In Jamal's case, because of his physically aggressive behavior, feelings of safety were important factors with regard to whether children in-
teracted with Jamal. Those children who did not feel safe in Jamal's presence during his final preschool year rejected and excluded him.

Helpee

We observed numerous social relationships in our research in which a student with disabilities was consistently the recipient of assistance or support
from another child. We termed these *helpee* relationships. A large body of
literature exists on peers without disabilities providing support to students
with disabilities (e.g., Haring & Breen, 1992; Hunt, Alwell, & Goetz, 1988;
Staub & Hunt, 1993). Although we observed help being provided in natural ways, we also found many examples of help being provided that was

planned purposefully by teachers and staff. The majority of helpee interactions in which we observed Jamal engaged, however, appeared to be incidental and age-appropriate in nature:

> Jamal is getting things out of his cubby to get ready to go home for the day. He is putting things in his backpack. He tries to grab his coat and drops everything. Tyrone, who has the cubby next to Jamal's, says, "I'll help you." Tyrone helps Jamal pick up his belongings and put them in the backpack. Out at the play court, Jamal sees the bikes and wagons and runs toward them. He climbs in the wagon and communicates by using gestures and vocal approximation, "Go, go, go." Tyrone rides by on a bike, then stops and pulls the wagon around the yard. Jamal smiles, laughs, and vocalizes to Tyrone.

We believe that these examples reflect the developmental differences between the concept of *help* at the preschool level versus *helping* at the elementary and secondary levels. Many young children have a natural inclination to help their peers, usually in a nondiscriminatory fashion. Too often in upper elementary and secondary school situations, help can lead to "unhelpful help." Peers without disabilities are sometimes unaware of the needs of students with disabilities to do things for themselves and may rush in to help in ways that interfere with learning. Older children who are in helping relationships with peers who have disabilities should receive direct guidance and support from teachers in making judgments about when help is needed and when it is not. Teachers of children at all ages can support helpee relationships by incorporating helping rules (Janney & Snell, 1996). These types of rules require children to seek out each other for help instead of going to an adult first. We have noticed a tremendous difference between classrooms in which relationships are supported planfully by adults and those in which children are left to figure out when and how to help.

In a teacher interview, Jamal's teacher talked about the types of important outcomes that are facilitated when children help each other in supportive ways in her classroom. She believed that it was especially important for children to be willing and able to help Jamal, given that he was occasionally aggressive toward his peers. As Jamal's preschool teacher pointed out, it is helpful to discuss the important learning opportunities that are available for all children in inclusive classrooms (Staub, 1996).

Helper

Helper relationships are relationships and interactions in which the student with disabilities provides support or assistance to another child. This type of relationship is relatively unusual for children with disabilities—an observation that we find distressing. Although Jamal seemed willing and able to help others, this category was not well represented in his data. Most of Jamal's helping interactions were with younger children, children with disabilities, and teachers or were attempts to help or influence the entire class, as in the following example:

> It is opening circle at preschool. Children are called up one at a time to pick an animal for the opening song. The teacher calls on Sally, a child with a disability who is sitting next to Jamal. She does not respond. After a few seconds, Jamal nudges her, then she stands up and takes her turn. The children are at the snack table, and they are celebrating Steve's fourth birthday. The teacher passes out birthday hats.
>
> They turn out the lights and light the birthday candles. Jamal jumps up and turns out the light in the bathroom that is adjacent to the classroom, then he returns to his seat. Everyone sings "Happy Birthday." Steve blows out the birthday candles. Jamal jumps up and attempts to turn on the lights. He cannot reach the switch. The teacher turns on the lights and tells Jamal to sit down.

Jamal's competence in negotiating his environment is evident when examining his helping examples. He knows who needs to be where and when they need to be there and is willing to share this information. These examples provide evidence of the importance of multi-age classrooms for children with diverse abilities. If Jamal were in a classroom in which all of the children were his own age or in a classroom with only other children with disabilities, he might not have had the opportunity to help his peers as highlighted in the previous example. Teachers and other adults may need to plan opportunities for children with disabilities to help others. There are many useful contexts in which children with disabilities can develop relationships in which they are the helpers. In our experience, however, adults seldom recognize the possibility and value of such relationships.

Conflictual

Students with moderate and severe disabilities, like their peers, have occasional conflicts with others. We observed, in a few instances, relationships in which there was repeated verbal or physical contact between the same two children. We termed such relationships *conflictual* or *adversarial*. In younger children, we found that conflicts arose over toys or games, especially within unstructured situations such as free time or choice time.

We found some examples of Jamal engaging in conflictual interactions. It is important to remember that Jamal had a history of aggression (e.g., biting) that at one point was quite severe. Because of this behavior, Jamal's teachers were not willing to let any potential conflictual situation progress too far without adult mediation. Some examples in this category of relationships follow:

It is opening circle in Jamal's preschool classroom, and Jamal is sitting next to Larry, who is wearing a visor. Jamal takes the visor from Larry. Larry says, "Give it back." Jamal ignores him and puts the visor on. A teacher mediates and tells Jamal to give the visor back to Larry. He does, and Larry gets up and puts the visor in his cubby.

It is snacktime, and Jamal is at a table with a teacher and three other children, including Abby, who is sitting next to him. The teacher tells Jamal that his mom will be happy that he is having a good day. Jamal gets up and does a little dance. Then Abby gets up and imitates Jamal's dance. Jamal becomes agitated and begins to demonstrate behaviors that are antecedents to aggression. The teacher says, "Abby is imitating your dance because she likes it." Jamal calms down and gets up and dances, then sits down and eats more of his snack.

Jamal's conflicts and aggression continued to interfere with his interactions and peer relationships. In the preceding examples, teacher mediation resulted in a calm ending; however, there are other examples in the data of Jamal's biting a peer or of peers' avoiding Jamal for a few days after an aggressive episode. Jamal, like other children who demonstrate such behavior, must be supported to communicate in a functionally equivalent but nonthreatening way to facilitate improved social relationships. A particularly problematic issue that we observed in our research involved the reluctance of many students without disabilities to provide direct and honest feedback to their peers with disabilities about undesirable or inappropriate behavior. Although many situations call for tolerance, understanding, and accommodation in supporting students with disabilities, in many situations tolerance may be viewed as a hindrance. Teachers have an important role to play in teaching children who do not have disabilities how to be honest and direct with their peers with disabilities. In many cases, this role involves helping students who are developing typically to appreciate the importance of their feedback in the learning process of their peers with disabilities.

UNDERSTANDING INCLUSION
AT THE PRESCHOOL LEVEL: HISTORY AND ISSUES

Since enactment of the Individuals with Disabilities Education Act (IDEA) Amendments of 1991 (PL 102-119), public schools have been required by law to provide a free appropriate public education (FAPE) to children with disabilities beginning at age 3 years, although all states extend these services to children from birth. The rationale for providing an inclusive education for young children with disabilities follows the same reasoning as that for older children with disabilities. First, the least restrictive environment (LRE) provision of the Individuals with Disabilities Education Act (IDEA)

Amendments of 1997 (PL 105-17) ensures that children with disabilities are educated alongside their age peers without disabilities to the greatest extent possible. Second, access to the general education curriculum and inclusion in classrooms with their peers without disabilities has proved to offer learning opportunities that do not exist in special education classes containing only children with disabilities (Bricker, 1995). Finally, many educators and families believe that educating children with disabilities in their community schools and neighborhoods is the ethical response to providing *all* children with a FAPE.

A single definition of *inclusion* within an early childhood context has yet to be provided. Our colleagues at the Early Childhood Research Institute on Inclusion, however, have offered a working definition that includes several features (cf. Odom et al., 1996). First, inclusion is the active participation in the same environment of young children with disabilities and children who are developing typically (e.g., Head Start programs, public and private preschools, child care programs, community groups). Second, services are provided to support the child in accomplishing the goals established as part of his or her individualized family service plan (IFSP) or individualized education program (IEP). Third, services are provided collaboratively by professionals from various disciplines (e.g., early childhood teachers, special education teachers, speech-language pathologists, family resource personnel). Fourth, evaluation of the effects of the inclusion program on children with disabilities is an ongoing activity of the IFSP or IEP team. Finally, the definition of *inclusion* extends beyond the school system to include the participation of young children with disabilities in family events and rituals and in community activities and groups (e.g., church activities, festivals, playgroups).

The inclusion of preschool children with disabilities parallels the inclusion of children with disabilities at the elementary and secondary levels in many ways; however, unique issues surround the inclusion of young children with disabilities:

1. Organizational structures: What is the natural setting?
2. Teachers' preparation, certification, and salaries: What is equitable?
3. Children's development, learning objectives, and teaching practices: What is developmentally appropriate?

Organizational Structures: What Is the Natural Setting?

When discussing inclusion at the elementary school level, an understanding of what *inclusion* means is fairly straightforward: a public school building in which children with disabilities spend all or most of their day in general education classrooms and settings. A range of preschool programs that can be characterized as inclusive may exist in a child's community and/or public school, however.

In an attempt to identify the range of preschool inclusion programs that may exist in a community and/or a public school, researchers conducted a study to establish an initial descriptive categorization of programs for preschool children (Odom et al., 1999). These authors found that inclusive classrooms for young children with special needs exist within a variety of organizational contexts. Indeed, one can describe a variety of inclusive placements that Jamal attended, including a public university preschool center, private child care at the care provider's location, private in-home child care, a blended public kindergarten class, and the church choir.

According to Odom and colleagues (1999), viewing inclusion from an organizational perspective provides a framework for examining policies that underlie the creation and maintenance of inclusive programs. Consequently, factors associated with the organizational context may serve as barriers to and facilitators of inclusion. When determining the best placement for a young child with special needs, one of the many considerations should be the organizational context and an analysis of the facilitators and barriers that exist within it.

Teachers' Preparation, Certification, and Salaries: What Is Equitable?

Public and many private school systems require that teachers meet certification standards that are established by their states. These standards usually include specialized coursework, a college degree, and supervised practicum or student teaching experiences (Odom et al., 1996). Staff at many private child care programs and even in preschools, however, are not required to be certified. In these programs, staff may have significantly less college preparation, with their training more likely to have been received in high school programs, community colleges, or child development associate programs such as Head Start (Wolery et al., 1994). In addition to differences in professional preparation, teachers in public schools receive higher salaries than teachers in private preschools and other programs such as Head Start. Unfortunately, these discrepancies mean not only that the quality of services for young children with disabilities varies greatly but also that training and salary differences sometimes lead to conflicts when early childhood education teachers and early childhood special education teachers collaborate.

Although Jamal and his family were fortunate to have access to high-quality early childhood education offered through a public university center, Jamal attended the infants and toddlers and preschool programs on a part-time basis. The rest of his day was spent first in a private home with a child care provider and later in a private child care center. Both of these placements were staffed by motivated, caring people; but children like Jamal are just as likely to attend a poorly run, poorly prepared program without the requisite motivation or expertise to handle severe behavior problems and learning needs such as those that Jamal experienced.

Children's Development, Learning Objectives, and Teaching Practices: What Is Developmentally Appropriate?

Another issue that surrounds serving the needs of young children with disabilities is related to providing learning opportunities that are developmentally appropriate. For preschool-age children with and without disabilities, educational objectives are most often referenced to language or cognitive development, social or motor development, or adaptive behavior (Odom et al., 1996). These developmental skills serve as the foundation for later learning in elementary and high school classes. Furthermore, teachers must enter the preschool environment with a thorough understanding of child development to support the inclusion of diverse learners (Grenot-Scheyer, Schwartz, & Meyer, 1997).

Teaching practices for preschool-age children also are different from those commonly used when teaching older children. For example, active engagement as compared with time on task (traditionally associated with measures used with older children) is a concept derived from classic child development theories that emphasize the importance of learning by doing in meaningful contexts (Tharp & Gallimore, 1988). Instruction strategies for young children encourage child-initiated learning as well as active engagement, whereas instruction at the elementary and high school levels is more likely to be teacher-directed (Wolery & Bredekamp, 1994).

Ms. B, Jamal's kindergarten teacher, struggled with her conflicting feelings regarding how best to support Jamal's educational experience. Her struggle centered on her belief that her expectations for Jamal were not developmentally appropriate. In some regards, she was operating under the skills-deficit model of learning. That is, the teacher teaches the child the prerequisite skills first before moving to higher-level tasks and learning. Our thinking today regarding recommended practices for young children, however, emphasizes providing appropriate supports and modifications to optimize the child's participation and learning. Furthermore, the range of support services and their intensity vary across children and settings, depending on individual students' needs.

CONCLUSIONS

Jamal's story provides us with important lessons about including young children with disabilities in early childhood and kindergarten programs. One of the ways in which Jamal's placement history differs from that of other children who are described in this book is that, with the exception of his kindergarten year, Jamal did not attend school in his community. In fact, the issue of neighborhood schools for young children is often moot. Many preschool-age children with or without disabilities attend child care and education settings that are not in their neighborhoods. They may attend schools that are closer to their parents' workplaces, church-sponsored preschools, or university-based preschools such as the one that Jamal attended. Inclusion apparently is not just a school issue but a community issue as well.

Another issue that is unique to preschools is related to the type of program that a child attends—namely, child care versus therapeutic versus preacademic. For many families, the child care issue is paramount, so parents may be more willing to have their child placed in a program that offers extended child care hours and flexible times as opposed to a program that is run only part time. Different types of programs typically employ staff with different levels of training. For example, child care providers generally have high school diplomas, early childhood teachers usually must have at least an associate's degree, and early childhood special education teachers need at least a bachelor's degree as well as teacher certification.

There are also issues related to the length of a program a child attends. In public elementary and secondary schools, the law requires a minimum and fairly standard number of hours that students must be served each year. In preschool programs, however, the number of hours of services provided to a child can vary from 2 hours per day, 3 days per week to a full-time placement of 6 hours per day, 5 days per week. This raises further questions regarding minimum hours of services, who pays for services that go beyond the minimum required hours, and who has the authority to make these decisions.

These issues will continue to be addressed and no doubt debated for many years to come. Given what is known about the importance of early intervention for young children with disabilities, however, the challenges that educators face in providing a quality early childhood program to all children are not nearly as great as the potential benefits for the children.

DISCUSSION QUESTIONS

1. Which settings in your community could provide inclusive early childhood programs?

2. How do the contextual features of the different settings affect the program for individual children?

3. What do you think are the most important domains of instruction for young children with disabilities?

4. Do the most important domains of instruction for young children with disabilities change as these children enter elementary school? If so, how?

5. Which types of interventions can be created to support the range of relationships described in this chapter for young children such as Jamal?

6. How can interventions address Jamal's aggressive behaviors as well as his need to develop appropriate social relationships?

4

Charlotte's Story

Getting Better, Happy Day, Problems Again!

Deborah L. Hedeen,
Barbara J. Ayres, and Angie Tate

It is the first day of school, and Angie wakes her three children in time for them to eat breakfast and get ready for school. There is excitement in their home as each child begins a new routine that will last for the next 9 months. Kiefer, who is beginning the fourth grade, is distracted by his new, small stuffed-toy animals. Gus is lying on the floor, mesmerized by his favorite cartoon show on the television. He will be attending afternoon kindergarten, so there is no pressure on Gus to hustle like his siblings. Not far from Gus in the room, Charlotte is wrapped in a quilt, sitting on the floor between the couch and the wall as she glances at the television while grabbing a handful of cereal from the bowl on the coffee table. Charlotte is beginning the second grade this year.

For most families, children's getting ready for school is as natural a part of every morning as their attending neighborhood schools. Angie's family, however, is experiencing some apprehension because they have asked that Charlotte be placed in a second-grade classroom with her peers. For other second-graders, this request would not be challenged; but in Charlotte's situation, because of her diagnosis of autism and because of some concerns of first-grade teachers, her placement is being questioned.

This chapter tells the story of Charlotte as she experiences the joys and challenges of autism and as her family works continually to create positive opportunities for Charlotte at home and at school. The chapter describes Charlotte and her education experiences from preschool through the second grade. Charlotte's family, friends, and educators have struggled with her behavior problems over the years, but they also have identified many of her strengths and aspects of her learning style that continually are being incorporated into a positive behavioral support plan. The support provided for Charlotte has evolved, which has been helpful in continuing effective strategies and discontinuing unsuccessful ones. No set plan works for all students, so it is important to try a variety of strategies until the right blend is created. Charlotte's behavioral support plan, which is detailed in this chapter, includes strategies for preventing problems whenever possible, teaching new positive skills, and responding to behavioral challenges in supportive ways. The chapter concludes with a description of the continuing challenges that Charlotte's parents face as they strive to create an enviable life for their daughter (Turnbull & Turnbull, 1998).

The information in this chapter comes from the collaborative efforts of the first and third authors, along with other family members and educators who have worked with Charlotte over the years. Because of apprehension of school staff regarding Charlotte's second-grade placement, Charlotte's family requested consultative support from the first author, who taught at a university in the same state, to assist with Charlotte's transition from first to second grade. After visiting the school briefly in the spring of Charlotte's first-grade year to plan for the transition, the consultant visited the school monthly during Charlotte's second-grade year to observe Charlotte's participation and to recommend and model alternative strategies. Observational notes were collected to develop additional techniques and interventions to assist with Charlotte's participation during classroom activities and increase her positive interactions with classmates and adults. In addition, videotaping was used as a strategy to provide opportunities for problem-solving challenging situations, and photographs were taken to document the strategies that were successful with Charlotte.

MEET CHARLOTTE

Charlotte is the second-born of three children in her family. She enjoys downhill skiing, hiking, boating, tandem bike riding, and rafting with her family. She also takes a ballet class and spends her free time playing computer games, jumping on the trampoline, and watching Disney movies. At times, Charlotte's autism as well as her behaviors have been misunderstood. Charlotte is often calm and happy, but her vocal loudness and quick movements can surprise people. Also on a few occasions, Charlotte has hit, grabbed, or bit adults who were working with her. Because Charlotte is nonverbal, expressing her needs and wants to others can be frustrating for her. The following sections describe Charlotte, starting with her early years as described by her mother (the third author of this chapter), detail her educational experiences during the first and second grades, and summarize some of the key features of Charlotte's learning style.

Early Years

As an infant, Charlotte rarely cried for attention, disliked being held, would not eat typical baby food, and appeared to be deaf. By 16 months of age, she had started private speech-language therapy and was enrolled in a preschool program at a child development center. When Charlotte was age 22 months, a team at the center diagnosed her as having pervasive developmental disorder (PDD). At 3 years of age, Charlotte underwent numerous evaluations conducted by psychologists, psychiatrists, and a pediatric neurologist.

During the same period, Charlotte received 10 days of intensive auditory integration training (Rimland & Edelson, 1995), which did not seem to affect or change her hearing ability or behavior. She also began an applied behavior analysis program (Lovaas, 1980) in a preschool program in which she received her education until she reached age 6 years. She was successful at discrete trial programs that involved matching, discriminating, and identifying objects and words. At age 6, Charlotte received a language and cognitive development assessment in Massachusetts (Miller & Eller-Miller, 1989). She was also introduced to the Picture Exchange Communication System (PECS) (Bondy & Frost, 1994) and quickly learned the program, which involves exchanging picture sentence strips for items. Charlotte continues to use PECS as a mode of communication in order to make requests and choices.

First Grade

Charlotte's family lives in the largest school district in a rural state. The district serves 27,000 students and employs more than 3,200 people. There are 34 elementary schools within the district. The neighborhood elementary school served 850 students at the time of Charlotte's initial enrollment. Charlotte's parents, Phil and Angie, did not know of any other children with severe disabilities within the district who were members of general education classrooms, but they wanted to give Charlotte the opportunity to attend her neighborhood school.

They met with the school district professionals several months prior to Charlotte's arrival in public school and immediately were told of other schools within the district that were considered more appropriate for Charlotte. After all of the hard work that Charlotte and her family had done in the early years, they wanted more than a classroom designed specifically for students with severe disabilities. Phil and Angie had attended state conferences that addressed inclusive education, and, from the information they had gleaned during the conference presentations, they believed that Charlotte's attending her neighborhood school was crucial to her further development.

Charlotte started attending her neighborhood school midway through her first-grade year. Her initial placement in the school was in a hallway where deliveries were made to the cafeteria. Charlotte started her day working at a desk in the hallway and ended the day in the first-grade classroom with her age peers. This is not exactly how the family had envisioned an inclusive placement, but they were pleased that at least Charlotte was enrolled in her neighborhood school.

Although the first-grade teacher had previous experience in special education, the paraeducator, who spent the majority of her time with Charlotte, had no formal training. The transition from a structured preschool program to her home school proved to be quite difficult for Charlotte. Within the first few months, she pulled the fire alarm twice, bit the paraeducator (a behavior that Charlotte had not displayed previously), and vocalized loudly in the first-grade classroom until she was physically removed. A variety of behavioral strategies (e.g., time-out, physical restraint, spraying Charlotte in the face with water) were used in an attempt to decrease Charlotte's inappropriate behaviors. The family was concerned about the aversive techniques that were being used and knew that school staff would need additional support and training in order for Charlotte to be successful. They believed that Charlotte's behaviors were a means of communicating and that Charlotte would need to learn alternative behaviors (Donnellan, Mirenda, Mesaros, & Fassbender, 1984; Evans & Meyer, 1985). At the end of Charlotte's first-grade year, the team was frustrated and angry, believing that they had been unsuccessful. Charlotte's family was still adamant that she should have the opportunity to learn alongside her peers without disabilities in her neighborhood school.

Second Grade

Many changes were made during Charlotte's second-grade year. One of these changes was that Charlotte would attend the second grade all day rather than sit in the hallway as she had for part of the day in the first grade. The education team had a fresh start, with all on the team except for the speech-language pathologist being new members. The new members included the principal, a special education teacher, a second-grade teacher, two half-time paraeducators, and the university consultant. Charlotte's second-grade class of 24 students included only three students from her first-grade class. The classroom was in a new location, and Charlotte needed to learn many new routines.

Even though there was a feeling of excitement about the opportunity to create a successful education program for Charlotte, concerns still were expressed at the school regarding her placement. Within 2 months of entering second grade, Charlotte's behavior problems had become quite intense. Each morning, whenever Charlotte said "Crackers," the paraeducator offered Charlotte a choice of snacks from her backpack. Once the snacks were gone, the paraeducator would show Charlotte the empty backpack, and Charlotte immediately would vocalize loudly, cry, and grab or hit the paraeducator. By 11:00 A.M. each day, Angie would receive a telephone call from the school asking her to pick up Charlotte because Charlotte was having a bad day. Charlotte also was struggling with other aspects of the school day: disconnecting from the adults and her classmates and responding with vocal and physical opposition to their efforts to include her in activities. Charlotte was confused, disgruntled, and unhappy for much of the time she was in school.

This is where Charlotte's story really begins. What did we know about Charlotte and her strengths? Under what conditions was Charlotte most successful in her learning? What was Charlotte trying to accomplish through her challenging behaviors? How could we take the answers to these questions and incorporate them into a positive behavioral support plan that would focus on preventing problems whenever possible, teaching new skills, and responding in supportive ways when Charlotte was struggling? The following sections describe Charlotte's learning style, outline steps that were taken to connect Charlotte with her peers, and detail the positive behavioral support plan that was created for Charlotte in the second grade.

CHARLOTTE'S LEARNING STYLE

Through careful observation of Charlotte when she was alone and/or interacting with others, the education team discovered many aspects of her learning style. The better people understood how Charlotte learned, the more conscious they became of addressing her needs within activities and routines. As the adults and students supporting Charlotte acknowledged her learning style, Charlotte became increasingly successful and comfortable in the inclusive second-grade classroom. In addition, these aspects of her learning style were incorporated into the positive behavioral support plan through strategies that were used for prevention, teaching, and responding.

One important aspect of Charlotte's learning style is that she is a visual learner. Charlotte learns best when visual and verbal directions are used simultaneously. She is also more successful at performing a task when she has an opportunity to observe the sequence of steps before being asked to demonstrate the skill. Charlotte likes the predictability of routines and wants to be informed of and prepared for any changes. In addition, she appreciates having breaks between activities throughout her day. Most important, she likes having a task broken up into manageable steps so that she can perform parts of the task successfully before she is required to complete it.

A wonderful example of Charlotte's learning style occurred when her father taught her how to downhill ski. He drove Charlotte to the top of the mountain, and they looked out at the ski area while sitting in the car. Charlotte was upset about being there, so they stayed for a few minutes and then went home. The next time, they stayed a bit longer while Charlotte watched some skiers. Each trip to the ski area involved adding one more step in learning to ski: getting out of the car briefly, walking in ski boots, wearing boots and skis, moving short distances on skis, and finally skiing long distances. As each step was added, Charlotte would become slightly upset because it represented a new experience. Once the routine became familiar to Charlotte, however, she would smile and vocalize when the family arrived at the ski area.

Charlotte also requires a great deal of movement within her day. It is difficult for her to sit in one place for any length of time, and she sometimes prefers to stand up rather than sit in a chair or to sit in a beanbag chair instead of in her classroom chair. In addition, Charlotte does not always look directly at the person to whom she is supposed to be attending (e.g., teacher, paraeducator, mother, peer). She is more likely to glance at the person briefly and then look away, but that does not mean that she is not attending to what the person is saying or doing.

TEACHING OTHER STUDENTS ABOUT CHARLOTTE

Because only three of Charlotte's first-grade classmates were also in her second-grade class, it was necessary to share information with the other second-grade students about Charlotte's interests, communication skills, and behaviors. Some students were curious about Charlotte's participation in second grade, and therefore class discussions helped to answer questions and problem-solve situations that were unique to Charlotte's learning style. The following sections describe strategies that were used to share information with students, problem-solve behavioral concerns through class meetings, and create positive interactions between Charlotte and her peers.

Sharing Information with Students

After school started in September and classroom routines had been established, Charlotte's mother, Angie, read the book *Feeling Left Out* (Petty & Firmin, 1991) to the second graders. (Each year Charlotte's mother selected a story to read to Charlotte's class that focused on including children with differences in activities.) The class had a discussion about how it would feel to be left out and brainstormed ideas to figure out how they could include their classmates during class activities and other school events. Angie then focused the discussion on autism and how specific characteristics of autism related to Charlotte. The students asked Angie a variety of questions: How can we talk to Charlotte if we call her at home? What does it mean when she makes certain noises? Why can't she talk? Why does she move her finger in circles in the air? Charlotte was not present in the classroom during this discussion, because the adults believed that the students would speak more freely if Charlotte were not there and that Charlotte might become anxious while students asked questions about her.

Angie also shared with the students a photo collage of Charlotte participating in a number of her favorite activities. The photographs showed her downhill skiing, jumping on a trampoline, swimming, and horseback riding. Because it was difficult for Charlotte to communicate her interests with her classmates, the photo collage clearly showed her many abilities beyond the classroom. Many classrooms require students to be able to sit for long periods of time, remain quiet and attentive while the teacher is talking, and complete detailed work assignments. Because these are not easy tasks for Charlotte, she was at risk of being viewed as incompetent by her classmates. It was necessary for students to understand all aspects of Charlotte's life so that she would be valued as a class member.

Class Meetings

It was important to have additional meetings with the students in Charlotte's class so that they could understand the meaning of some of her behaviors. The first behavior that needed to be explained was Charlotte's occasional vocal loudness. When students were asked about this, they could identify two types of loud sounds that Charlotte made. One sound was a "happy" sound, and they gave examples of occasions when they heard her making that sound. The second sound was a "mad" sound, and they knew that she made that sound when she was frustrated or did not want to do something. One student said, "I'd make that sound, too, if I couldn't talk."

Another issue that needed to be addressed during a class meeting had to do with the few instances when Charlotte slapped students in the face. Many times during the day, students sat huddled together on the floor to hear directions from the teacher for the next assignment. A few students sat very close to Charlotte, and sometimes a classmate put her arm around Charlotte's shoulders. Usually, Charlotte looked at her classmate and smiled, then looked at the teacher while the teacher was talking. The next thing that Charlotte would do was move her head in the opposite direction of the classmate and make a quiet sound. She would make this motion a few more times, then she would slap the classmate on the cheek. The classmate would then quickly remove his or her arm from around Charlotte's shoulders and look at Charlotte with surprise.

The students later were asked why they thought Charlotte had slapped one of her classmates in the face. At first, they were not sure; but after further problem solving and reminders about Charlotte's movements and vocal sounds before the slap, they were able to figure out that she probably was bothered by her classmate's arm around her shoulders. The classmate then said, "But she smiled when I put my arm around her." It was explained that Charlotte probably did like the arm around her shoulders, but only for a little squeeze, and then it would be important to give her some space so that she was free to move around. Once students started paying closer attention to Charlotte's body movements and vocal sounds, Charlotte's slapping behavior decreased. The students were problem solving and taking responsibility for interpreting Charlotte's behavior and responding by giving her more physical space.

Through class meetings, students also were taught how to involve Charlotte in activities. For example, each time students left the classroom, Charlotte ran halfway down the hall to get a drink at the water fountain. Because the water fountain was in the opposite direction of where the class was going, Charlotte always was left walking by herself to music, gym, or lunch. Through brainstorming with the students, it was decided that Charlotte's partner would wait right outside the classroom for her or would go with her to get a drink of water. Students also were shown how to take a picture symbol of the class's next activity to Charlotte so that she could see visually and understand what would happen next.

It was critical to include students in class meetings because, regardless of whether Charlotte's concerns were discussed, students still were aware of the issues and were coming to their own conclusions about Charlotte's behaviors. A proactive approach to involving students as team members was a respectful way of valuing the students' perspectives and inviting them into Charlotte's life.

Creating and Supporting Positive Interactions with Peers

It was evident that students wanted to interact with Charlotte. Charlotte's family, however, was concerned that because Charlotte could not talk and thus could not initiate interactions with her peers, it would be difficult for her to develop friendships. To assist Charlotte in establishing friendships, a formal process was conducted with all of the students in her class. During the second month of school, Charlotte's second-grade class participated in a Circle of Friends meeting (Forest & Lusthaus, 1989). At the beginning of the meeting, students described activities that they enjoyed doing with their friends. The following activities were listed on the chalkboard: playing at a friend's house, going to birthday parties, watching videotapes, talking on the telephone, eating lunch together at school, and playing outdoor sports.

As part of the Circle of Friends process, students listed the names of people who were important in their lives based on the relationships that they had with these people (e.g., family members, close friends, other friends, people from organizations, service providers). The students were encouraged to talk about how they made close friends and were asked to consider that Charlotte, their classmate who could not talk, displayed some behaviors that might cause her to have difficulty with initiating friendly contacts with others. Four students had identified Charlotte as a friend, and additional students asked to be included in Charlotte's circle of friends. Further discussion ensued about students' remembering to include Charlotte as they planned to do the activities that were listed on the chalkboard.

The Circle of Friends activity made students more aware of Charlotte, and they began including her during activities that took place at school (e.g., eating lunch, playing at recess, choosing Charlotte as a partner). Charlotte was invited to many of her classmates' birthday parties, and her own birthday party was well attended. Despite these structured and predictable routines being in place, spontaneous elements of friendship such as stopping to visit a friend at home, calling a friend on the telephone, and inviting a friend for lunch were limited. It is possible that one formal meeting to address Charlotte's circle of friends was not enough to assist with creating ongoing friendships for her that would be generalized into her home life. Additional meetings with students were planned, but the educators found it difficult to maintain the momentum that had been initiated at the first meeting. This area needs to be addressed more carefully as the team plans for Charlotte's inclusion in third grade (Grenot-Scheyer, Harry, Park, Schwartz, & Meyer, 1998).

POSITIVE BEHAVIORAL SUPPORTS

Because Charlotte's behaviors were placing her at risk of being removed from her neighborhood school, it was imperative to create a positive behavioral support plan that not only would be used when Charlotte was having difficulties but also would be the foundation for developing her education program (Evans & Meyer, 1985; Hedeen, Ayres, Meyer, & Waite, 1996). The purpose of the positive behavioral support plan was to identify ways to prevent problems from occurring, teach Charlotte new behaviors that would assist in her successful participation with others and in activities, and respond to her behaviors in supportive ways (Ayres & Hedeen, 1997; Janney et al., 1989; Topper, Williams, Leo, Hamilton, & Fox, 1994; see Figure 1 on pp. 58–59). The plan provided a way for all team members to be consistent with their proactive procedures so that routines became predictable and safe for Charlotte and so that she could see the inherent value of interacting with others (McGee, Menousek, & Hobbs, 1987).

A strong component of the positive behavioral support plan for Charlotte was the use of visual strategies. Gray (1995) and Hodgdon (1996) reported that students are more likely to follow routines and transitions when verbal directions are paired with visual representations such as picture symbols, words, or objects. Individuals with autism who have written stories about their lives have shared that sometimes so much is going on in the environment that it is difficult to filter out the verbal directions that they are asked to follow (Grandin, 1995; Williams, 1992).

Picture and word symbols helped to cue Charlotte visually so that she could have greater success during daily routines and activities. They provided visual cues for Charlotte when she was having difficulty with focusing on a task, following directions, or performing the actions required during a routine. The following sections provide examples of how visual strategies, coupled with other proactive supports, were incorporated into a prevent–teach–respond format to facilitate Charlotte's participation in second-grade routines and increase her positive interactions with peers.

Preventing Challenging Behavior

Prevention consists of minimizing the occurrence of challenging behaviors whenever possible. It may be necessary to change the environment or the materials in the environment. The steps of the routine or the people in the routine may need to be changed. These subtle differences can prevent the behavior from occurring so that the student experiences successful interactions and participation. Through preventive efforts, attention is focused on creating a positive learning environment rather than on waiting for the student's behavior to occur and then responding to it. The examples described in the following subsections were used on a daily basis to assist Charlotte with following the steps of an activity, making the transition from one activity to another, increasing movement within routines, and making active choices (see Figure 1, "Prevent" column).

Visual Strategies   A picture schedule was used to assist Charlotte with knowing the sequence of events (e.g., math, reading, music, lunch) that would take place during the school day (Hodgdon, 1996; McClannahan & Krantz, 1999). Prior to establishing a picture schedule for Charlotte, she was not as successful in following typical routines and directions with only verbal cues. The horizontal schedule (18 inches by 3 inches) was taped across the top of Charlotte's desk. The picture symbols, which were laminated black-and-white line drawings (1 inch by 1 inch), were attached to the schedule with Velcro and placed in sequence from left to right to reflect the daily classroom routine (see Figure 2). Mayer-Johnson's (1981) Picture Communication Symbols, which are available in book form or in software format, were used as the drawings for the picture schedule.

When Charlotte was ready to engage in an activity, she moved the picture symbol to the "Now" box on the lefthand side of the schedule. When the activity was completed, Charlotte placed the picture symbol in an envelope attached to the side of her desk. Once Charlotte was comfortable with her desk schedule, a laminated paper clock face was added to the lefthand corner of the schedule. The paraeducator asked Charlotte to look at the clock on the wall in the classroom and then draw the hands on the clock face on her desk. This was a functional way to integrate teaching Charlotte about time with natural teaching opportunities during the daily routine.

Whenever new strategies were added to Charlotte's routine, the materials were introduced in a step-by-step process. For example, when the clock was first introduced, the paraeducator pointed to the classroom clock and then drew the hands on the clock. Charlotte was allowed to watch the new routine for a few days before she was asked to participate. Charlotte was less frustrated and more willing to participate when the adults in the classroom gradually introduced new routines by modeling them first.

A portable schedule was used when Charlotte left the classroom, because it provided easy access to the pictures depicting upcoming

Name: Charlotte

Behaviors: Using loud voice, pinching, hitting, biting

Purposes:
1. Frustrated because she cannot communicate needs, wants, or ideas.
2. The routine has changed without notice or it is difficult to wait.
3. Escape/avoidance—would prefer not to participate or would like to take a break.

Prevent	Teach	Respond
Use a picture schedule to help Charlotte know plan for the day, and carry portable schedules in school.	Have Charlotte indicate her need to take a break before she becomes anxious or frustrated and then return to complete work.	Use a calm voice while showing picture and/or word cards to explain routine or task.
Provide mini-schedules for content area activities to assist Charlotte with focusing on and completing tasks.	Teach Charlotte to use picture symbols to make choices among desired activities, objects, or lunch options.	Provide time for Charlotte to respond. She may need a moment to focus, think, and visually scan the materials and directions.
Consistently carry and use schedules because we cannot predict when Charlotte will become frustrated or confused by routine or activity.	Have Charlotte participate in small and large group activities with curricular modifications when necessary.	When Charlotte begins to initiate a response, provide verbal praise and positive facial expression.
Balance schedule with seatwork and active activities (go for a walk, deliver mail, use computer, and movement activities).	Teach Charlotte to initiate needs, wants, and interactions by selecting pictures and giving to adult/student or moving pictures on schedule to "now" spot and then into "done" bag.	Offer Charlotte an option of where to work when she is starting to get agitated (table in back of classroom, beanbag chair, or table between classrooms).
Recognize when Charlotte is becoming anxious (unhappy sounds or movement) so that choices can be provided in order to understand her need.	Have Charlotte participate in turn-taking activities with peers that will teach Charlotte to wait (standing in line for drinking fountain, slide, or getting on school bus).	When Charlotte is frustrated, use materials that are predictable and comforting (Disney books, stickers, counting cards).

Prevent	Teach	Respond
Use social stories to introduce new events and activities or a change in routine (substitute, recess bells). Provide toys (little stuffed animals) as a way to interrupt routine of eating crackers. Establish predictable routines to begin and end each day. Allow Charlotte to observe new routines to begin and end each day. Allow Charlotte to observe new routines before participating while adult models the steps.	Teach Charlotte to use schedules and social stories. Have Charlotte model peer behavior for following school rules and routines (getting in line, sitting at desk, circle time). Teach Charlotte the difference between work time and free time. Teach Charlotte to use wait cards and visual time keepers.	If verbal cues are not working, guide Charlotte with light assistance to area or provide gestures by pointing to object. Bring materials to Charlotte to get her interested before moving to the activity. Take short breaks by walking around classroom and then returning to work. Ignore the behavior while redirecting to activity and then provide reward (positive gestures and feedback) for any attempts at participation.

Figure 1. Charlotte's positive behavioral support plan.

NOW

Figure 2. Charlotte's picture schedule. (The Picture Communication Symbols ©
1981-2000 Mayer-Johnson Co. are used with permission.)

activities. The paraeducator carried the portable schedule at first, and
eventually Charlotte was responsible for carrying the schedule. The
portable vertical schedule (2 inches by 6 inches) had four picture
symbols attached to the card with Velcro. These picture symbols were
of the next three or four activities that would occur during the day.
For example, the class would attend music class, get books at the library, take a bathroom break, and return to class. The picture symbols
for MUSIC, BOOK, BATHROOM, and CLASSROOM were attached to the portable schedule. When Charlotte completed one of the activities, she
removed the picture symbol and placed it on the back of the card.

Another type of schedule that was used during the day was a
minischedule (Hodgdon, 1996). The minischedule was similar to the
portable vertical schedule in size but was used for a different purpose. The minischedule had three or four picture symbols that represented specific activities within the lesson. The paraeducator would
check the teacher's lesson book in order to determine which picture
symbols would be used on the minischedule. For example, the following activities were listed for the reading lesson: Write words for
the story on the chalkboard, students read silently at their desks, students complete a worksheet, and group discusses what students have
read. Those four activities were then represented by the following
picture symbols: CHALKBOARD, STORY, WORK SHEET, and GROUP TALK (see
Figure 3). Each picture symbol represented time as well. Because
each part of the lesson lasted about 10 minutes, the four pictures
equaled approximately 40 minutes. The sequence of pictures provided Charlotte with an easy way to understand which tasks needed to
be completed before she could take a break. As each activity was
completed, the corresponding picture symbol was removed and
placed on the back of the card, and a smiling face picture was added
to the minischedule to provide Charlotte with positive feedback.

A partner reading card was another visual strategy created for
Charlotte in second grade. Each morning the teacher would call out
students' names to be partners for reading. During this time, students
usually were talking and moving around the room. As students approached Charlotte to read with her, Charlotte would push or hit

Figure 3. Charlotte's minischedule. (The Picture Communication Symbols © 1981-2000 Mayer-Johnson Co. are used with permission.)

them. Students were confused by Charlotte's reaction to partner reading because they knew that she liked reading books. In order to assist Charlotte with the transition to partner reading, an index card was used to show Charlotte's picture, a plus sign, a picture of the other student, an equals sign, and a picture symbol denoting READING (see Figure 4). As soon as the paraeducator knew who Charlotte's partner was for a particular reading activity, that student's picture was attached to the card. Charlotte was shown the card, and she was supported to get the reading book from her desk and, with the card in her hand, search for her reading partner. Once the card was added to the partner reading activity, Charlotte could anticipate the plan, and she no longer needed to push or hit the other students out of frustration.

Another frustrating situation for Charlotte developed when there was a change regarding which person was scheduled to work with her. There were times when the teacher or one of the paraeducators was absent and other times when scheduling changes would affect which adult was assigned for that time period. Usually, Charlotte was provided with no preparation to anticipate the change. Charlotte liked her routine to remain the same, and these changes caused her to become upset and frustrated. A change-of-routine card similar to the one used for partner reading was designed to be used when different people would assist Charlotte. The card had a picture of Charlotte, a

Figure 4.   Charlotte's partner reading card. (The Picture Communication Symbols ©
1981-2000 Mayer-Johnson Co. are used with permission.)

plus sign, the other person's picture, an equals sign, and a picture
symbol of the activity. An instant camera was available so that a pho-
tograph could be taken of the person who would assist Charlotte on
a particular day, which was then attached to the card. The card allowed Charlotte to anticipate the change in routine so that she could
look forward to being with the person rather than become anxious
about reading with a new, unfamiliar person.

Finally, a computer card was created to ease Charlotte's transition from the computer room to the classroom. During the day, Charlotte would take breaks from her classroom activities to use a computer in a small room located near the office area in the school. The
plan was for Charlotte to play one game that lasted about 10 minutes
and then return to the classroom. At some point, Charlotte began extending her break to approximately 40 minutes and playing four
computer games each time she took a break from the classroom. She
was starting to spend more time in the computer room than in her
classroom. When the paraeducator told Charlotte, "You can play two
games, and we will go back to class," Charlotte would play two
games and then, instead of turning the computer off, begin to play a
third game. The paraeducator would remind Charlotte that it was
time to stop, and then Charlotte would become loud and upset.

The computer card consisted of pictures of the computer games
cut from the original software boxes. Charlotte would select two
games to play and then attach the two choices to a larger vertical card
that cued her to play two games and then turn off the computer (see
Figure 5). This visual device assisted Charlotte in seeing the expected
outcome of computer time. After the new routine was established,
the number of computer games that Charlotte played during break-
time was reduced, and she was once again playing one game and
then returning to class.

Social Stories   The purpose of a social story is to outline the
steps of an activity or routine so that the student can understand and
rehearse the expected behavior during a social situation (Gray, 1995).
These stories are extremely helpful in providing information about
new routines, explaining how the student might feel during and after
an event, and describing how the student can participate during an

activity. It is difficult for some students with autism to understand the emotional context that is linked to behavior (Grandin, 1995). Reading and rehearsing a story that describes the process of a new classroom routine or activity may lower the student's anxiety level so that he or she can complete the activity successfully. A variety of social stories were used with Charlotte to introduce new routines and field trips and to assist with times of the day that were challenging for her (see Table 1).

Predictable Routines Establishing comfortable and predictable routines to begin and end the day is crucial to students' making smooth transitions to and from school. For many students with autism, these are stressful times of the school day, and the predictability of knowing what will happen at these times has a calming effect for them (Barron & Barron, 1992; Grandin & Scariano, 1996; McKean, 1996). Because Charlotte had difficulty with her morning transition into school, a routine was established whereby she would arrive at school each morning, hang her jacket and backpack on the coat hook in the hallway, then go to her desk to have a snack. A snack would be placed on her desk prior to her arrival, and she would eat the snack as the teacher took attendance and completed the daily lunch count. At the beginning of the school year, some difficulties

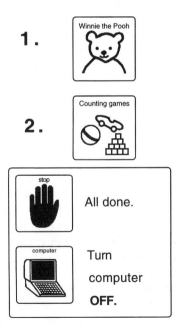

Figure 5.   Charlotte's computer card. (The Picture Communication Symbols © 1981-2000 Mayer-Johnson Co. are used with permission.)

Table 1.   Social stories

Group Time

When the bell rings at 8:40 A.M., it is time to sit at my desk and have my snack. The teacher will take lunch count and check which students are at school. Next, the teacher will say, "Up front and on the floor," and I will go to group time. All the students will sit on the floor and listen quietly as the teacher tells us about the calendar and explains what we will do in school today. I like sitting with my friends and listening to the teacher tell us about the fun things I will do in school.

It's Time to Work

Sometimes my teacher wants me to do work that I don't want to do. My teacher will show me the work I should do and tell me when I can have free time. It's okay because my friends have to work, too. I will try to get my work done when they are working so that we can play later. I can't wait to have free time! I feel happy when I get my work done.

arose from the use of food as a reinforcer for Charlotte throughout the day. Therefore, a change was made so that Charlotte did not have to earn food; instead, it was just given to her during natural snacktimes. After finishing her snack, Charlotte would walk to the computer room, play a game, and return to the classroom to start her day.

Charlotte's afternoon routine did not go as smoothly. Charlotte would have a snack and go to the computer room about 15 minutes before the end of the day. Then she would return to the classroom to put her chair on her desk, take the papers out of her cubby box, and get her coat and backpack from her coat hook. Often there was a lot of movement in the classroom at this time, and the other students would inadvertently block a clear pathway for Charlotte to get to her desk, her cubby box, and then her coat. She would become quite loud and upset at these times, and sometimes she pushed students out of her way to complete her routine. Her anxiety level increased during this time, perhaps because she was confused and unsure of how to complete her routine when so many students were in her way. A possible solution that was not implemented during second grade would have been for the other students to have remained seated until Charlotte entered the classroom, went to her desk and cubby box, and started walking toward her coat hook. This procedure could have been the afternoon cue to all students that it also was time for them to get ready to go home.

Creating Opportunities for Movement   As stated previously, Charlotte requires a great deal of movement in her day. During Charlotte's second-grade school year, a number of opportunities were created for her to move around the classroom. At times, it was necessary to use the school as a resource to create additional opportunities that would blend Charlotte's movement with her learning. During the morning, when students in the classroom spent long periods of time completing seatwork, Charlotte delivered mail to some of the teachers in the school. This provided an opportunity to address a number of Charlotte's goals, such as following a sequence of directions and interacting with others. The activity also provided the physical movement that Charlotte needed each morning. A new routine that was established for Charlotte near the end of the year involved reshelving library books. These activities lasted about 15 minutes and provided a way for Charlotte to take a break from the classroom routine for some movement but still allowed her to learn from a structured activity.

Teaching New Skills

Teaching new skills involves determining what a student needs to learn to replace challenging behaviors. Therefore, it is necessary to understand the purpose of the student's challenging behavior so that a replacement skill can be selected. For example, if a student is grabbing a peer's clothing at recess and those around the student hypothesize that he or she is trying to get the other student's attention, an appropriate replacement skill is to teach the student to tap his or her peer on the shoulder to get the other student's attention. A combination of good prevention and teaching new skills provides the student with more successful ways to interact with and respond to others. The skills that are identified are often used as goals on the student's individualized education program (IEP). The skills described in the following subsections were actively being taught to Charlotte to increase her ability to participate during class lessons. These skills included turn taking, waiting, and communicating wants and needs (see Figure 1, "Teach" column).

Participating Through Curricular Modifications   The second-grade curriculum was adapted through the use of modifications and materials that were interesting and meaningful to Charlotte and tied to the classroom lessons. It was necessary to have a variety of hands-on materials available during assignments and activities so that Charlotte could participate in lessons alongside her peers (see Figure 6). A four-tier basket was used to store materials for reading, writing, spelling, and math. The adults in the classroom had easy access to supplies that could be used to enhance these lessons as well as to modify lessons across other subjects, including science and social studies.

Turn Taking and Waiting   At times, Charlotte was so intent on continuing an activity that it was her only goal, to the extent that if anyone tried to interrupt her plan, she would become very upset. It would have been much easier to let Charlotte complete the activity just one more time and keep the peace than to ask her to stop. It was very important, however, for Charlotte to learn and understand the steps of turn taking and waiting. Charlotte was supported to take turns and wait through the use of visual strategies. When Charlotte was engaged in an activity successfully, she was handed a small card with the word *wait* printed on it to interrupt the routine so that Charlotte would wait a few seconds before continuing the activity. Once Charlotte became familiar with a routine, her wait time increased within the activity. This strategy was extremely helpful during times of the day when the paraeducator needed a few minutes to organize materials, when Charlotte needed to listen while the teacher explained directions, or when a student was interested in showing Charlotte something. Other possibilities that were not addressed in Charlotte's second-grade experience included asking Charlotte to use the *wait* card when she was lining up, getting a drink at the water fountain, and waiting for the bus.

Another strategy that was used to teach Charlotte to wait was the use of a visual timekeeping card (adapted from materials available through Pyramid Educational Consultants). This card was used to indicate to Charlotte when she could gain access to a preferred item or activity. The card had a picture symbol of the item or activity that she had selected for free time. The picture was attached to the card with Velcro. Below the picture symbol on the card were three empty circles. Each time Charlotte completed a part of the task, a small eraser was attached with Velcro to one of the circles. When all of the circles were filled, the activity was completed, and then it was Charlotte's turn to have free time. This strategy was especially helpful when the lesson materials could not be used to indicate closure. The visual timekeeping card also helped Charlotte learn to take turns and differentiate between the adult's request to complete an activity (adult's turn) and Charlotte's turn to engage in an activity of her choice (Charlotte's turn).

Communicating Wants and Needs   Charlotte's method of communication required that she give a picture symbol of what she wanted to an adult or another student in exchange for an item or an activity. She used picture symbols in both informal and formal ways. Sometimes picture symbol choices were presented to Charlotte informally, based on which materials or activities were available during a given lesson, so that she could make a selection. Charlotte also used Picture Exchange Communication System (PECS; Bondy & Frost, 1994). Her PECS book had more than 150 picture symbols from which she could select to tell someone what she wanted. She would

Start each lesson with second-grade curriculum materials (worksheets and books). Use the following ideas to enhance learning for each lesson.

Reading

1. Follow with finger.
2. Use picture symbols to create sentences related to the story.
3. Match picture symbols with photographs in the story.
4. Verbally repeat words/phrases.
5. Practice flashcard words from story.
6. Point to and read main point attached to the bottom of each page.
7. Complete sentence by selecting answer from three choices.

Writing

1. Hand-over-hand writing
2. Trace letters
   a. Outlined R—trace inside.
   b. Dot-to-dot.
3. Templates—write alphabet.
4. Use whiteboard with marker.
5. Backward chaining—play - pla
6. Journal—combination of writing and picture symbols from Charlotte's weekly activities
7. Select words from dictionary to write in journal.

Spelling

1. Choose functional words from spelling list.
2. Match spelling word cards.
3. Use yellow highlighter marker over each word.
4. Match spelling pictograms with words.
5. Color pictures to match words.
6. Cut and glue letters to form words.

Math

[Count, trace number, and say number]

1. Number dot cards (follow with finger)
2. Use manipulative (bears, dinosaurs).
3. Use stickers to count each number.
4. Use numberline.
5. Use flashcards to match numbers.
6. Use touchpoint math numbers.

Figure 6. Second-grade curriculum modifications for Charlotte.

attach two picture symbols to a sentence strip (e.g., I WANT next to DRINK) and give the sentence strip to the other person while being encouraged to repeat the sentence verbally. Charlotte usually would point to each picture symbol while verbalizing the words.

Charlotte also needed a way to communicate her desire to take a break when she was becoming frustrated with an activity or when she simply needed to get up from her desk for a few minutes. At first, the adult had to anticipate when Charlotte needed a break in order to present the correct picture symbol choices (e.g., WALK, DRINK, BEAN-BAG CHAIR). Later the picture symbols were placed on top of Charlotte's desk, but over time the pictures interfered with Charlotte's ability to work successfully at her desk. The picture symbols were then attached with Velcro to the side of Charlotte's desk so that she could select a picture easily and hand it to the adult. Once Charlotte could communicate her desire to take a break, her level of frustration during seatwork activities decreased.

Charlotte also had longer scheduled breaks throughout her school day. For these breaks, she enjoyed walking outside around the school, going to the computer room, and relaxing in the beanbag chair. Her scheduled breaks usually lasted about 10 minutes. It was important that her breaks remain as free-time options instead of assigning her other work expectations during that time. A break was a time for Charlotte to calm down and relax before returning to another structured work time.

The beanbag chair provided a way for Charlotte to remain in the classroom during her break. Thus, she could listen to what the teacher and other students were doing while she relaxed. It also seemed that Charlotte liked to get away from the physical closeness of everyone and everything in the classroom for short periods of time, and the beanbag chair allowed her to view and listen to the class from a distance.

Responding to Challenging Behaviors

A positive behavioral support plan emphasizes prevention and teaching rather than reacting once the student's behavior has occurred. Instead of focusing energy on selecting appropriate consequences for behaviors that adults in the classroom want to increase or decrease, the behavior is approached in a more holistic manner (Hedeen et al., 1996; Topper et al., 1994). It is important, however, to plan for the occurrence of behaviors that have not been prevented so that teachers and paraeducators can remain calm and supportive while redirecting the student to the task at hand and rewarding his or her attempts to participate and interact (McGee et al., 1987; Topper et al., 1994; see Figure 1, "Respond" column).

In supporting Charlotte while she was experiencing difficulties, it was important to use a calm, supportive tone of voice. In some situations, the adult could refer Charlotte to the visual schedule, the *wait* card, or other modifications, and this visual information helped Charlotte relax. It often helped if the adult noted Charlotte's increasing anxiety or frustration and simply prompted Charlotte to request a break. Allowing Charlotte a few minutes to walk around or to get a drink could prevent a situation from getting worse.

At other times, the situation quickly developed into a struggle between Charlotte and the adult. In such cases, the adult needed to give Charlotte some space while helping her feel safe and secure. Occasionally, it was helpful to ask Charlotte to leave her seat and sit in the beanbag chair, which provided a comfortable spot for Charlotte to regain her composure. Once Charlotte was settled, the materials could be brought to her to continue the activity that had been interrupted at her desk. At such times, it was important to encourage any attempts that Charlotte made at participation and to infuse value into the situation (McGee et al., 1987; Topper et al., 1994). At times, it was difficult to engage Charlotte in the task at hand, and in those situations the task was switched to something that she enjoyed doing and found more predictable and comforting. Charlotte would be brought back to the original activity once she was more relaxed and ready to work.

Charlotte's frustration while participating in activities may have been her best attempt at making sure that there were still boundaries within her learning environment and that the adults were providing the structure underlying the routines that sometimes seemed confusing to her. It was clear that as the adults responded by providing consistent support and predictable visual strategies, Charlotte became more tolerant of the demands and even calm in her responses to the changes that took place in her classroom and school environments.

CONCLUSIONS

During Charlotte's second-grade year, much information was gathered on her learning style, a positive behavioral support plan was created to address her needs, and she responded positively to the strategies included in her education program. The general and special education teachers, paraeducators, and Charlotte's classmates received ongoing in-service training and in-class technical assistance. Charlotte's third-grade teacher had been selected toward the end of Charlotte's second-grade year, in-service training had begun for team members, and Charlotte was spending small portions of each day visiting the third-grade classroom. Unfortunately, even with all the support provided and the active involvement of her parents, Charlotte's placement in second grade in her neighborhood school continued to be challenged throughout the school year. In fact, Charlotte's last day of second grade arrived a month sooner than it did for the rest of the second-grade class because her parents were concerned about some of the second-grade parents' reactions to Charlotte's behaviors as well as her participation in the classroom. Because of the climate that was created around Charlotte, it was extremely difficult for Charlotte's parents to endure further questioning of her school placement. As a result, they had Charlotte stay home for the remainder of the year to prevent any additional problems.

Yet, though the school district administrators and teachers as well as the parents of some of Charlotte's classmates struggled with her inclusion, the other students in Charlotte's class were teaching Charlotte to cross the monkey bars, slide down the slide, and play crack the whip. She began to ride the school bus with her brother and children from the neighborhood. Charlotte had been invited to several birthday parties and was growing more socially than she ever had in her previous school settings. Charlotte's parents expressed their awareness of how important peers are in Charlotte's life and the contribution that Charlotte makes to her peers' lives:

> Charlotte brings diversity to our school community while teaching others about tolerance, acceptance, and compassion. Charlotte needs these children to show her how kids do things. The children who have shared their days with Charlotte have learned that although we are not all the same, we are all supported and valued.

Whether Charlotte had a successful second-grade year depends on one's perspective regarding Charlotte's behaviors. Charlotte's behavior problems were the major concern of the school community throughout the school year for two reasons: 1) Charlotte's behaviors made her different, and 2) members of the school community had differing opinions on how to address her behaviors. In the future, each time an issue arises regarding Charlotte's behavior, it will be important that the team problem-solve how to support Charlotte rather than question her placement. It will be necessary for the school to provide ongoing support and training for staff, parents of classmates, and classmates themselves regarding awareness of autism and other disabilities as well as positive behavioral supports. It will be important for the team to be supportive of one another in order to create optimal learning experiences that will assist Charlotte with interacting with her peers and adults in the classroom and with participating in her school community.

Charlotte's family's dream is that in the future, Charlotte will be welcomed into her neighborhood school along with her brothers and other children from the community. Charlotte's parents say it best:

Our family hopes to see more educators become willing to take the risk of including an excluded child. Inclusive education takes courage—the courage to change and commit to those who challenge traditional teaching. We want the entire school to triumph in Charlotte's accomplishments and understand that some days will be better than others but that she is not continually on her last chance before being removed from the school. We want staff and parents to look beyond the autism and see the little girl who is trying to be successful in a school where the rules don't always make sense to her. We want the educators to take pride in the support they offer and understand that they make a big difference in the life of Charlotte and our family.

Quick-fix and intrusive interventions are not the solution in providing a student with successful life skills. An important goal of positive behavioral supports is to create greater interdependence between the student who exhibits challenging and misunderstood behaviors and classmates, teachers, paraeducators, and service providers in the classroom (Vittimberga, Scotti, & Weigle, 1999). Students with behavior problems are at risk in schools and communities because their best attempts to communicate and participate may be different from how other students respond in similar situations. It is essential that administrators, educators, parents, and students collaborate to create positive learning environments for all instead of simply valuing the few who understand and can follow the rules successfully. We must broaden our perspective of belonging and participation so that individuals with diverse learning styles can feel safe to learn and practice new skills in school settings. It is through the support and commitment of others that educators have a positive effect on how all students are accepted and valued in school communities.

DISCUSSION QUESTIONS

1. How did the team determine Charlotte's learning style?

2. Why was it necessary to understand Charlotte's learning style?

3. How can information about how a student learns be used in a positive behavioral support plan?

4. Describe why it was important to involve classmates in understanding Charlotte's interests and behaviors.

5. The one formal Circle of Friends class exercise was not enough to ensure that students would involve Charlotte in activities outside school. Describe other strategies that would have been helpful in connecting Charlotte with her classmates after school and on weekends.

6. Why was it important to develop a positive behavioral support plan to address Charlotte's challenging behaviors?

7. Discuss the importance of the three key elements of a plan: prevention, teaching new skills, and responding.

8. Which elements of Charlotte's second-grade year will be critical to implement for her in third grade?

9. How would you plan for Charlotte's successful transition from second to third grade?

10. Describe some additional strategies that will assist the third-grade teacher and Charlotte's third-grade classmates.

11. How would you address the possible concerns of the parents of classmates if a child with behavior problems were a member of your class?

5

Cecilia's Story

Learning
Opportunities and Obstacles

Marquita Grenot-Scheyer
and Susan Leonard-Giesen

As 13-year-old Cecilia was expressing her frustration with school, her
mother, and what was happening at home, she confided to a special
education support teacher that what she really wanted to do was be
finished with school so that she could get a job. Anne, her support
teacher, advised her to stay in school, work hard, and "keep the peace"
with her mother.

The challenges that Cecilia faces are similar to the challenges that all young
people face as they make the transition from childhood to adolescence.
Adolescents strive for autonomy and seek to establish themselves as separate, self-governing individuals, which means that they rely less on their
parents for directions and guidance (Berk, 1999). Cecilia faces additional
developmental, social, and structural barriers as she proceeds through the
education system, however. She is a Hispanic girl with long dark brown
hair and brown eyes. She has a profound hearing loss that has resulted in

her use of hearing aids. She has mild cerebral palsy and has been diagnosed as having developmental delays. We came to know Cecilia as a result of her participation in a longitudinal investigation of the social relationships of children and youth with and without disabilities (Meyer et al., 1992a). During a 4-year period beginning when Cecilia was 9 years old, we had the opportunity to observe her at school in an inclusive education program. It soon became clear in our research that the education service delivery model had a tremendous impact on Cecilia's education and her social relationships. The manner in which Cecilia's education was structured and delivered is particularly important with regard to understanding it.

IMPACT OF SERVICE DELIVERY

Inclusion is typically viewed as the placement of students with disabilities in their neighborhood schools, in general education classrooms with appropriate supports and services, and alongside their age peers (Grenot-Scheyer et al., 1996). Cecilia's educational placement may be better understood in light of varying patterns of placement of students with disabilities in local school districts across the United States.

As Lipsky and Gartner (1997) suggested, there is not a general pattern of how inclusive education programs are initiated in school districts. Rather, programs are established in a variety of ways:

- Efforts of parents, general and special education teachers, administrators (school principals and district superintendents), clinicians, and providers of related services
- Statewide or local district reform initiatives
- Federally funded systems change projects
- Court decisions

Although systemic models of inclusive education may be influenced by how particular inclusive education programs are initiated, a student's individual placement also is influenced greatly by his or her disability label. For some students, their disability label becomes their defining characteristic. From a sociological perspective, the student's disability achieves master status. That is, those who interact with the student with a disability may have trouble seeing a person first and instead see a person with a disability and all of the disability's associated stereotypes (Biklen, 1989). The disability label in effect becomes the focal point for the student's educational placement. The more significant the developmental delays associated with the disability labels applied to children and youth, the less likely that they will be afforded the opportunity to learn among their peers without disabilities.

U.S. Department of Education (1995) data reveal that though nearly 82% of students who receive a label of speech-language delays attend general education classes, 66% of those who receive a label of mental retardation attend separate classes or other restricted classrooms. This placement pattern is even more striking for students of differing ethnicities who have disabilities. For example, in one California school district, students of differing ethnicities compose 65% of the total school population but represent only 37% of students with significant disabilities who are included in general education classrooms (Roach, Ascroft, Stamp, & Kysilko, 1995). Roach and her colleagues stated that for students of differing ethnicities with disabilities, special education is "tantamount to the inadequate separate but equal education system that was outlawed by the Supreme Court in 1954" (Roach et al., 1995, p. 11).

As is often the case, the genesis of the inclusion program in Cecilia's urban school district was the result of the hard, persistent work of several families to secure inclusive education for their sons and daughters with disabilities. During a period of 1½ years, four sets of parents met with district personnel and faculty from a local university to convince the district to develop and support an inclusive model of education and to plan collaboratively with district personnel to bring these students back to their neighborhood schools. Permission to include first 4 and later a total of 20 students with severe disabilities during a 4-year period was obtained from district personnel. An inclusion support teacher was identified to plan, develop, and evaluate the education programs of these students. As more and more families requested inclusive educational placements for their sons and daughters with disabilities, the district grew in its expertise and experience with this model of education and began identifying potential students for inclusion.

This notion of eligibility runs counter to many moral and educational beliefs and legal requirements regarding inclusive education (Falvey, Grenot-Scheyer, Coots, & Bishop, 1995; Lipsky & Gartner, 1997; McGregor & Vogelsberg, 1999). The reality is that the implementation of inclusive education for students with disabilities remains uneven and appears to be dependent primarily on a student's age, a student's disability, and state education practices (Lipsky & Gartner, 1997; Roach et al., 1995). This pattern of placement has not changed significantly since the enactment of the Education for All Handicapped Children Act of 1975 (PL 94-142). More than 25 years after passage of that major federal legislation, segregated placement patterns continue despite reform efforts, research priorities and findings, the development of effective inclusion practices, and advocacy efforts by professionals and by families of students with disabilities.

CECILIA'S BACKGROUND AND SCHOOL PLACEMENT

Although many students in Cecilia's school district are eligible for an inclusive school placement under IDEA, few are actually placed in inclusive classrooms because of notions of criteria. Cecilia's placement history is somewhat atypical of what other students with disabilities in our project experienced. Cecilia was born in Mexico and moved to the United States when she was 3 years old. Cecilia began school in a general kindergarten class at Second Street School. Second Street is a small but growing elementary school in an urban school district in southern California. The kindergarten through fifth grade elementary school serves a primarily Hispanic population, the majority of whom are eligible for services under Title I, including free and reduced-cost lunches.

One feels a sense of community when one walks onto the Second Street School campus. Parents and young children are present on campus as school-age children are dropped off in the morning and picked up in the afternoon, and many community activities are held on the campus. School administrators and faculty exhibit a strong commitment to support community involvement and participation in this mostly working-class neighborhood.

During Cecilia's kindergarten year, school officials suspected that she had developmental delays and a hearing impairment, and a referral for special education services was made. Cecilia's parents were informed that there were no classes for students who were labeled as deaf and hard of hearing at the school and that Cecilia would have to be transported to another school within the district to receive such services. Because Cecilia's parents wanted her to remain at the neighborhood school, the individualized education program (IEP) team decided to place her in a special day class for students with severe disabilities. She remained in a special day class until the end of the second grade with in-class support from a speech-language specialist with training in supporting students who are deaf and hard of hearing.

Cecilia was nominated by the district inclusion support teacher to be included in the third grade. Her parents agreed to this placement but did not actively seek it. During the fourth grade, Cecilia was nominated by her general education teacher to participate in English language development (ELD) transition classes. ELD classes have as a primary goal providing students with comprehensible instruction in the core curriculum and increasing these students' English proficiency (California Department of Education, 1997). A resource specialist teacher was assigned to Cecilia in the fourth grade. This teacher used a pull-out service delivery model to work on specific goals in Cecilia's IEP. Cecilia's participation in the ELD class and the resource specialist class, as well as support from the inclusion support teacher in the general education classroom, provided us a window through which to view the complex interaction and often counteracting nature of these service delivery models.

METHODS

The best way to tell Cecilia's story is to provide accounts of actual activities that were observed throughout the school year. This story is constructed from the numerous observations and interviews that were completed during the course of research that supported this study (Meyer et al., 1992b). Cecilia was included in general education classes but was pulled out on a regular basis for various support services throughout the time we observed her. During the third and fourth grades, she was pulled out for ELD classes for most of the morning. During the fifth and sixth grades, she was pulled out for speech-language and counseling services on a weekly basis and for instruction in the resource specialist program on a daily basis.

Procedures and Analysis

During the 4-year study, data were collected primarily through participant observation of a range of school activities. The project used a participant observer model to gain an insider's perspective on the lives of children and youth with disabilities (for a detailed description of methodology, see Meyer, Park, Grenot-Scheyer, Schwartz, & Harry, 1998a, 1998c). Trained community members, all parents of children without disabilities in the school or community, followed and observed children in a variety of in-school and after-school activities that yielded a comprehensive picture of typical days for these children. The participant observers watched target students and their peers without disabilities for approximately 30–40 minutes at a time and then left the classroom or other setting to tape-record their observations. For Cecilia, a total of 95 observations of varying length were made. These observations were then transcribed and analyzed. In addition, comprehensive and longitudinal interviews with some of these students, their families (including Cecilia's), and their teachers helped to complete the picture regarding the nature of the participants' social relationships and schooling.

The authors of this chapter and other project staff independently reviewed the transcriptions to identify salient themes regarding social relationships. These themes were reviewed and independently organized into categories using a constant comparison method (Strauss, 1987). Categories were formed by placing similar responses together. As responses that did not fit existing categories were found, new categories were formed. In order to limit bias that might arise from reliance on a single rater's perspective, the raters then met to compare themes and came to a shared understanding regarding salient themes that emerged across the observations. An analysis of demographic information (e.g., activity, nature of activity, setting, peers present) related to Cecilia's day also was completed. The excerpts presented in this chapter emerged from this data.

FINDINGS

As indicated previously, the outcomes that we observed were categorized into broad themes and subthemes that, in their entirety, provide an empirically grounded conceptual framework. From this framework, we can describe Cecilia's development across many educational domains, with an emphasis on her social development. Several major themes of particular importance to Cecilia are presented and discussed in this chapter, including the following:

- Importance of belonging: A view from the inside and the outside
- Peers: Developmental necessities
- Mismatch of support services
- Increasingly difficult and complex curricula
- Contextual structures and learning

Importance of Belonging:
A View from the Inside and the Outside

A sense of belonging is an important theme in the child development, school reform, and inclusive education literature. Relationships, especially friendships, are developmental necessities with regard to the acquisition of skills and competencies that are essential to a child's cognitive, social, and emotional growth (Newcomb & Bagwell, 1996). When students believe that they are valued members of the school community, the school itself becomes more effective at fostering growth and development in all domains of learning (Grenot-Scheyer, Staub, et al., 1998; Schaps & Solomon, 1990). Similarly, a guiding principle in the literature on inclusive education emphasizes the importance of including children and youth with disabilities in the life of the school, both within and outside the schoolyard (Meyer et al., 1998a; Stainback & Stainback, 1990). Cecilia's interaction with her peers without disabilities, as described in the following excerpt from an observation during physical education class, is a painful and bittersweet mix of belonging and being on the outside:

Observer's comment: At one point, [Cecilia] did walk over to the next team, where Rosa and Carmen were sitting, awaiting their turn. They were sitting there talking, and Cecilia walked over and said something in Spanish. The two girls looked up at her and never responded to her and then looked away to talk about whatever they were talking about. Cecilia just stood there for a minute and then walked back to the team.

Throughout our observations of Cecilia, we saw a complex mix of peer acceptance and rejection that is reflective of the developmental progression of children's relationships, Cecilia's poor social interaction skills, and the lack of adult support for these relationships. Throughout her school experience, Cecilia alternated between being an insider and an outsider. Lunchtime is a particularly difficult time for Cecilia, as the following excerpts illustrate:

As the class is waiting in line on the playground for their lunch, the girls in front of Cecilia are sort of grouped together as the line is progressing. Cecilia is still on the outside of this group, standing behind. It almost looks as if when she moves closer to become part of the group, the girls don't acknowledge her. They ignore her, then she falls back away from the group and just looks around the playground while she is waiting in line for lunch. During the time I observed Cecilia waiting in line for lunch, she didn't talk to anyone, and none of the other girls spoke to her.

When she finally reached the kitchen window and got her lunch tray, the rest of the girls just left the area, and Cecilia was left there alone to eat her lunch. She did follow the girls to where they were sitting; however, none of the girls without disabilities acknowledged her presence. She just sat and began eating her lunch. The girls were involved in their own conversations, and Cecilia was just sitting there eating her lunch and not talking to anyone. Alma, who was seated to her right, did turn to Cecilia, and they had a brief conversation. Cecilia was still left alone at the lunch table after this brief conversation, however. Cecilia continued to eat her lunch and did not talk to anyone.

During childhood, children demonstrate a strong desire to belong, to be part of a peer group. A peer culture exists within these groups, as evidenced by a specialized vocabulary, a mode of dress (Berk, 1999), and behavior that can be characterized as hanging. Some examples of Cecilia's moving in and out of the peer group and hanging are illustrated by the following excerpt:

Once on the playground, Cecilia immediately headed over to talk to one of the playground supervisors, with whom she appears to be acquainted, since she gave the woman a hug. Cecilia stood and talked to this woman for a couple of minutes, then they were joined by two Hispanic girls without disabilities. These two girls stood and talked to the playground supervisor for a couple of minutes, and Cecilia just stood there, listening to their conversation. Shortly thereafter, another Hispanic girl without disabilities, Martha, approached Cecilia and the supervisor. While Martha was talking to the supervisor, Conchita came over to where Cecilia was standing. This time, she started talking to Cecilia and Martha in Spanish. While Martha was talking to the supervisor, Cecilia started poking Conchita, and then Conchita poked her back. They then began chasing each other around the playground supervisor. Cecilia had a big smile on her face and was laughing. The other girls were smiling and laughing, too. So, it all appeared to be in fun. Martha soon walked away, leaving Cecilia and Conchita with the playground supervisor. While the supervisor continued to talk to the other Hispanic girl, Conchita and Cecilia started kicking sand at one another and then began chasing each other around the playground supervisor. In a few minutes, the bell rang, indicating that the lunch period was over.

This rough-and-tumble kind of interaction is characteristic of the play that children without disabilities were observed to engage in frequently. Too few instances of Cecilia's participating in this manner were observed, however, compared with her peers without disabilities. The majority of the observations were of Cecilia on the outside looking in.

Peers: Developmental Necessities

The importance of having a peer to talk with, to learn from, to giggle with, and mostly just to hang out with is well documented in the literature and validated in daily life experiences (Belle, 1989; Bukowski, Newcomb, & Hartup, 1996; Hurley-Geffner, 1995; Meyer et al., 1998). Peer relationships are influenced by cultural and contextual norms, children's social interaction skills, their experiences with a wide variety of people, and the adults who either interfere with or support children's relationships and subsequent learning (Grenot-Scheyer & Leonard-Giesen, 1997).

We observed few instances of Cecilia's just being one of the girls, with all the lightness, silliness, and teasing of boys that are characteristic of this developmental period. The following excerpt during physical education provides this illustration. The girls had just finished playing volleyball and were sitting down to rest. After the teacher had gotten all the girls back in the game for a second round and they had played for a bit, they sat back down in the same group to watch the game. Then a boy diverted their attention:

> As they were watching the game after they were pulled out again, there was this one boy—he seemed like a character—and he had sweats on. He pulled his sweats down, and he had shorts on underneath. Then he came up to the girls and said, "Hey, girls, you wanna see something?" One of the girls said, "Oh, Steve, you just think you're so hot!" He pulled down his sweatpants, and he was showing that he had his shorts on and was being a real clown. The girls were saying, "You think you're somebody famous." They mentioned some singer in Spanish—I didn't catch the name, but they were saying, "You think you're something good," and they were just shouting at him. The more they shouted at him, the more he would do the show for them. Cecilia said, "He's so stupid. He thinks he's funny and he's not."

The girls continued to tease and shout at the boy for several more minutes.

Observer's comment: They got along really good, they talked and laughed, and Cecilia laughed with them. They were making fun of the boy together.

In the following observation, Cecilia and her peers are just hanging. Children without disabilities frequently engaged in this type of interaction, and here Cecilia was included. The opportunity to be with a group, to share food and laughter and sometimes secrets, is an important aspect of students' school culture and a developmental necessity. The following observation during lunchtime in Cecilia's fifth-grade year illustrates this point:

> So [Cecilia] was sitting with about four girls, and they were eating slowly. Everybody else finished real fast and got up and went out to play, but those four girls stayed at the lunch benches for awhile, and they ate very slowly. Then Cecilia got up with them and went toward the playground. I went slowly to let them get ahead of me, and then I went around to see if they were going to participate in any of the games or not, but it seemed like they were in that little group of girls. Then they went toward a lawn area in front of their classroom. They sat there in a little circle. They got up and ran toward the bathroom. I didn't go into the bathroom, but they all went in together and stayed for a couple of seconds. Then they came out together again. Then they went toward the field where the baseball diamonds are. They stayed there for the rest of recess. They were playing with each other,

tagging each other, and pulling each other's sweaters, and they stayed out there until the rest of the lunch period was over. They weren't really doing much in the way of getting involved with any of the games or the playground equipment; they were really just keeping to themselves. When the bell rang, Cecilia and the other girls came toward the classroom.

The primary focus of our research was peer interaction, but we were also interested in the educational contexts that supported or mediated such interactions as well as students' learning. The three themes presented in the following sections emerged as strong areas of concern for Cecilia.

Mismatch of Support Services

Numerous supports and services are often required to ensure the success of students with disabilities in inclusive classrooms; indeed, they are required by law. Lack of articulation and collaboration among personnel who deliver such services necessarily affects the daily schedule of students and results in a complicated service delivery pattern. As Grenot-Scheyer, Harry, Park, Schwartz, and Meyer (1998) suggested, the nature of education services is often directed by historical service delivery practices and patterns that do not always focus on the needs of the whole child.

During the third and fourth grades, Cecilia received her education primarily from the general education teacher and the inclusion support teacher. In addition, speech-language services and the expertise of a specialist in education of deaf and hard-of-hearing students were identified on Cecilia's IEP, but no observations of these were included in her data set. As indicated previously, beginning in the fourth grade, ELD and the support of a resource teacher in the resource specialist period (RSP) were added to Cecilia's IEP. The combination of all of these support services resulted in a highly complicated schedule during the several years that we observed Cecilia. As is true of many children with disabilities labeled as having limited English proficiency, Cecilia was served by a pull-out model, which removed her from her general education classroom for approximately 2 hours each school morning. This fragmented model of service delivery appeared to contribute unnecessarily to a lack of articulation and transition between teachers, a mismatch of curriculum and individual objectives, and interruptions in Cecilia's social interactions with other children. Cecilia's participant observer provided a description of this fragmentation of curriculum and instruction in the general education classroom, the transitional ELD class, and the resource teacher's class:

This particular time of day is allocated [to] language and reading. Mr. F, a general education teacher, told me that he has had [Cecilia] placed in the transitional reading class. This is the class where English is taught as a second language. So, while her classmates in Room 1 [a general education classroom] are having their lesson in reading and language, Cecilia leaves the classroom and goes to Room 16 [the ELD class] with a group of students.

While Cecilia's peers are engaged in a reading and language lesson, Cecilia is working on cursive writing, which indicates the curriculum mismatch identified previously. The participant observer continued:

> They are sitting at their desks in the classroom. The teacher puts an assignment on the board in cursive writing, and they are to copy that down. This is their first procedure of the day. Cecilia's got her back to that board. That's the position of her desk. She's turning around and looking at the board to copy what the teacher is writing. The teacher says she can do the assignment. It takes her a little longer than the other kids, but she can do it. Cecilia is writing, and she's also holding two one-dollar bills in her hand at the time. She's having a little bit of difficulty. I saw her fiddling with the two dollars, and I was kind of wondering what it was for. They're going to go to a swap meet. The sixth-grade class is going to hold a swap meet today, so [Cecilia's class is] going to buy some things. The teacher asks Cecilia if Cecilia would like her to hold the money until it's time to go, and Cecilia says "Yes."

The apparent mismatch of curriculum in the RSP continued, as well as a lack of teacher collaboration, as indicated by the following observation:

> So I follow her to tutoring (i.e., the RSP) again. This time I got to stay in her classroom. She was going to do some of her corrections in math, and then they were going to read. She goes in there to do her special math and reading. Now I understand why Mr. A (the general education teacher) sometimes skips her in the classroom, because she has special math that she does, and special reading. Mr. A is supposed to look and see if her tutor gave her any extra work in the classroom for her to do while Mr. A is teaching the other class (of general education students). That's what her tutor instructor had said. Maybe I should volunteer and get up and look through her math book or her reading book and see if there are any papers there that her tutor had and tell her that she needs to do that while Mr. A is teaching the rest of the class.

The apparent disconnection between the general education classroom and the resource class and the resulting effect this may have on Cecilia's socialization and sense of belonging is also evident in the following observation:

> She sat down, and there were about three students from her general
> education class in this tutoring class. They got placed in four differ-
> ent groups, and they were doing different things. Some were reading
> words from the bulletin board, and the teacher was reading a story to
> one group. Cecilia's group was studying the definition of the oppo-
> sites of things and pairs. A young man came into the classroom and
> asked me if I knew where Cecilia and the other two kids that were in
> her general education class were. I showed him where she was sit-
> ting, and I noticed that the two boys were in another group, and I
> pointed them out also. He said that they had Popsicles in their class
> today, and they brought Cecilia and the boys their treat in their tu-
> toring class. The tutoring teacher said, "It's very nice, Cecilia, that you
> got a treat from your class. I think your ice cream is going to melt if
> you wait until recess. Why don't you guys go ahead and step outside
> and eat your ice cream?" All three of them stepped out at about 1:40,
> and they stayed together in a little group at the end of the building.

The complexity and mismatch of education services increased as Cecilia moved from grade to grade. Perhaps because of the number of personnel involved in her education and the lack of collaboration across the
IEP team, Cecilia's education services did not improve over time as one
might expect. Rather, the fragmentation of services increased over time.

Increasingly Difficult and Complex Curricula

The longitudinal investigation allowed us to observe the changes in both
Cecilia and the curriculum over time. As indicated previously, observations
of Cecilia began in the third grade and continued until the end of the
seventh grade. As the following observations illustrate, the nature of the
curriculum and expectations began to increase in degree of difficulty and
became more complex in the fifth grade. There appeared to be a lack of
structure and problem-solving strategies to ensure Cecilia's active involvement with the curriculum. The data indicate that as the curriculum became
more complex, the amount of time that Cecilia spent in general education
classrooms decreased, and ultimately she was placed primarily in special
day classes in the seventh grade and was included only for physical education and one elective class, a practice that seems all too common at the secondary level. The following excerpt is indicative of the level of complexity
of the curriculum that existed in the fifth grade for Cecilia:

> They went back to their classroom. I went in their classroom, and Ce-
> cilia just went in and sat down and then got up and went to the trash
> can and threw in a piece of paper and came back and sat down. She

seemed like she got out her book. Mr. A said, "Get out your math book and quietly sit down and look up at the board, because we're going to continue finishing our math." Cecilia got her book, but she really was not paying attention to the board. She was playing with her calculator. It didn't seem like she was using the calculator for her math. She really wasn't doing anything. She was just sitting there, playing with her calculator, and that was about it. The rest of the class was trying to continue finishing their math. Cecilia was just real quiet and sitting there, looking down at the book and really not looking at the board or at what Mr. A was writing on it. She was really into playing with her calculator.

As students progress through higher grade levels, they are expected to be able to work more independently. Directions are more general in nature and may contain an increasing number of steps, and guidance from the instructor tends to decrease. Students with disabilities who are included in general education classrooms at higher grade levels need to receive varying and sometimes complex support in order to be successful. Such support does not necessarily have to come from an adult, as is evident in the following excerpt:

[The science teacher] was writing some instructions on the board, and the class seemed very quiet compared to the other class that I was in. The other class was loud and unorganized. I spotted Cecilia; she was sitting quietly. I noticed that everybody else had paper and pencils out on their desks and were writing what Mr. P was writing on the board, but Cecilia did not have any paper or pencil on her desk. Mr. P finished writing on the chalkboard and said, "Everybody get that down. It's important that you do get all this information because this is part of your grade for next month." Everybody said, "Yes, we have all the information," and then he shouted loudly, "Cecilia, do you have everything written down? Do you understand?" She nodded her head and said "Yes," and he said, "Okay." Students who didn't finish their science homework from the day before could continue their science. If not, they could continue on their rock project that they had to turn in. Then he walked toward the middle of the classroom and said, "Make sure you put the rocks in the right place and do everything the way it's shown on the sample," and then he approached Cecilia and asked if she understood and asked where her assignment was that she was supposed to do yesterday. She didn't say anything and just opened her book. A boy in the same group said, "Mr. P, I'll help her." He came over and sat right beside Cecilia and started helping her do her work, and then she turned around and screamed across the room: "Neomi, I want you to come and sit over here with me," and Neomi said "No." I guess Cecilia didn't want this little boy to help her, but it was really nice of him to offer to help. Mr. P got a buzz on the intercom, and then it was time for Cecilia to go.

In the following observation during the seventh grade, the participant observer was watching Cecilia in the ELD room. The teacher was working with a small group of students at a table using basic word flashcards. After they had finished with these cards, the teacher asked Cecilia about some work that she had to complete for her teacher:

"Cecilia, I know you have a book report for tomorrow in Mr. P's class. Have you started on it?" Cecilia's friend said, "I did. I have some of it done. All I need is a title." The teacher said, "Good. Did you help Cecilia?" The girl said, "Yeah, but she said she did not want to do it, because she was going to the library or she had something all ready to copy, but I don't really know. I've got to get mine finished, too." The teacher said, "I'll go get some information for you. I'll help you because I really want you to turn something in because it's not going to look good if you don't turn anything in." So, the teacher went to get some information. The teacher came back into the classroom and told Cecilia to go sit in the back where she could concentrate and write some paragraphs on a piece of paper and start doing her report. The teacher said, "I made it very simple for you. I got all the materials you need. All you have to do is copy it and find a title for it. You have only 15 minutes to work on it before you go back to the classroom." Cecilia went to the back of the classroom and sat there, and then she tapped me on the shoulder and told me in Spanish, "*Ven conmigo* [Come with me]." I said, "Okay, I'll be right there." I didn't want to distract Cecilia by moving really close to her, but I did want to see if she was going to work on her book report. She made a mistake and crumpled her paper and started over again, and she did that one more time. The teacher told Cecilia, "Cecilia, you're just playing. You're not doing your book report," and Cecilia said, "Oh, I'm tired, I don't want to do this." The teacher said, "Come on, Cecilia. This is not the first time. We go through this a lot."

The participant observer concluded her observation by commenting that Cecilia continued to complain about the work and stayed in at recess to complete it. This observation reflects the apparent lack of training of the general education teachers in how to provide appropriate supports for students with disabilities who are included in their classes. As the teacher commented, "We go through this a lot"—this appears to be a signal that Cecilia needs additional or different forms of support.

Contextual Structures and Learning

The socioecology or context of the classroom and school has a major impact on the successful inclusion of students with disabilities in the life of the school community (Grenot-Scheyer et al., 1998). This became evident to us as we followed Cecilia over time. She changed and developed in many areas, and the changes that occurred in her education program year after year were striking. It was apparent in our observations and interactions with school personnel that all of them cared about Cecilia. It was also clear, however, that the level of understanding regarding the goals of Cecilia's inclusive placement and the methods necessary for its success varied tremendously across staff throughout the years of the project. This variability clearly affected Cecilia's learning and development, as indicated in the following observation, which occurred in the resource room:

> The teacher was writing spelling words on the board for the students. They were supposed to have studied over the weekend because they were going to have a spelling test. They were refreshing their spelling words. The teacher was going around the room, asking everybody if they could come up with a sentence containing the spelling words. Then it came to Cecilia's turn. Her word was *path*. Cecilia said, "I went on the path." She knew how to make a sentence with the word she was asked to use. Then the teacher noticed that Cecilia didn't have her hearing aid in her ear, and she said, "Cecilia, you don't have your hearing aid. What are you doing? You're supposed to have it on. You're supposed to be listening because we're going to have a test with these words." Cecilia was cleaning out her desk and really not paying attention. When it came her turn, she knew the word she was asked about, and she knew how to form a sentence containing the word. Cecilia continued cleaning out her desk, and then she finally put everything back and put her hearing aid on. The class continued studying the words over and over again. Then they went up to the chalkboard, and each one got a turn. The teacher would tell them a word, and they would write it on the board. Cecilia got to write a word on the board when she got it right. That's mostly what they were doing.

During this school year, Cecilia was placed with two general education teachers who team-taught. Contrast the previous observation with the one that follows, in which the observer is watching Cecilia in her sixth-grade general education classroom:

Cecilia is at her desk doing her math project. She's interested in her paper. There are a lot of activities going on around Cecilia in the classroom. Some of the kids are up and about. Some of them are sitting on the floor, working on their projects. Some of them are at different desks, coloring their drawings. They have already finished with their math. Cecilia runs into a little problem with her multiplication. She gets out of her seat. She goes over to the math chart on the wall in the back of the classroom. Using a multiplication table, Cecilia puts one finger on the number that she needs and one finger on another number and then crosses it to find out what the answer is. She goes back to her desk and works hard on her math paper. The teacher noticed which kids were working as they were supposed to. She called Cecilia's name. Cecilia looked up because she was doing what she was assigned to do. The teacher called for a show of hands with regard to who hadn't finished their math work. Cecilia's hand went up. The teacher requested that the students put their names at the top of their papers and that they turn in their papers to her and then start their science projects. Cecilia put her name on the front of the paper and took it up to the teacher, and she asked the teacher if she could finish the problem, and the teacher said "Yes," so she came over to the desk in the rear righthand corner of the classroom, where I was sitting. She finished that one problem. She took her paper and placed it on the teacher's desk. She put the calculator in a box with all the calculators in it, and she went over to her file box to pick out her paperwork. (Students had individual work folders where they picked up assignments.) Cecilia was unable to find her paperwork in her file, so she approached the teacher and asked the teacher if she knew where her paperwork was, and the teacher told her it should be at her table. Cecilia went back and rechecked the file and was unable to find her paperwork.

In the following observation made during Cecilia's fifth-grade year, the participant observer watched Cecilia in the resource room, where she was engaged in a math activity. The requirements, the nature of the support provided, and the reinforcement provided were different here in contrast with those in the general education classroom:

Cecilia was doing some of her math problems. She did well, so the teacher told her, "You can go to the box of goodies." She picked out some of the toys for a prize because she had done very well on her math problems. Cecilia was thrilled about her prize. Then all of the students went back to their desks to see which papers they had to get together for their homework. The teacher gave them a couple of sheets for their homework, and Cecilia said that she already had done that; but the teacher said, "It doesn't hurt to do it all over again. That way you can just keep recording it in your mind, and you can refresh it."

CONCLUSIONS

Cecilia's lament at the beginning of this chapter sounds so typical, yet her needs are not typical. We continue to believe that a quality inclusive education program is the best way to prepare Cecilia and other students with disabilities to become active, participating members of their local communities. For Cecilia, whether the education system was successful in moving her toward that goal is questionable.

We know what inclusive education can and should look like in real-world classrooms. Recommended practice as presented in the literature is not always as neatly in place as we would like it to be for all students at all times. Cecilia's story at least in part demonstrates the variability and fragility of inclusion in one school that is reflective of national patterns. We have learned much about the complex interplay of often-competing service delivery models. We hope that Cecilia's story has shed light on the complexity of inclusion and can inform others as they continue their efforts to educate students with disabilities successfully in general education classrooms.

DISCUSSION QUESTIONS

1. What were the positive characteristics of Cecilia's inclusion? What was done well?

2. Evaluate the role of the inclusion support teacher. What did she do that was consistent with recommended practice? Which areas of support could she improve?

3. Analyze the nature of the curriculum modifications and adaptations provided for Cecilia in one of the excerpts. What would you do differently?

4. Discuss the nature of collaboration among all of the support personnel. How could their collaboration be improved to ensure Cecilia's academic and social success?

5. What is the optimum model of service delivery for a student such as Cecilia, who has both learning and language development needs?

6

Andre's Story

Frames of Friendship

Mary Fisher

It is 9:00 A.M., and I am observing Andre and Miranda. When I enter the classroom, the class is excited about the play that they are putting on for the school that day. Jason, who is playing the wind, is pretending to fly around the room with his arms spread out, practicing. I walk over to Andre and ask him if he is ready for the play. Andre looks up at me and starts laughing out loud. I say, "What's so funny?" Andre points his fingers toward Kamisha, who is sitting not far from Andre. Kamisha says, "You laughing at me, Andre?" Andre shakes his head from side to side, but he is still laughing. Mr. S gives the class a pep talk about speaking their lines out loud, not moving around on the stage, and not chewing candy or gum. The lights are turned down, and Jason makes the introduction. Miguel rocks Andre back and forth in his wheelchair as the class sings a song.

Observer's comment: I really think Andre enjoys being in the show and on the stage, because the look in his eyes as he gazes out at the auditorium and the smile on his face are indescribable. All of the teachers and paraeducators — too numerous to name — talked about the smile on Andre's face.

The author was affiliated with Syracuse University at the time this research was conducted.

Andre's wheelchair has an umbrella attached to the handle, and when it is Andre's time to perform, Miguel pushes Andre around and around the stage as if he were walking in the park. The wind comes, but it is a mild wind; of course, the wind is being played by Jason. The children in the auditorium laugh, and a few of the children shout, "Look at Andre onstage!" (Atlantic Avenue School, Spring 1995, third grade)

Andre was born and grew up in Barbados. When Andre was 6 years old, his family moved to the United States because his mother believed he would receive better schooling here. Andre has cerebral palsy related to a blood incompatibility detected only after Andre was several days old that resulted in a condition that causes mental retardation, cerebral palsy, and other health issues. Despite receiving a pessimistic prognosis for Andre from a doctor, Andre's mother educated herself about Andre's physical needs and taught him how to eat and chew. Having been both a parent and a teacher and not holding high expectations with regard to education programs for Andre in Barbados, she opted to move.

The place where Andre's mom has seen inclusion pay off for her son is in an urban public school in the Northeast. Atlantic Avenue School serves about 850 students in prekindergarten through the fifth grade. The demographics of the school's student population represent a typical urban U.S. public school: 65% of students are African Americans, 28% are Hispanics, 5% are European Americans, and 2% are Asian Americans. All of the children are eligible for free lunches. Fifteen percent of the children are eligible for special education services.

INTRODUCTION

This chapter describes various aspects of Andre's experience during his third- and fourth-grade years at Atlantic Avenue School, providing one picture of the social relationships and friendships of a student with disabilities. This picture presents a focal point for the examination of the potential effect of social interaction opportunities on students' general development as well as the setting events and adult behaviors that facilitate or hinder those social interaction opportunities—in particular for students with significant disabilities. Friendships are considered to be supportive contexts for development. Such relationships set the stage for engaging in behaviors related to social, emotional, and cognitive growth (Newcomb & Bagwell, 1996). Through careful consideration of Andre's experiences, we may illuminate better the ways in which adult caregivers—including teachers and paraprofessionals—can act responsibly on behalf of children in inclusive settings, attending not only to children's academic and intellectual development but also to their well-being and social development.

ANDRE'S SCHOOL EXPERIENCE

Andre began his U.S. school experience in a self-contained special education program situated at Atlantic Avenue School and operated under a separate district special education administration. The special education program existed as an entity apart from the neighborhood general education school, Atlantic Avenue School. Andre was enrolled in the special education preschool program and attended the program for 1 year. By a special collaborative arrangement between the two school administrations (Atlantic Avenue School and the citywide special education program), the next year 14 families from the special education program were invited to enroll their children in the neighborhood school. Families were invited because they already resided within the catchment area designated for Atlantic Avenue School. This inclusive arrangement was initiated jointly by both principals, one representing the general education program and one representing the special education program. This program is supported through staff development provided by the state's systemwide change initiative, the purpose of which was to bring children home to their neighborhood schools. The initiative involved school districts across the state that had competed for and received minigrants to support inclusive schooling task forces and planning team activities within their districts. These task forces functioned at various levels within the districts, including the district level, the building level, and the team level. Selected sites were awarded up to $3,000 to implement action plans with regard to policy, service delivery, and staff development initiatives.

Since his arrival at Atlantic Avenue School, Andre had been assigned to general education classes with special education supports and services. He was eligible for special education support under the categorical label *student with multiple disabilities*. In keeping with recommended practice, one teaching assistant was assigned to supplement the classroom teaching staff in Andre's classes throughout the school day (Ayres, Meyer, Ervelles, & Park-Lee, 1994). One other student with significant learning disabilities also was assigned to Andre's class. Both students received direct push-in support (i.e., support in the general education classroom) from a special education teacher for 10 hours per week. Each student was provided with physical, occupational, and speech-language therapy as pull-out services three times per week for 30-minute sessions. The support team and classroom staff met every other week and shared progress notes and recommendations, again implementing a recommended practice for supporting students with identified needs in an inclusive setting (Pugach & Johnson, 1995a; Villa & Thousand, 1995).

Andre's individualized education program (IEP) goals and objectives for both third and fourth grades addressed communication, academics, and mobility. Targeted activities included communicating with augmentative and alternative communication (AAC) devices, responding to "who" and "what" questions, using a calendar, sightreading, participating in class, receiving grade-level sex education, completing prevocational industrial tasks, grasping a peg and putting it in a hole, travel training within the building, ambulating in a gait trainer, sitting upright in a chair, propelling and maneuvering a wheelchair in a specified direction, participating in team and individual sports, and toileting. The special education teacher was accountable for paperwork; but at appropriate times throughout Andre's daily school routine, all of the adults in the school were expected to implement procedures to achieve the objectives established for Andre, sharing and exchanging traditional roles and responsibilities using a transdisciplinary framework (Orelove & Sobsey, 1996; Rainforth & York-Barr, 1997).

The principal and a number of faculty members at Atlantic Avenue School were especially keen to pursue support for children's social relationships in this new setting. These teachers believed that friendship was a significant factor in teaching and learning and understood that social integration required planned opportunities for interaction. In addition, they were interested in friendships for their classes as a whole and were willing to move beyond traditional ideas that had focused mainly on the need to teach social skills only to students with disabilities (i.e., addressing *their* individual impairments while ignoring the potential for group or community change).

THE CONSORTIUM

A nucleus of teachers and the principal from Atlantic Avenue School became involved with the Consortium for Collaborative Research on Social Relationships of Children and Youth with Diverse Abilities (Meyer, Grenot-Scheyer, et al., 1992) and its 5-year research endeavor. With encouragement from the school, Andre's family agreed to participate along with the remaining 13 "invited families" as well as "general education" families. During the 5 years of the research project, Andre and his classmates participated in several studies about friendships between students with and without disabilities. The studies were designed using a participatory research model and examined four major questions:

1. What *frames* or perspectives do children and youth without disabilities have regarding their peers with severe disabilities?

2. How do significant others view and value *frames*? Who sees each frame as negative or positive, and why?

3. What setting events and adult behaviors in the environments that children and youth experience either support or hinder the different frames?

4. What naturalistic interventions effectively discourage disliked or devalued frames and encourage liked or valued frames?

The term *frame* as used in the preceding questions simply represents a category that emerged in the Consortium analyses—one of the pictures or ways of seeing peers with disabilities that surfaced as we observed and talked with children and their families about social relationships inside and outside school. We established a set of six frames that represented the social relationships between students with and without disabilities (Meyer et al., 1998c). Table 1 presents a list of the frames with sample quotes and codes from our data analysis. Briefly, the frames included Ghost/Guest (Black, 1996), Inclusion Kid/Different Friend, "I'll Help ____," Just Another Kid, Regular Friend, and Friends Forever.

Each of these frames was supported by data collected over a period of 4 years on 40 students who lived in urban, suburban, and rural areas. Through our participatory model, we established agreement that these frames resonated with our own experiences and were representative of social interactions for students or family members whom we knew. We came to appreciate, however, that the desirability of each frame differed across groups of significant others, who were our constituencies. Depending on who did the observing, a frame was valued either positively or negatively. For example, some of us determined that our goal must be to achieve or demonstrate reciprocal friendships for children with severe disabilities because we saw children without disabilities engaged in reciprocal friendships. We wanted social relationships between children with and without disabilities to include the same kinds of best friendships that we believe exist between peers who do not have disabilities. Some of us, however, were happy with "I'll Help ____" relationships for children with severe disabilities. It is enough for us that other children without disabilities can appreciate and learn to help children with disabilities. This helping relationship is valued as an opportunity for children with severe disabilities to participate partially in activities or to be with a peer; help is considered far more important than play or best friend relationships. The general education constituent groups, including teachers and school principals, consistently reported that having a child with severe disabilities in the classroom teaches the other students to be kind and gentle.

Ultimately, then, the test of the validity or credibility of our findings and ideas is not how strongly we can argue for or against particular interpretations but how compelling those interpretations are for those who read examples from the data and share knowledge of similar situations (see Meyer et al., 1998, p. 198).

Table 1. Frames that children without disabilities have regarding their peers with disabilities

Frame	Example quotes	Example codes
Ghost/Guest (Black, 1996)	"Nothing to do with us!"	Invisible/ignore Exclude
Inclusion Kid/ Different Friend	"He's weird."	Differential treatment by everyone
	"He's so cute!"	Affection
	"It's not nice to tease special kids!"	Polite
"I'll Help _____"	"Can I push him to science?"	Helping
	"It's my turn to help her!"	Like a teacher
Just Another Kid	"It's no big deal." *"Una vida típica"* [A typical life] "Like everyone else" "An acquaintance, not my friend"	Performance expectations and typical consequences
Regular Friend	"Polite" "He's just my friend." "He's got my back."	Hanging Affection Outer circle of friends Invited to parties Humor or having fun
Friends Forever	"Part of my life" "Best friend" "Trust with anything " (e.g., secrets)	Hanging Humor or having fun Affection

From Fisher, M., Bernazzini, J.P., & Meyer, L.H. (1998). Participatory action research: Supporting social relationships in the cooperative classroom. In J.W. Putnam (Ed.), *Celebrating diversity in the classroom: Cooperative learning and strategies for inclusion* (2nd ed., p. 145). Baltimore: Paul H. Brookes Publishing Co.; adapted by permission.

DATA

The data from which these frames emerged included observations in school, students' responses to friendship surveys, small-group student interviews, and family interviews. Trained participant observers (or fieldworkers) who lived in the school community conducted the school observations. These people included parents, aunts, grandparents, and bus drivers of general education students as well as members of the community who did not have children in school. Our fieldworkers were "hired hands" in that they were paid by the hour to collect data. Yet, they were also members of our research team who were conducting short, informal interviews with students and teachers to obtain more information about their observations and offer analytical comments related to their observations that emerged in our analyses. Our participant observers were assigned to classrooms and instructed to collect information about children's social interactions with one another and not to focus on information about teaching procedures unless the teacher in some way mediated social interactions between the children. Observers watched and often participated in the classroom for about 40 minutes and then left the classroom to find a quiet place to record what they had seen into a hand-held tape recorder. Their recorded comments were later transcribed and analyzed at the regional research site. (A more complete description of this process can be found in Biklen & Larson [1998] and Meyer, Minondo, et al. [1998].)

The observers followed individual students during their weekly school activities and routines, from arrival through dismissal. Observations were scheduled so that the minimum number of observations of each student captured all of his or her typical routines within a 2-week time frame. The actual number of observations of each student varied, depending on the student's attendance, school calendars, and the number of years the student participated in the project. For Andre, these 2-week segments were collected at least once in each 9-week school quarter that he was involved in the research project.

Students' responses to friendship surveys were collected during Project Years 3 and 4. For elementary school–age children, this survey was introduced and conducted by a graduate research assistant. Children were asked to do the following:

1. Name their circle of friends and indicate why those children were selected.

2. Name three children with whom they would like to work and indicate why those children were identified.

3. Indicate with whom they might play at recess and what they might do together.

4. Generate a list of children whom they would invite to a party.

When target children with severe disabilities were not nominated in any category, the research assistant conducted a quick follow-up probe regarding two or three classmates who did not make the list: "I notice [*child's name*] is not on your list. Are you friends with [*child's name*]?" For affirmative responses, the research assistant then asked, "Why?" The probe was first asked regarding a nontarget student and then was asked about the target student. Small-group student interviews were conducted with middle

school students during Years 3 and 4. The family interviews were conducted at least once within the time frame during which school observations were conducted for a particular child. The interview with Andre's
mother was conducted at the end of Andre's fourth-grade year at Atlantic
Avenue School.

In the next section, the frames are described in some detail as they
were reflected in Andre's third- and fourth-grade school experience. These
frames reflect the view of Andre that his classmates held during this time
frame. The data represented in this chapter include school observations,
students' responses to friendship surveys, and the interview of Andre's family. Ideally, this presentation of Andre's experience will generate a thought-
provoking response by readers about both the setting events and the adult
behaviors that supported or hindered the different frames. As educators, we
must examine carefully what adults can do differently about our environments and our behaviors to encourage liked or valued frames and to discourage disliked or devalued frames. How can we support the emotional
well-being, social and personal development, and intellectual development
of all children?

ANDRE'S FRAMES

In order to acquaint the reader with Andre's school experience, this section
presents snapshots from Andre's days at school during the spring semesters
of third and fourth grades. The snapshots are intended to capture representative social interactions on any given school day within the identified
time period. The interactions are presented as they were categorized using
our frame analysis, beginning with Ghost/Guest.

Ghost/Guest

The Ghost/Guest frame ranges from an invisible social status to one in
which the student's presence is acknowledged, but he or she is clearly
viewed as an outsider rather than as a member of the classroom. In Andre's
data, we saw some examples across the year in which Andre was ignored. In
other examples, Andre's classmates presumed to know his needs without
checking with him to verify their presumption, or their comments about
Andre were directed to someone other than Andre. In our qualitative
analysis, this kind of interaction was coded as "invisible/ignore."

> **Math**   Andre is in his seat. No one is talking to him at all. They
> are all too busy pushing their pencils across their desks to each other.
> They are busy interacting among themselves. They know Andre is
> there, yet they are not talking to him.

Observer's comment: I noticed that students' chosen seats had changed from the last time I was in Mr. P's room, and I was looking particularly at Andre's table. Franco now sat next to Andre, and I decided to sit right next to Andre to see if I could hear any conversations that would include him directly.

Reading   They have reading centers. I've mentioned this before, that the children change their seats according to their reading groups. At Andre's table, we have Anna, who is on the right side of Andre. Across from Andre, we have a boy named Ricky. The children have to open their readers. They are going to read a story. They all have their readers open in front of them. Andre's notebook is still open on his desk from the previous work they were doing. His reader is closed. It is sitting on his desk in front of him. Anna reaches over Andre, closes his notebook, and opens his reader. Ricky tells her, "Leave his notebook open so he can write." Anna says, "No. He has to read now. I have to close it so that he can follow." Neither child looks at Andre or asks him if he needs or wants some help [spring semester, third grade].

Aquarium Field Trip   The hostesses, Ms. Matz and Suzy, are giving numbers out to the children—Andre is number 4. Ms. Matz lines up the children into groups of four and five each. Andre's group includes Larika, Tash, Crystal, and Andre. In the groups, the 3s and 4s receive gloves. Ms. Heath [the special education teacher] gives Andre a glove. When he doesn't put it on, Ms. Heath puts it on for him. Andre keeps saying "No," but Ms. Heath puts it on Andre's hand anyway. The "number 5s" [children] in the group receive bags, and the "number 1s" receive writing pads to write notes. We proceed out of the wildlife conservation building to the beach to pick up the garbage on the sand. Ms. Heath, Andre, Larika, and Crystal are close to the boardwalk. The other classmates are near the water with Ms. Crowley [the paraeducator], Mr. Jordan [the classroom teacher], and the hostesses, Ms. Matz and Suzy. Ms. Heath is holding the garbage bag. Crystal is writing the notes while Tash and Larika are picking up the garbage from the sand. Andre has his gloves on and is just sitting in his wheelchair, looking on as his group and Ms. Heath do the work. The group is picking up paper, glass, and plastic garbage from the sand. Once they pick it up and put it into the bag, they have it weighed. The weather is clear, sunny, and windy. Ms. Heath is trying to move the wheelchair on the sand, but she can't. Andre is sweeping the sand, making a hole with his foot. When he sees something in the sand, he makes a screeching sound and points with his right foot. No one seems to notice [spring semester, fourth grade].

In comments and logs made over the course of Andre's third- and fourth-grade year, the participant observer who made the previous observations shared her concerns about the lack of interactions between Andre and his peers without disabilities. She attributed this problem to Andre's inability to speak. Andre faced at least two issues regarding communication. First, he had experienced the loss of his native language and cultural base. Many educators would argue that Andre needed a culture-centered approach in his learning community (cf. Cronin, 1998). During Andre's first year in an inclusive placement, a teaching assistant who was fluent in Spanish was assigned to his class. This requirement was dropped from Andre's IEP after the first grade, however, because the consensus of Andre's IEP team was that Andre was not using Spanish to communicate his needs and wants. Second, he was dependent entirely on nonvocal alternatives to communicate and interact with classmates and teachers because of his cerebral palsy. All children have a right to communicate, and it is the responsibility of adults to identify and eliminate or minimize any barriers to children's communicative interactions (Beukelman & Mirenda, 1998).

Although the professionals in Andre's education environment were searching for an effective and efficient communication strategy, no alternative was used consistently. In addition, Andre's classmates were not taught any specific steps to verify that their interpretations of his initiations or responses were accurate. It was quite natural for Andre's classmate Anna, for example, to presume to close Andre's book without confirming his thoughts on the matter. Even when challenged by another classmate, neither Anna nor her challenger, Ricky, thought to check with Andre. At the aquarium, Andre is screeching to communicate and trying his best to participate by using his feet rather than a gloved hand to find garbage. Andre attempted to make his preference for not wearing a glove understood, but the special education teacher seems to have interpreted his response as noncompliance, and consequently Andre was ignored.

Inclusion Kid/Different Friend

This frame was about "being there, but. . . ." Classmates did acknowledge children with disabilities. This acknowledgment, however, was based on how the child with a disability differed from peers without disabilities rather than on how they were alike. For example, classmates and children throughout the school knew the name of the child with a disability, but that child was not a member of any student social groups. Even in the teacher's perception, the name of the child with a disability appeared on the list of students with an asterisk next to it, or in bold print, or at the bottom of the list, out of alphabetical order to indicate special status. The child with a disability belonged only because he or she was *different*. Everyone intentionally treated him or her differently, held the student to different standards, and applied different consequences for the student's participation in the usual curriculum, activities, and routines of the classroom.

The comments and interactions from which this frame emerged represented positive statements such as "She's so cute!" and negative comments such as "He's a little weird." Although some interactions with students with disabilities were affectionate, they seemed generally characteristic of interactions between children of different ages—for example, that between an older sibling and a younger sibling.

> **Reading** Andre is sitting alone at his desk in the back of the room. Tomás looks over toward Andre and yells out, "Yo, Andre, do you want to read?" Andre looks at Tomás and starts laughing and moving around in his wheelchair. Tomás goes to Andre's desk and sits on a chair next to Andre. Tomás puts the library book on the desk and starts reading to Andre, but I don't think Andre wants to hear anything that Tomás is reading, because Andre grabs the book from Tomás and places it in front of him. Andre then tries to turn the pages with his hands, but he cannot get his fingers to work. Andre's fingers are very stiff and straight. When Tomás tries to open the book, Andre shakes his head from side to side very quickly, indicating that he doesn't want anyone to help him. Tomás says to me, "Watch this, Miss Snow," and lets the book drop on the floor. When Tomás picks up the book, Andre is also trying to pick up the book by reaching over the side of his wheelchair. Tomás puts the book on the table, but this time Tomás has opened the book.

> *Observer's comment:*   *I believed that Andre knew what Tomás had done, because Andre looked at Tomás and started laughing loudly for about 5 minutes. Tomás said, "I didn't fool Andre" [spring semester, third grade].*

> **Reading** Andre says something that sounds like "Let's go," and a boy named Ricky who sits at the table with Andre says "I want to go" and starts laughing, and so does Andre. Another boy is sitting at Andre's table. I don't know his name, but he has a brown complexion and short, black hair, and he wears a green-and-white sweater with beige pants and black sneakers. He says to Ricky, "Where are you going, Ricky?" Ricky says, "I don't know, but Andre said 'Let's go,' and I told him I wanted to go with him." Ms. C, the para[educator] assigned to help Andre, comes over and tells Ricky to stop talking with and teasing Andre and to do his work. Ms. C also takes Andre's notebook out of his desk and puts it on the desk in front of him and

puts a pencil in Andre's hand and walks away [spring semester, third grade].

At 1:30, the children are settled into their seats, and Mr. J is giving out separate tests to two reading groups. Allie [another student with a disability] calls me to do her test for her. Andre returns from the bathroom with Ms. C [paraprofessional]. After the reading test, they're going to take a spelling test. At 1:35, Ms. G [the reading teacher] is taking her group to the reading center. Andre is wheeling around the back of the classroom from desk to desk, looking at his classmates doing their tests. Mr. J leaves because he has prep. Mr. F [another building substitute] comes into the classroom to watch the students. By 1:45, students are taking the spelling test, and Andre is still wheeling around the classroom. No one requires that he stop moving about or that he take the test. At 2:00, the test is over. Mr. F lines up the children because they are going to gym. The para takes Andre and Allie downstairs to leave on their bus [spring semester, fourth grade].

Spelling   At 9:30, as I enter the classroom, it is time for a spelling test. Andre is wheeling around the classroom, bothering his classmates while they are doing their test. He is wheeling beside them, trying to grab their pencils. At 9:45, the test ends [spring semester, fourth grade].

Summary   According to the three observers' comments and the logs that they compiled, the social interactions that did occur between Andre and his classmates appeared to be different in kind from the interactions that occurred between peers without disabilities. Social interactions between a student without disabilities and Andre often conveyed a sense that the student without disabilities was assuming responsibility for, was protective of, or was teasing a younger child or sibling. For example, it is unlikely that Ricky would knock another classmate's book off his desk or that he would seek the attention of an adult to witness his interaction with any other classmate. The observers noted also that the adults in the school treated Andre differently from the way they treated students without disabilities. Despite his distracting behavior during a spelling test, Andre was not reprimanded by classmates or by adults; he was not even required to take the test. Everyone at the school had expectations for Andre that were separate and distinct from those they had for students who were developing typically.

"I'll Help ___"

Social interactions represented by this frame were those in which students without disabilities offered assistance to their peers with disabilities. Interactions were prompted by the opportunity to do something for the child or youth with a disability. This included assisting with mobility and routines (e.g., getting around the room or building, picking up something dropped, getting out materials, opening a book to the assigned page), completing school tasks, and teaching something new. These kinds of interactions were coded as "helping" and "like a teacher." In "like a teacher" occurrences, children initiated the interaction as their teacher might, in some cases even imitating the exact tone of voice and interactive posture modeled by their teacher. These interactions included correcting, helping, and tutoring, and they were positive (i.e., friendly, supportive), neutral (i.e., matter of fact, directive), and negative (i.e., scolding, condescending).

Reading   Ricky and the boy in the green-and-white sweater, Daryl, are arguing over who is going to copy Andre's reading sentences into Andre's notebook. Daryl grabs the book from Andre's desk and says, "I'm going to write down Andre's work." Ricky yells out to Ms. C [paraeducator], "Who's going to copy the sentences down for Andre?" Ms. C says, "I am writing them down now." She is across the room. She shows the book that she is writing in to the two boys. Ricky says, "I just wanted to help Andre." Then Ricky asks Ms. C who are the helpers for the day. Ms. C says, "Jamela and Tomás." Ricky repeats, "I wanted to be a helper, too" [spring semester, third grade].

At Lunch   When Andre and his helper get their lunch, they walk to their assigned table, with Andre sitting at the end of the table in his wheelchair. Andre's lunch is pork and beans, franks, an apple, and milk. The lunchroom is so noisy that you can hardly hear yourself speak. Even though one of the helpers, Camilla, is sitting next to Andre, there is no interaction between them [spring semester, third grade].

Aquarium Field Trip   Andre is with Larika, Tash, and Adrian at the box looking at a shell, a starfish, and a lobster that workers found in the sea. Larika is holding the shell close to Andre's right ear so that he can hear the sound of the shore in the shell [spring semester, fourth grade].

Summary   Helping is clearly an expected behavior in school for the children without disabilities. In Andre's fourth-grade classroom, helping Andre is a "room job." Two students are selected each day to push Andre to special classes and to the cafeteria. The opportunity to help Andre is sometimes a conditional reward for appropriate behavior. On the friendship survey administered in Andre's class in the middle of third grade, four classmates responded that they had chosen Andre as a friend because they could help him in the following ways: "teach him how to walk," "help him read," and just "help him." Students also take advantage of many natural opportunities to help without prompting from adults, as Larika did at the aquarium.

Just Another Kid

The Just Another Kid frame depicted membership in the classroom community. The student with a disability was first and foremost a "kid" or a "third-grader." Although he or she may have had a difference (e.g., cerebral palsy), it was not a big deal. The disability was not a singular, defining characteristic as in the Inclusion Kid/Different Friend frame. Rather, children were observed hanging together at school and participating in classroom activities and routines. Observed interactions that provided the basis for this category were coded variously as "affection," "humor" or "having fun," "playing together," "hanging," "advocating," "including," and "safe teasing."

Arrival   The class is glad to see Andre back after an extended absence because of illness and a move. Anna asks Andre if he has moved yet. Andre says "Yes" by shaking his head. Anna asks, "Where do you live now?" Andre stares at Anna, starts laughing, and shakes his head from side to side to say "No."

Observer's comment: Andre was telling Anna he didn't know where he lived [spring semester, third grade].

Listening to a Story   Mr. J is left with eight students in the classroom, including Andre. Andre is arm wrestling with Brian, one of his classmates. After that, Andre wheels around the classroom. Brian follows Andre around until Liza goes up to Andre and says, "I'm going to read you a storybook about Hanukkah." Andre sits beside Liza and Brian, and behind Andre is Larika. Liza is about to read the book to Andre, but Andre does not stay long. He then starts to move away from Liza and wheels around the classroom, and Brian follows [spring semester, third grade].

Science   Once the class enters the room from lunch, the children settle into their seats. Andre is already at his desk. He rode up the elevator ahead of his class. The lesson at this moment is science. They are learning how to create tornadoes in a plastic bottle. The paraeducator leaves to get a plastic bottle for Andre. Tony, who sits across from Andre, is showing some magic tricks, pretending he is swallowing a pen by sliding it down the side of his mouth. Andre starts to laugh hysterically. Tony's display of his magic trick continues until the paraeducator returns with the plastic bottle [fall semester, fourth grade].

Reading I see Sergei with his arms around Andre. Andre is giggling and leaning on Sergei's shoulder. They are taking out their readers. Sergei gets out Andre's book and opens it to the lesson page. Andre is leaning over his desk. With his right hand, he is turning the pages. Then he stops to look around at his classmates for a few minutes. After about 15 minutes, Andre begins making moaning sounds while looking toward Sergei. As Andre turns the page, Sergei is reading a paragraph. Andre's left arm is on the back of Sergei's shoulders [fall, fourth grade].

Planting Trees Two teachers and five students are outside the front of the building to plant six trees. The first one to plant a tree is Ms. C [the paraeducator]. Andre smiles and helps Ms. C kick dirt into the ground as she is patting down the dirt. Andre is laughing a lot after this. Mr. J waters the tree. Ms. C says to the students that they will be in charge of watering the trees once each week. Each classmate (Roshan, Natasia, Anthony, and Jared) then plants a tree. Andre plants his tree using his right foot to push dirt into the hole as Ms. C fixes the dirt around the plant, patting it down. The fourth tree is Roshan's. Andre helps Roshan push the dirt into the hole to pack it down. When they finish, they put up a plaque [spring semester, fourth grade].

Regular Friend and Friends Forever

No school data for Andre fell into the Regular Friends and Friends Forever categories. According to the literature on children without disabilities, though third- and fourth-graders may still rely on their parents for many functions of social relationships, the majority identify one or more best or regular friends (Fiering & Lewis, 1989; Hartup, 1996). Several other children with disabilities who participated in the Consortium studies did engage in interactions that were the basis for this frame (Meyer, Minondo, et al., 1998). On the friendship survey conducted during the spring semester of Andre's third-grade year, two children named Andre as a best friend ("I could do stuff with him," "He's nice"), and two others identified him as a regular friend ("He's funny," "He can wheel himself in his wheelchair"). These data indicated that Andre was a regular or best friend, yet none of the observed interactions between Andre and these particular students or between Andre and other classmates validated the self-reports of friendship. Several observations were categorized as Just Another Kid, but an overall review of the school observations during Andre's third- and fourth-grade years indicated that the frames of friendship that Andre's classmates held for him fell evenly across three categories: Ghost/Guest, Inclusion Kid/Different Friend, and "I'll Help ____." This interpretation of Andre's school interactions was validated by participant observers and classroom teaching staff.

ANDRE'S LIFE OUTSIDE SCHOOL

In contrast to the school data, Andre's mother described his after-school life as being rich in social relationships. She reported that Andre had a number of friends in the neighborhood as well as family friends. This section includes two vignettes of events involving Andre outside the school environment to provide a more rounded picture of his life. The information was obtained through parent interviews at the end of Andre's third-grade school year.

Life at Home

"He's very outgoing. He makes lots of friends." According to Andre's mother, these two statements accurately capture her son's interactions at home and in the neighborhood and also how she sees his life at school. At home, Andre likes to play with his older brother, his cousins, and the kids in the neighborhood. Card games are among his favorite indoor activities. Andre's mom describes how Andre's card games are "modified":

They may not play it exactly how it's played. I don't play cards myself, so I don't know. He can't use his hands properly. He can recognize figures as they go higher in sequence, so sometimes he will point to the cards and somebody's going to be there to help him pick them up, or however they arrange it. Instead of the traditional way of actually playing, they develop new little games and stuff.

Hanging with Friends

Andre loves to go to the park with his friends. He likes to go on the slide [his mother or his brother stands near the slide to provide support], and he likes to race the kids on bicycles, speeding along with them in his wheelchair. According to his mother, some of the things Andre does when he hangs out with his friends from the neighborhood include "wheelies" and "hanging 10":

Andre rides with his friends when they ride their bicycles, and he goes along with his wheelchair. Sometimes the guys do wheelies on their bicycles, and he attempts to do it with his wheelchair. Last year he had two accidents from trying this on his wheelchair. But he's a little champ. He likes to do things the other kids do. Last summer he had a great time. They were playing handball, and he was able to use his feet instead of his hands to propel the ball. So he has lots of activities. Yes, I'm satisfied with his creativity. He has always been that way. He will find a way to do whatever—find his version of the activity—with a little help, of course, but he's very outgoing. That's why I can't keep up with his friends. He makes a lot of friends. One day I go out there, and he brings me somebody. Next day he brings me somebody else.

Another example of Andre's creative play maneuvers occurred at the neighborhood playground. One day, when Andre and his friends were outside playing on the blacktop with skateboards, someone lent Andre his skateboard. Andre turned the skateboard crossways with both feet on it and tried to move his wheelchair with it, and it didn't work. Then he turned the skateboard sideways, lengthways with one foot on the ground, propelling both the wheelchair and the skateboard. Andre's persistence, flexibility, and strong desire to be a part of the neighborhood playgroup resulted in his participation by riding a skateboard with the rest of the kids.

HOW OTHERS VIEWED THESE FRAMES

As part of our participatory research process, we checked our frames with various constituent groups, including

- The teachers, parents, and children at our school sites
- Researchers, educators, employers, parents, and advocates at regularly scheduled regional and national consortium meetings
- The teachers, parents, advocates, and researchers who gathered at regional and national conferences

We found widespread agreement that a rich social life would be reflected by the existence of at least some relationships representing each of the six frames. Our research group then agreed that if a student's relationships were limited to the first three frames (Ghost/Guest, Inclusion Kid/Different Friend, "I'll Help ____"), thus excluding the Just Another Kid, Regular Friend, and Friends Forever categories, we should try to intervene. Interactions with peers without disabilities must not be limited solely to frames in which peers view children with disabilities in terms defined by the categories Ghost/Guest, Inclusion Kid/Different Friend, or "I'll Help ____." On the contrary, we believed that students' disabilities were not the salient feature of their interactions with others, that everyone needs help sometimes, that everyone should have a network of pals, and that everyone should have at least one best friend (Fisher et al., 1998).

We also determined that we would identify interventions that addressed groups of children rather than target children who had difficulty with initiating certain identified social skills for individual remediation. In designing our intervention plans, we were determined to identify multiple measures as indicators of meaningful change for children with and without disabilities. Increasing the specific knowledge and performances for target children and youth with disabilities could be two such indicators of meaningful change in making and keeping friends. Asher, Parker, and Walker (1996), for example, identified 10 knowledge and performance factors that are useful for moving from acceptance to friendship. These include initiating interactions outside the setting, being perceived as a fun, resourceful, and enjoyable companion, recognizing the spirit of equality, self-disclosure, expressing caring, concern, admiration, and affection in appropriate ways, being able to help friends when they are in need, reliable partners, managing disagreements and resolving more serious conflicts, being able to forgive, and recognizing that friendship can be embedded within the broader social network of the peer group and the classroom.

It is necessary to move beyond this traditional focus on one child's knowledge and performance—an individual child's skill repertoire—and also address the knowledge and performances of his or her peers and the adults in these settings. For many children and youth, initiating activities outside school necessitates parent involvement with respect to scheduling and transportation. Furthermore, children acquire new friends through networks. Preliminary steps must address proximity and introduction so that children can begin to identify commonalities and shared interests. The teacher's beliefs and understanding of his or her role with respect to children's friendships also have many implications for the ways in which a classroom is structured and consequently whether conditions for making friends exist and whether opportunities are nurtured. Each classmate's understanding of his or her responsibility to others in the classroom community has significant implications for membership and the possibility of friendship. We have learned that in order for an intervention to be likely to succeed, it must have a broader focus than an individual student's repertoire and must consider other criteria for naturalistic intervention; that is, it must be doable with available resources, sustainable over time, constituency owned and operated, and culturally inclusive (Meyer, Park, et al., 1998a).

Based on the summary in this chapter of Andre's interactions at school, and given the Consortium's intervention perspective, some manner of intervention for Andre would be more than appropriate. Although our analyses yielded many interactions represented by the frames Ghost/Guest, Inclusion Kid/Different Friend, and "I'll Help ____" and several interactions that were categorized as Just Another Kid, there were no examples in the Regular Friend or Friends Forever category. Andre "sort of" belonged as a member of his class, yet he was not connected within a smaller group or with one or two peers in particular. Although he appeared to have connections with his classmates and to be well liked by classmates—for example, they initiated affectionate interactions with him and he with them—Andre did not have Regular Friend or Friends Forever frames operating at school. Children in third and fourth grades still depend on parents for many functions of social relationships, but the majority also report Regular Friend and Friends Forever relationships (Fiering & Lewis, 1989; Furman & Buhrmeister, 1987; Hartup, 1996).

In addition to the school observations, our collective information regarding Andre suggested that many opportunities existed for possible interactions that could have resulted in his attaining valued frames. For example, Andre's mother pointed out that Andre is exceedingly motivated to hang with his peers. He does in fact hang with friends when he visits his old neighborhood. Furthermore, three different observers commented on several occasions when they perceived that adults' behaviors had interfered with Andre's interactions with his peers. In student surveys conducted during the spring semesters of third and fourth grades, peers' responses specific to Andre suggested that several children were interested in inviting Andre to parties, yet invitations were never extended. Teachers and observers described Andre as a "most likable kid." This chapter's opening vignette captured Andre partly in the Inclusion Kid role—Andre has name recognition and is widely known at school—and also as Just Another Kid—having a great time playing his role in a class production with his classmates. It seems, then, that further analysis and reflection on at least the issues described in the following section possibly could cement Andre's status as Just Another Kid as well as move him in the direction of Regular Friend and Friends Forever status.

DYNAMICS OF HELPING INTERACTIONS THROUGHOUT THE CLASS

When one student is singled out as the student to help, he or she may become "the helpee" (Van der Klift & Kunc, 1994). Help is a critical and valued skill that creates opportunities for people to be better citizens. The next step for educators is to design classroom communities in which help is an underlying value that is often demonstrated, a classroom in which each child both gives and receives help.

Effects of Adult Behaviors in Supporting, Blocking, or Hindering Interactions

At the aquarium, Larika naturally supported Andre by holding a seashell close enough for him to hear the ocean. Andre attempted to help his group by locating trash with his foot and vocalizing to get their attention, but this helping interaction was "missed" by the adults assigned to support him. Andre's peers teased him during reading, and the paraprofessional intervened, presumably to stop the teasing and get the boys back "on task." While emphasizing the importance of an academic task, how might an adult reshape his or her mediation so that such an interaction builds connections and solidarity between students with and without disabilities? Andre went to lunch with two classmates, yet no interactions between the children resulted during the lunch period, despite the students' proximity. A quick assessment of the cafeteria situation regarding seating for adults and children may indicate that moving Andre nearer to the group of third-grade boys would improve Andre's chances for lunchtime chitchat.

Information that Andre's Peers May Need to Communicate Effectively with Andre

In the series of Ghost/Guest vignettes, Andre is at a disadvantage in some cases simply because peers and teachers neglect to verify his need or his perspective regarding their interpretation of events. Anna and Ricky might simply have asked Andre to indicate whether he wanted to read his book by nodding or shaking his head. This strategy may be another possible next move for Andre's instruction team.

Additional Curricular Redesign and Adaptations

Andre seems to be wandering during spelling tests. This may be a time during the day when alternative assignments are required for Andre, or maybe an alternative means for responding to the same test could be designed for Andre.

Information from Andre's Family Regarding Friendship Opportunities that Occur Outside School

Are there boys from Andre's new neighborhood who are his classmates or members of other fourth-grade classrooms? As a next move, teachers and peers could identify these children and determine when during the routine of the day at Atlantic Avenue School Andre might meet up with them. Andre's family might like to have some names and telephone numbers to help Andre pursue friendships outside the school day. Given our responsibility for children's well-being and social development as well as their academic and intellectual development, these are a few of the possible promising next moves for Andre and his learning community.

DISCUSSION QUESTIONS

1. Observers noted in their comments that teachers often seem to get in the way of Andre's interactions with classmates. How can the adults (teachers, paraprofessionals, and parents) in these vignettes replay their roles so that Andre moves from being Just Another Kid to Regular Friend and Friends Forever?

2. The adults in the school vignettes seem to place a high priority on helping Andre. How might the class as a community consider the varied aspects of social relationships for *all* students? And teachers?

3. Andre's mother and older brother seem to be "naturals" in facilitating Andre's social interactions at the park. How might schools connect with families with regard to social relationships both inside and outside the school?

4. Andre appears to be at a disadvantage with respect to communication. What steps would you recommend that Andre's teachers take regarding the development of a culturally relevant learning community and AAC? Are there ways in which the general curriculum (or Andre's IEP) might be expanded to ensure that these steps are considered or taken?

5. What recommendations can be made to Andre's elementary-to-middle school transition team? Andre's mother has great expectations for Andre's education in the United States. How can the school community continue to validate her decision to immigrate and maintain her sense that, indeed, inclusive schooling pays off?

7

Cole's Story

Outcomes in Membership, Relationships, and Skills

Debbie Staub

In comparison with last year, when Cole would do everything he could to get all attention directed to him, when he was breaking things and ripping pages out of books, now he can move in and out of small groups, be by himself, work with his buddies, and understand what it means when someone tells him, "Please be quiet." I think his understanding is great, and his sense of humor is leaping off the charts. I think a sense of humor often does great things with understanding how kids are really capable. But, you know, Cole still doesn't write his name, and he doesn't do all the things that we want in measuring kids' academic attainments. How do schools measure the Coles of the world? I don't think anybody feels overly comfortable with this kind of question. But on the humanistic side of the coin, it feels right to have him in my class. I just know that somewhere in all this confusion and looking for answers, Cole has benefited and so have I. (Cole's fifth- and sixth-grade general education teacher)

Cole, a young man with severe disabilities, would not be considered a "poster child" for inclusion. With a long history of aggressive behavioral outbursts and other challenging issues, Cole is the type of student about whom some educators might say, "Inclusion is fine, *except* for students like Cole." Yet, having known Cole for more than 5 years and having observed him in inclusive school settings from his sixth-grade school year into high school, it is difficult to imagine what Cole's life would be like if he had not had the opportunity to be educated alongside his peers without disabilities. This chapter tells the story of Cole's life in inclusive education settings from his sixth-grade experience in elementary school until the end of his ninth-grade year in junior high school. Westling and Fox defined the term *inclusion* as the practice of "providing the supports necessary to promote the learning of every student in the neighborhood or home-zone school without the use of separate special education classrooms" (1995, p. 228). Cole's story is about the outcomes he experienced, the challenges and issues that his family and his teachers faced, and the perceived meaning that Cole's inclusion experience had for Cole and his peers.

COLE

Cole was born without complications into an upper-middle-class European American family in February 1980. Cole showed typical developmental growth until 11½ months of age. At that time, he contracted spinal meningitis, resulting in early paralysis and severe seizures. Many of the milestones he had reached prior to his illness, including walking and beginning talking, were lost. He did not walk again until he was almost 5 years old, and he did not use words again until he was 6 years of age, and even then he used them only sporadically and inconsistently. Both of Cole's parents hold professional jobs, and his family lives in an upscale suburban neighborhood in the Pacific Northwest. Cole has one brother, Ryan, who is 3 years older than Cole.

When Cole returned home from an extended hospital stay while he had meningitis, Cole's parents, Marty and Sue, realized the devastating impact of Cole's illness on his development. They began their long journey toward ensuring that Cole received the best educational opportunities available in, as Sue phrased it, "environments that would provide better role models for him." Cole attended first a self-contained infant-toddler program for 18 months and then a segregated preschool in his home school district, which served preschool-age children with moderate and severe developmental delays, until he was 5 years old. After preschool, Cole attended a segregated elementary school that formerly had served children with moderate and severe disabilities from the entire school district. Between Cole's first- and second-grade school years, the school district decided to select several elementary schools that would house self-contained classrooms for children with moderate and severe disabilities. Children were placed in these classes based on their disabilities and on where they lived. Although not all students with disabilities necessarily attended their neighborhood schools, it happened that Cole's neighborhood elementary school (the same school that his brother attended) served the needs of students with moderate and severe disabilities in its self-contained program. Cole began attending his neighborhood school, Jane Austen Elementary, as a student in the self-contained program when he was 7 years old.

Jane Austen Elementary School is located in a middle-class suburban neighborhood. The school enrolls 800 students in preschool through the sixth grade. Approximately 94% of the school population is European American, and 6% are of other ethnicities.

Interview data and individualized education program (IEP) documents indicated that Cole's behaviors in his self-contained classroom included "mimicking other students with special needs," "throwing temper tantrums during which he could not be reasoned with," and "physically assaulting the teacher and paraeducators by kicking, biting, and pulling their hair." Marty and Sue were discouraged with Cole's behavior problems and slow growth in critical skill areas such as communication and self-help. So overwhelmed were they with just trying to find some balance among Cole's behavior problems and making it through everyday life that it did not occur to them to be worried about Cole's lack of social interactions with his peers. When the principal at Jane Austen Elementary School announced at the end of Cole's second-grade year that the school was moving to a "full inclusion" education model, Marty and Sue were intrigued and excited about the possibilities for their son. They attended the year-long planning meetings and participated on the core team that would be responsible for developing a school mission statement and a plan for implementing inclusion at Jane Austen for the following school year.

Cole's parents described his first inclusive school experiences as moderately successful. Cole continued to exhibit many of the same problem behaviors that had been identified in his self-contained class. Although his inappropriate behaviors were never eliminated fully, they decreased over time. By the middle of his fifth-grade year, Cole had established several positive relationships with classmates without disabilities and had improved his skills in receptive and expressive communication. Unfortunately, the last 3 months of his fifth-grade year were marked by his poor health, including the recurrence of seizures, which led to prolonged absences from school. In addition, a gastrointestinal tube was inserted into Cole's abdomen to provide him with much-needed nutrition.

Research assistants and I began observing Cole in the fall of his sixth-grade year, which was a difficult time for him because he still was experiencing health problems. When I first met Cole, he was a thin, frail 12-year-old boy coming out of a period of frequent seizure activity. There was a lot of concern regarding his medication. For a good part of his fifth-grade year and early into his sixth-grade year, Cole spent a lot of time sleeping. A combination of frequent seizures and high dosages of medication to control the seizures was exhausting him. Cole's alert behavior was characterized by frequent behavioral outbursts such as tantrums or physical aggression toward the paraeducator who was assigned to work with him full time. A month into the Consortium's research and observations in Cole's class, however, his behavior shifted and he began experiencing fewer seizures. Many exciting outcomes were noted at this time and documented across a series of observational studies. They are described herein within a conceptual framework that the Consortium's research group formulated. The following is a description of the conceptual framework used to describe these outcomes.

CONCEPTUAL FRAMEWORK FOR UNDERSTANDING OUTCOMES OF INCLUSION FOR INDIVIDUALS WITH MODERATE AND SEVERE DISABILITIES

In an effort to describe outcomes that occur for students in inclusive school programs, from fall 1992 to summer 1996, colleagues from the Consortium for Collaborative Research on Social Relationships: Inclusive Schools and Communities for Children and Youth with Diverse Abilities (Meyer et al., 1992) and the Inclusive Schools Research Group (Peck, White, Billingsley, & Schwartz, 1992) collected and analyzed data from multiple sources that included classroom observations, interviews with teachers, parents, peers without disabilities, and paraeducators, videotape recordings and documents such as IEPs, and examples of children's work. An important feature of this work has been the Consortium's effort to construct an understanding of outcomes for students with disabilities in active dialogue with parents, teachers, and students (Carr & Kemmis, 1986; Freire, 1985; Torres, 1995). In these conversations and in the more "objective" data the Consortium collected, Consortium researchers confronted again and again compelling evidence of change in children's lives that was not described adequately in terms of the simple acquisition of skills. The outcomes documented for Cole were no exception. Consortium researchers used the inductive category formation techniques that Lincoln and Guba (1985) described, as well as the cross-case analysis techniques that Miles and Huberman (1994) set forth, to analyze hundreds of excerpts from observations and interview data. From these analyses, the Consortium researchers developed a conceptual framework that describes the types of outcomes they observed for students with severe disabilities in inclusive school settings.

Conceptual Framework

The types of outcome patterns that have emerged in the Consortium's follow-along data set are conceptualized in terms of three broad domains. The first domain of outcomes that Consortium researchers observed had to do with the extent to which children with severe disabilities achieved *membership*, or a sense of belonging, in the formal and informal groups that made up the social fabric of the classroom and the school (Ferguson 1994; Schnorr, 1990). Second, Consortium researchers observed that children in inclusive classrooms may develop a wide variety of *personal relationships* with other children. Third, the Consortium's findings suggest that many of the children whom the Consortium researchers studied were learning many of the same types of *skills* that have been the traditional focus of special education outcome assessment. These include social-communicative skills, academic skills, and functional skills. Each of these broad outcome domains had strong effects on the others. Moreover, each of the domains may be viewed in terms of its relationship to a higher-order outcome that Consortium researchers conceptualized as *increased participation in valued roles, activities, and settings of the community and culture* (Bronfenbrenner, 1979; Lave & Wenger, 1991).

Membership

The term *membership* is used in this chapter to refer to the phenomenological sense of belonging to a social group such as a classroom, a cooperative work group, or a friendship clique. Membership cannot be observed directly. People can and routinely do, however, make inferences about the extent to which a child is treated as a member of a group by observing aspects such as accommodations that group members make to include a child, shared symbols that the group uses (e.g., special T-shirts, team names, uniforms), and rituals that occur in the group context (e.g., special greetings, activities, or roles performed only by group members).

Membership is an important outcome in and of itself in the lives of children, including those with severe disabilities. In fact, membership outcomes generally have received the highest importance ratings from parents and teachers in social validation studies of the Consortium's outcome framework (Peck et al., 1994). In addition, membership sets the stage for additional opportunities. For example, the extent to which a student with severe disabilities is viewed as a member of the classroom can affect the kinds of opportunities that he or she is likely to have for participating in social relationships as well as other classroom roles and activities (Schnorr, 1990). These opportunities for participation can have an impact on the child's skill development and the formation of classroom relationships, as became evident in Cole's story.

Relationships

The domain of outcomes referred to as *relationships* includes the character-istics and the extent of dyadic personal relationships between children with disabilities and their peers without disabilities. Consortium researchers categorized relationships between students with disabilities and other indi-viduals (both with and without disabilities) on the basis of 1) consistencies in their social interactions over time, 2) interviews with teachers and parents, and 3) when possible, informal interviews with the students themselves. As in most relationships, the qualitative features of the social relationships that Consortium researchers observed between individual children were not static but often varied across specific contexts (Fiske, 1992).

Clearly, a high-priority outcome for children with severe disabilities, as is true for any child, is the development of friendships. Friendships—more specifically, the lack of friendships in the lives of individuals with se-vere disabilities—in fact have been the focus of most analyses of social re-lationships in the professional literature to date (Haring, 1993; Meyer et al., 1998b). Other types of relationships, however, also play an important role as sources of learning and support for students with severe disabilities. The Consortium's observations of the variety of relationships that emerged be-tween children with disabilities and their peers without disabilities led us to identify four types of relationships: play/companion, helper (giver), helpee (receiver), and conflictual. Each of these types of relationships offers im-portant learning opportunities for children (see Richardson & Schwartz, 1998).

Skills

The third domain in the outcome framework included descriptions of the behavioral competencies that children develop over time. These have been the predominant focus of traditional outcome assessment in special educa-tion. Skills—particularly social and communicative skills—can strongly af-fect (but do not exclusively determine) the extent to which students with severe disabilities are able to participate in a variety of social roles, activi-ties, and settings. The Consortium's analysis of what children learned in in-clusive settings and how they learned it suggested that many critical skills are acquired within the context of social activities in which personal rela-tionships and membership play an important part (Grenot-Scheyer, Staub, Peck, & Schwartz, 1998). Consortium researchers observed children learn-ing new skills in the context of counting materials for distribution to class-mates, checking off the names of children for a lunch count, reading a sim-plified script for a role in a class play, and many other social activities.

Linkages Among Outcome Domains

The relationships among the outcomes described in the previous section are transactional. That is, the quality of a child's social relationships with peers is affected by and affects the child's status as a member of the group and also is affected by and affects the skills that he or she develops. All of these factors contribute to the student's access to and participation in valued roles, activities, and settings in the school and the community. The richest examples of inclusive educational practice suggested that multiple positive outcomes are likely to accrue to the students involved in an inclusive education program.

COLE: A CASE ILLUSTRATION

In this section, the outcome framework is used to describe and evaluate Cole's outcomes regarding membership, relationships, and skills beginning in his sixth-grade year and during the next 3 years as a member of an inclusive junior high school. In particular, the reader is encouraged to note the critical functions that Cole's *social relationships* played in providing him with opportunities to learn new skills, and to achieve a sense of *membership* in or belonging to valued social groups and as a means of supporting participation in valued roles, activities, and settings.

Sixth Grade

Cole attended the sixth grade in Mr. H's multi-age, fifth- and sixth-grade class with 30 other students who were developing typically and another student with moderate developmental delays. Mr. H's education philosophy was based on a belief in self-directed learning, primarily by using literature as a catalyst. The stress on literature in this classroom was evidenced by bookshelves that were overflowing with reading material for students of all ability levels. When students in Mr. H's class were not engaged in independent expert studies or working on small-group projects, they could be found in a large group discussing topics of current interest.

As noted previously, Cole was experiencing many seizures, and his medications exerted considerable influence over his daily activities in the beginning of his sixth-grade year. As the year progressed, Cole's medical issues appeared to stabilize, and he was having fewer seizures. In fact, his paraeducator commented, "This is the best he has ever been." The following subsections describe the types of membership, relationships, and skills outcomes that Consortium researchers observed in Mr. H's class.

Membership

Observer's comment: Cole sat down between two of his class-mates who did not have disabilities and started eating his lunch. He talked to Phil and sat listening to peers as they talked. He occasion-ally repeated things they said, and they all laughed.

As a sixth grader, Cole was very much a member of his class. The Consortium's data revealed consistent indicators of Cole's member-ship within the class. He usually followed the class schedule, includ-ing library visits, music and physical education classes, lunch, recess, and some academic activities.

Observer's comment: Cole got up from the computer, picked up his stuffed dog, and goofed around by his peers for a few minutes until the teacher came over and asked Cole to read silently like the other students were doing.

Although Cole's academic skill level prevented him from performing many of the same academic activities as his classmates, adaptation attempts were made successfully to have Cole engage in the same content areas. For example, an observer commented that when the class was doing a math activity, Cole sat at the back of the room, "working with a [teacher's aide] on a counting activity or on the com-puter doing a numbers game." Unfortunately, many times Cole's health problems placed physical boundaries on his access to classroom ac-tivities.

Observer's comment: During a whole-class art activity, Cole is walking around the room getting supplies with peers helping him. Cole is about to get started on his art project when he has a seizure and has to lie down for awhile.

Cole also participated in daily classroom routines and transi-tions, including doing morning check-in, taking the attendance list to the office, preparing for lunch, and cleaning up at the end of the day. Cole often needed direction to perform classroom routines.

Observer's comment: Students are walking around the classroom, cleaning up before they leave school for the day. A peer tells Cole he can empty the garbage. Cole picks up the garbage and empties it into a large trash can.

Cole was included in class meetings and discussions, popcorn sharing, writing, and class votes, though he was not always engaged. Cole's ability to participate actively in the classroom seemed to increase during the course of his sixth-grade year.

Cole's paraeducator's comment: [Before Christmas,] he was just so . . . quiet, you know? Now he is singing, wants to have a turn in music class to get up and perform. Like in a large group, when he raises his hand [he does this lots of times], he does have something to say about what they are talking about.

Also noted was an increasingly consistent pattern of Cole's membership in small groups, both teacher- and peer-developed. These groups developed primarily during informal times, such as during recess with limited to no adult direction. Groups formed for academic activities were often marked by Cole's lack of engagement.

Observer's comment: Looking at a book, Paul [a peer] says, "You've got to pick out a part to play, Cole. Do you want to be that one? Cole, you have to pick!" Cole is not choosing.

Cole became accustomed to small groups of peers helping or encouraging his academic progress, and his paraeducator noted, "When there's a peer working with him, you get a lot more out of Cole." As his sixth-grade year progressed, recess and lunchtime offered a glimpse into Cole's developing inclusion in peer-developed groups.

Observer's comment: Cole sat down between Phil and another one of his classmates without disabilities and started eating his lunch. He talked to Phil about something. . . . Cole sat listening to peers talking around him, repeating what they said occasionally and laughing, and eating his lunch.

One observer captured Cole initiating a small-group activity during recess.

Observer's comment: Cole walked over and stood right next to the boys [three classmates without disabilities] and handed the ball to one of them. Cole started to walk away, back to the basketball court. His friend Phil came over and asked Cole what he was doing. Cole said, "Playing ball!" Phil said, "Do you want me to play ball with you?" Cole said "Yeah" and ran to the court—kind of jumping along the way like he was excited.

There was little evidence of school membership outcomes for Cole and only a few examples of Cole's participating in extracurricular activities. Interviews with Cole's teachers and parents indicated that his medical issues contributed significantly to his lack of participation in outside activities.

Relationships

Observer's comment: Aaron [a classmate without disabilities] walked right over to Cole and started talking to him. He said, "We're making a new rule — no being mean." Then he walked with Cole to the front of the room and told him to tell another boy what the new rule was. Cole tapped the boy's shoulder to tell him, but the boy walked away. Aaron smiled and put his hand on Cole's shoulder and walked with him a ways.

Consistent with his strong showing of class membership during his sixth-grade year, Cole also developed relationships with several of his peers without disabilities. His teacher commented, "Cole has had friendships or is sort of related with almost everybody in this class." Sue, Cole's mother, noticed that he was "more interested in trying to interact and have some sort of a relationship with the other kids" than he was before the sixth grade. Initially, most of the interactions between Cole and his peers were typical of a helper–helpee relationship wherein Cole was the recipient of help.

Observer's comment: A friend of Cole's from his class meets him at the bus and walks him to class. This same friend helps Cole get ready for class when they get to the classroom.

Observations later in the year showed that Cole had established play/ companion relationships with Aaron and Phil. He often sat with them during lunch and sought them out at recess and in the classroom. There was only one recorded example of friendship activities extending beyond the school environment: Aaron visited Cole at his home, where, according to Aaron, they "ate a snack, watched about 5 minutes of TV, then played karaoke for the next 4 hours."

Skills

Cole's paraeducator's comment: When [Cole] used to get a cold, for example, he would expect someone to get him a tissue and either wipe his nose for him or at least talk him through the process of doing it himself. Now if he has a cold, he gets up, finds a tissue, and blows his nose. He won't even let you do it for him; he'll get it by himself.

During the latter part of his sixth-grade year, Cole's social development showed considerable progress. In part, this may be attributed to the stabilization of his medications and seizures. His interactions with peers, according to Cole's mother, demonstrated that "he has grasped the concept of sharing and trading." His paraeducator noted, "He is like a different boy. . . . You can reason with him." Cole's progress in this area was even noticed by a classmate without disabilities, who commented to an observer, "Cole is listening more, and his behavior is better." Cole also began to share his sense of humor with both peers and adults who surrounded him. While playing basketball with Phil at recess one day, for example, Cole intentionally threw the ball into a mud puddle, seeming to wait for Phil's reaction.

Observer's comment: Phil took [the ball] out [of the puddle] and Cole said, "Ball in puddle" and made a funny face. Paul laughed and said, "Because you threw it in the puddle, Cole." Cole laughed. Cole walked with Paul to class and said to [the observer], "Threw ball in the mud puddle" and laughed again.

During the sixth grade, Cole's academic tasks were concentrated on his recognition of numbers, letters, colors, and picture communication symbols. There were numerous examples of Cole's love of picture books and, though he was unable to read them on his own, many observations showed that he listened intently and examined the pictures while being read to. Reading sessions with his peers sometimes included Cole's retelling the story and/or identifying relevant information about the books.

Observer's comment: While sitting with his friend Phil, Cole opens his favorite book, Beauty and the Beast, and announces, "The Beast is sad." Later, Cole sniffs a picture and says, "The Beast smells!"

Cole's paraeducator commented that she believed "Cole processes a lot of stuff. . . . [I]t will come out in a couple of weeks."

Cole's ability to listen during class presentations and discussions progressed considerably in sixth grade, such as his participation in literature sharing: "Cole 'pops in,' stands up, and shows his magazine" [observer's comment]. His ability to monitor himself also appeared to improve: "While building a birdhouse, Cole was visiting with peers, and his paraeducator noted that he stayed focused and she had to warn him only once to be careful" [observer's comment]. The task of filling the staff soda machine provided a successful opportunity for Cole to practice listening and problem-solving skills.

Observer's comment: Cole successfully loaded the machine and followed directions from his paraeducator. Cole put cans into the machine by looking at their color. He opened the machine door wider and moved a chair over to put by the door.

Cole's ability to respond to his environment without constant redirection from a peer or a paraeducator improved throughout the year.

Observer's comment: When the bell rang for the end of recess, Cole lingered behind, finishing his snack. When he was done, he put his trash in the can and walked to the door.

Summary   Throughout his sixth-grade year, teachers, peers, parents, and observers witnessed a gradual increase in Cole's participation in his school environment. There was a direct connection between this development and the stabilization of his complex medical issues as well as a classroom setting that offered Cole the freedom to interact socially with his peers. Consortium researchers hypothesized that the loosely structured classroom, the reasonable and defined expectations, and the acceptance of Cole by both his peers and the adults in the classroom contributed significantly to his success in this inclusive environment. In an interview, Mr. H stated,

In order for Cole to be accepted in the classroom, he had to be accepted as a person, not [an] anomaly. And I thought that the kids took that on. They learned that if he had one of his tantrums and wasn't going to get up, they could walk over him, step over him, get into the class, and life went on.

Likewise, Cole influenced Mr. H.

I have to give and take. . . . It seems like we all have a role, we kind of move in and out of circles. . . . There's permission, there's a lot of permission for kids to interact with him.

The end of Cole's sixth-grade year was marked by celebration of his achievements in communication, reduction in his behavior challenges, his relationships with his peers, and his membership in his class and school community. Cole attended the sixth-grade overnight camp with his classmates, and he participated in the sixth-grade graduation ceremony.

Junior High School: Grades 7, 8, and 9

Cole's parents were very pleased with Cole's growth, and they were excited about his transition to Kennedy Junior High School. A primary reason for their enthusiastic attitude regarding Kennedy Junior High was the smooth planning and preparation for Cole's transition to this school. A great deal of planning and preparation occurred in the spring of his sixth-grade year: Cole made several visits to the junior high, where he met his future teachers and got to know the school's physical environment.

Kennedy Junior High School is Cole's neighborhood school, which is both middle-class and suburban as is Jane Austen Elementary School. The school enrolls approximately 900 students in seventh through ninth grades and serves a predominantly European American student population. When Cole first began school at Kennedy, it was in only its second year of operation. The mission of Kennedy Junior High is to ensure that every student, regardless of ability level, is able to perform successfully and is challenged in general education classes. It was the only junior high school out of six others in the school district that followed a full inclusion model (see Staub et al., 1996, for a more detailed description of this school). Since its inception, the faculty at Kennedy have been committed to providing a curriculum that accommodates all learners (Jorgensen, Fisher, Sax, & Skoglund, 1998; Staub et al., 1996). Adaptations to the curriculum were just as likely to occur for slower learners as they were for accelerated learners. The curriculum also reflected the use of recommended practices in education, such as cooperative learning strategies, multiage grouping, thematic instruction, and student-directed learning techniques (Eichinger & Downing, 1996; Putnam, 1998).

Given Cole's history of behavior challenges and health issues, the special education teacher and staff at Kennedy made a concentrated effort to prepare the Kennedy community for Cole's arrival. This preparation included the special education teacher's providing ability awareness training for students and faculty:

When I provide the ability awareness training, I try to talk openly about what might be some of the more uncomfortable issues such as bladder control, or what if Cole burps out loud in class. I always receive per-

mission ahead of time from the parents to discuss these things. No question is forbidden at this point. I also help the students discuss how they should behave like themselves around their peers with disabilities and what to do in the event of a seizure or something like that. (Staub et al., 1996, p. 199)

Cole's participation at Kennedy also was facilitated by the student aide program. The student aide program was developed at Kennedy because of the small number of special education staff available to support the needs of students with disabilities in the general education classrooms. A student aide was assigned to attend a scheduled general education class for a student with disabilities. Each student with disabilities had a different aide for every class period. Each student's schedule was based on individual need and choice. For example, Cole required classes that offered him the opportunity to be active and move around. Therefore, his schedule included drama, band, home economics, physical education, and leadership. Each of these classes met the criteria of sufficient opportunity to move about and offered appropriate contexts for addressing Cole's IEP goals.

The responsibilities of the student aides varied considerably and were influenced by subject matter, the needs of the student with disabilities, the general education teacher's expectations, and the student aide's personality. Student aides were monitors, helpers, friends, and/or teachers. For example, in Cole's case, many student aides had several roles, as one of them described:

One thing I do is to make sure that Cole behaves appropriately. I try to remind him not to make noises, which is hard because he always wants to do rude things, and so I had to teach him not to do that.

The Consortium's analyses suggested that Cole's experiences and outcomes during his years at Kennedy were affected by several factors: the student aide program, a continuation of medical problems, changes in his home environment, and his developing desire for independence. Although Cole had student aides accompany him throughout the day, his health issues still required adult aides to be nearby. Adults did have fewer interactions with him, however, because the student aides provided both the physical assistance needed and the peer contact that Cole desired. Changes in medication and other health problems (e.g., surgeries, seizures) continued to influence Cole's behavior during school hours. Because of his increasingly aggressive behaviors and his growing physical size, Cole's family decided to move him first into a group home at the beginning of his eighth-grade year and later into foster care. As Cole began to assert his desire for independence, he experienced frustration. His mother suggested that this was a disadvantage of his inclusion: "Cole is there at school with these kids who have all this freedom; they get to make so many decisions for themselves, and he can't do that." In spite of these upheavals in Cole's life, he continued to experience positive outcomes in his inclusive school environment.

Membership

Special education teacher's comment: This year [eighth grade] I've noticed that he has social connections to a group of four or five guys. He sits with them. They joke together. They laugh appropriately. I don't think he initiates conversation that much, though he might initiate some interaction — like pointing to someone's hat — or he'll initiate some verbal jokes — it's the kind of thing that any teenager might do. He looks as if he feels he's one of the guys.

During his first year at Kennedy, Cole followed a schedule similar to that of his classmates. His time in general education classes gradually decreased over the 3 years, however, for a variety of reasons: Teachers decided that certain activities were inappropriate for him, Cole came to prefer the special education room, and Cole's medical and behavior problems continued to limit both his participation and his engagement. Although the teachers appeared supportive of Cole's inclusion, according to several observations, Cole's teachers sometimes asked him to return to the resource room when he was scheduled for general education classes. These requests seemed to coincide with class activities such as testing, long lectures, and science labs.

Observer's comment: As Cole and his student aide arrived at his math/science class, the teacher told Casey [the student aide] that it would be better if Cole worked outside class today because they were going to be doing a science lab.

There also were several observations in which Cole refused to leave the resource room and attend his general education classes.

Observer's comment: Cole's teacher asked Cole if he was ready to go to his math class. Cole said "no" and walked toward Brandt [a student aide]. Brandt said, "Come on Cole, let's go to math, okay?" Cole put his head down.

Interview data revealed the effect that Cole's medications had on his participation: One of his afternoon student aides reported that "a lot of times, he's sleeping." Despite such barriers, Cole enjoyed membership in the school, in his classes, and in teacher-developed small groups. He was well liked, prompting one of his general education teachers to comment that Cole is "probably one of the most popular students at our school." His popularity was not limited to his peers. In one incident, his popularity caused him to miss his physical education class.

Observer's comment: Carrying a guitar that one of his student aides gave him, Cole was walking to class when the band teacher stopped Cole and said, "Oh, you got a guitar." And Cole said, "Yeah, you want me to do a concert?" And [the teacher] said, "Yeah, come on in."

In an effort to prevent Cole's tendency to become distracted (and/or to distract others), his teachers expected and encouraged him to participate in class activities. Playing instruments in music, "directing the curtain" in drama, cooking in home economics, and performing duties in leadership class were examples of Cole's participation in his classes. The physical freedom of physical education class sometimes triggered Cole's inappropriate behaviors, but the gym teacher took advantage of Cole's desire for attention.

Observer's comment: A boy from the class holds a bullhorn and talks into it. . . . Cole follows him around. . . . [The teacher] gives it to Cole and tells him to repeat what she says.

There was much evidence of Cole's progress as a small-group member. He participated in role-playing scenarios in drama, squad activities in physical education, community field trips, and brainstorming sessions in the resource room. Many of the examples reflected his developing understanding of his role in a teacher-led small group but also showed his tendency to imitate others' behaviors.

Observer's comment: In foods class, Cole is stirring some ingredients in a large bowl. There are three other students in his cooking group. They all watch Cole, and when he is finished, they take the bowl, stir it a little more, add more flour, and dump the dough onto the table. Cole watches them . . . and dumps the flour container onto the table.

Examples of Cole's participation in a peer-developed small group were minimal at first but increased during his time in junior high. One of his teachers described Cole's role in small groups.

He seems to be hesitant to interact with a group of kids at first, but then usually one of his buddies says, "Hey, there's Cole. Cole, come sit with us." And before long he's laughing and hanging out with the group, looking very comfortable.

Relationships

Observer's comment: Cole sees Chris [one of his student aides] walk into the room. As Chris walks toward Cole, Cole gets very excited and says in a distinct voice, "There's Chris! Look, he's back!" Chris smiles and says, "Hi, Cole." Cole says, "He's back, he's back!"

A paraeducator succinctly summed up Cole's outcomes in this area during his years in junior high: "He is quicker to make relationships." Indeed, the data support this assertion and provide many examples of Cole's friendly interactions with peers. Cole's improved ability to interact even caused one of his peers to comment that Cole's "friendships look like guy friendships." The student aide program at Kennedy provided a consistent format for Cole to develop relationships with his peers who were developing typically. As expected (Murray-Seegert, 1989), these relationships initially were of the helper–helpee type, with Cole receiving the assistance. Increasingly over time, however, Cole pursued a helper role with other students and adults. Often he transported a student in a wheelchair, opened doors for people, offered to help with class or group activities, and sometimes took on responsibilities voluntarily.

Observer's comment: Cole walked across the room and picked up Erin's school bag. Erin said, "What are you doing, Cole? Do you want to put my folder in my bag for me?" Cole said, "Yeah."

Cole's popularity in school was highlighted by his relationships with individual students. He usually greeted peers by name, especially during passing time, and several observations recorded Cole participating in a high-five and an "Arsenio Hall call." Similar to many of his classmates without disabilities, Cole practiced behaviors such as whispering, talking loudly, and joking with friends during classtime. There are several examples of Cole chatting with his student aides about nonschool subjects such as magazines, after-school activities, and family pets.

Consortium researchers found many instances of Cole's emotional attachments to his student aides. Initially, the student aides' interactions with Cole were activity-oriented, but data supported Cole's gradual development of friendship with many of his aides. Often Cole would get excited when he saw certain student aides.

Observer's comment: Cole goes into the room, takes off his coat, and sees Ryan. He runs across the room with his arms out, calling, "Ryan! Miss you, miss you!"

Cole's commitment to his friends was demonstrated on several occasions. Once one of Cole's student aides did not show up to take him to his class because the student aide had gotten into trouble.

Observer's comment: Cole asked one of the boys in the hall, "Where's Mike?" The boy answered, "I think he's in the office." Cole walked toward the office.

Sometimes Cole was concerned about both his student aides and his classmates in the special education program. The following observation was made during a community field trip.

Observer's comment: Cole got out of the van and stood by the van, waiting for Jessica to get into her wheelchair. The paraeducator asked Cole to walk with other peers into McDonald's. Cole continued to wait for Jessica.

Unfortunately, there also were incidents involving Cole's aggressive behavior toward his peers. These behaviors included cutting a hole in a boy's sweatshirt, breaking a student's eyeglasses, knocking a hat off a student's head, and pushing a girl in the hallway. The reactions of Cole's peers and/or student aides included admonishment and a lack of understanding. When Cole knocked the boy's hat off during lunch, an observer noted, "The boy looked at Cole, laughed a bit, shook his head, and then continued talking to his peers." The following incident illustrates the influence of Cole's peers on his aggressive behaviors.

Observer's comment: After Cole snipped a hole in Blake's shirt, he agreed to apologize to him. Cole stood up and walked over to Blake. Another boy, Brian, walked over and said, "Cole, are you going to say 'sorry' to Blake?" Cole put his head down and said, "Yeah," but he didn't say he was sorry.

Sue, Cole's mom, and teachers acknowledged in an interview that "Cole's move into the group home resulted in his learning some obnoxious behaviors."

Skills

Cole used to be real shy. He'd duck his head and not say a word and close his eyes if someone came close. Now he can talk about anything! (a friend without disabilities)

As in sixth grade, Cole's most significant growth during his junior high experience was in social communication. He learned how to interact more appropriately with his peers, how to share, and how to wait patiently for his turn. He also displayed improvement in receptive communication skills, which were reflected in his increased ability to follow directions. Cole began initiating more social interactions with his use of complete sentences to express his feelings or to describe his day. Cole's sense of humor also remained constant. One of the most dramatic examples of Cole's increased ability to communicate was described by one of his peers: "He had these little seizures and he's, like, dazed, and he doesn't know what he's doing, and I said, 'Cole, what's wrong?' And he'd say, 'Mike, I think I had a seizure.'"

Initially, Cole's actions seemed dependent on the influence or the guidance of nearby peers, but over time Cole demonstrated a gradual tendency to practice these behaviors on his own. In one example, Cole was alone outside the cafeteria.

Observer's comment: A drama group was on stage, working on their performance. Jim [the maintenance man] stood near the stage, watching. Cole called his name loudly and ran into the cafeteria, then was quiet when he saw what was going on. Cole watched the practice quietly and respectfully.

There was evidence also of Cole's inappropriate behaviors during his junior high years. Fights with both his paraeducators and student aides and occasional temper tantrums continued to occur, often because of a request by others to stop a particular behavior. His tendency to mimic the inappropriate behaviors of some of his peers created an environment that began to threaten his successful social interactions. In an interview, one of his general education teachers noted that "some of Cole's peers were questioning his remarks (e.g., 'shake your bootie') and wondering, 'What is he saying? Why is he doing that?'"

In addition to growth in the social communication area, Cole exhibited growth in functional skills. In the classroom, he learned to monitor his participation by waiting his turn, following directions, and performing tasks, both within a group and individually. Cole adjusted quickly to junior high school routines such as moving to different classes, getting his own lunch and cleaning up afterward, and packing his backpack. He learned to complete his jobs with little assistance (e.g., cleaning up the lunchroom and performing recycling tasks as part of his leadership class). Cole's participation in courses such as foods class also helped him to develop some self-help skills (e.g., cooking).

Observer's comment: Cole, Andy, and Joan get a skillet. Joan shows Cole how to crack and scramble an egg. Cole begins to stir. Joan prompts Cole to stand up and stir the egg.

Like many of his peers, Cole struggled with his desire to be more independent. He started to resist assistance from paraeducators and student aides. Fewer of his activities demanded constant redirection; for example, he learned to tie his own shoes and wipe his nose. In one situation, without any assistance, Cole assumed duties typical of an adult.

Observer's comment: The special education school van arrives. Cole hurries to open the front and double passenger doors. He tells the adult aide, "Hop in." As the aide starts to fasten Jessica's seatbelt, he tells her, "I'll do that," and she says, "Okay," and thanks him after he's buckled and tightened it with a few tugs. He asks, "All set?" and shuts and locks the door.

As the academic levels of his peers in his general education classes increased, Cole gradually began to spend more of his school day in the resource room and/or the community participating in functional skills development activities. There are no traditional academic test results that documented success for Cole, although he seemed to grasp and desire the concept of learning and doing academic tasks such as reading, writing, and math. One day in his language arts class, Cole picked up a big, heavy textbook. A classmate asked if he was going to read it to the class. Cole said, "Yes." He walked to the front of the class, opened the book, looked at it for a few seconds, and promptly closed it. Cole mumbled something. A peer asked him to repeat what he said, more loudly this time. In a clear voice, Cole said, "I can't read it. It is Spanish."

Summary   Cole's junior high years were marked by celebration of his achievements as well as concern for his future. Cole's moves, first to a group home during his eighth- and ninth-grade years and then into a foster placement, were not easy transitions for either himself or his family. As Cole grew bigger, his physical aggression became a significant concern of the staff at Kennedy Junior High, and it became necessary to develop a behavioral support plan as part of Cole's IEP. Cole had never seriously injured another person at the school, yet there always was an underlying threat of danger when Cole was acting out. His health continued to fluctuate, with an increase in seizures again at the end of his eighth-grade year and into his ninth-grade year. Cole appeared to be much more aware of how he was different from his student aides and from his other peers, and this realization led him to experience frustration that manifested itself in behavior problems. He began wanting to spend more and more time in the resource room at Kennedy, which was meant to serve not as a classroom but as a transition area for students with disabilities.

Cole also showed remarkable improvement in many areas, however. His participation in all valued roles, settings, and activities of the school and classroom communities was critical for his development and growth in the outcomes of membership, relationships, and skills. More important, his participation in groups and school activities was instrumental in the development of positive perceptions by Cole's peers with regard to his membership, relationships, and skills.

CONCLUSIONS: SUPPORTS, CONTEXTS, AND PRACTICES PERCEIVED TO FACILITATE OUTCOMES

According to the Consortium's analyses, Cole's participation in inclusive settings during the time of the Consortium's research was influenced primarily by two factors: the engagement of peers as a support system and the attitudes and perceptions of teachers and administrators. Peers played an important role in Cole's behavior changes and socioemotional development. His desire to be around peers led him to behave in socially appropriate ways. Daily interactions with his student aides provided many opportunities for Cole to practice communication skills in context, modify his' behaviors, and express his emotions. The use of peers without disabilities as a source of support continues to receive wide attention in the field. Social skills acquisition (e.g., Haring & Breen, 1992; Staub & Hunt, 1993), conversational turn taking (e.g., Hunt, Alwell, & Goetz, 1988), and academic skills development (Staub et al., 1996) for students with moderate to severe disabilities have been associated with elementary and secondary peer support programs.

The adults who worked with Cole, including his special education teachers, his paraeducators, his general education teachers, and the principals at Jane Austen Elementary and Kennedy Junior High were instrumental in creating an inclusive environment for Cole that allowed him to realize positive outcomes in membership, relationships, and skills. Their supports ranged from strong administrative leadership and the use of collaborative models of communication at the building level (see, e.g., Salisbury, Palombaro, & Hollowood, 1993) to specific classroom-based strategies, including cooperative learning groups (Hunt, Staub, Alwell, & Goetz, 1994), teaching teams (Thousand & Villa, 2000), and curricular adaptations (Jorgensen, 1998). For instance, many of Cole's teachers adapted their classroom activities so that Cole could participate at different levels. In turn, the principals supported the peer programs and ensured that teachers and paraeducators received appropriate training and support, particularly with regard to Cole's behavioral support needs. The willingness and ability to let go of some power issues with regard to Cole was critical in the role that adults played in Cole's education. Interpreting Cole's desire for attention as a functional behavior that should be addressed rather than viewing it as a disruption proved to be a critical contextual factor. Most important, the acknowledgment of Cole's ability to contribute to the dynamics of a classroom and the school were key to the perceived reciprocal benefits of Cole's inclusion.

Cole often presented intense challenges to those who facilitated his inclusive education experience, yet not once in the 4 years that I spent in the Jane Austen and Kennedy school communities getting to know Cole and the significant people in his life did I hear anyone talk of giving up on Cole's inclusion. Furthermore, there was a true sense of appreciation of the gifts that Cole had provided these communities.

DISCUSSION QUESTIONS

1. How can a student aide program such as the one at Kennedy Junior High School be structured to ensure that everyone involved (e.g., students with disabilities, student aides, teachers) receives benefits?

2. What are the potential positive outcomes for teachers of a student aide program such as the one at Kennedy? For students? For administrators?

3. What safeguards should be implemented to ensure a balance of both social and task-related interactions between student aides and students with disabilities?

4. What types of curriculum decisions were important to Cole's IEP team?

5. How might a team working with a student like Cole make decisions about the type of curriculum in which Cole participates?

6. How can the team ensure that Cole receives valued roles in inclusive classroom environments?

7. How important is the issue of age-appropriateness in determining curriculum for students such as Cole?

8. In which ways did adult mediation (i.e., assistance from the paraeducator, general education teachers, consulting special education teacher) affect outcomes for Cole in the areas of skills, membership, and relationships?

9. What should the classroom adult's role be in situations in which there is a student aide program such as the one at Kennedy?

10. At what point can adult mediation become adult interference?

11. What are some ways in which an IEP team might address the adult mediation issue?

12. As Cole became older, he began to reveal a greater sense of awareness of his disability and the ways in which he was different from his peers without disabilities, and occasionally he displayed this awareness by behaving inappropriately. How can educators address this issue with students, and what might Cole's team do specifically to help Cole maintain a positive self-image?

13. How might a team address the issue of a student's self-esteem when that student's curriculum and expectations are different from those of his or her peers without disabilities?

Ro's Story

Planting the Seeds and Reaping the Harvest in Middle School

Rosalind M. Vargo and Joseph C. Vargo

Why do you want Ro included? Middle school kids . . . they don't even like themselves. Why would they like your child?

In those few moments of conversation with a middle school special education teacher, the stage was set and the obstacles clearly articulated for (or against) middle school inclusion. This chapter tells our family's story about inclusive schools. We hope to put a human face on the notion that parents can and should assume their rightful role as partners in their children's education. We believe strongly in the value of partners and partnerships. We believe, in fact, that the only way to make a difference for our child, or for any child in our schools, is through a cooperative and collaborative approach that focuses on the child. We believe that in order to achieve a sustained effort that works for kids, all members of the team must have the desire to put the needs of kids first. Parents are often the missing link in the

---

Note to the Reader: Rosalind M. Vargo, the first author of this chapter, is the mother of Ro, the young woman with Rett syndrome who is described in this chapter.

chain, the last piece of the puzzle. Parents are integral to the notion of a collaborative education team.

RO

Let us begin by introducing you to Ro with a one-word description: Personality! She is our oldest daughter—15 years old at the time of this writing. She has Rett syndrome. Ro has participated in general education classes and curricula with support from special education and related services throughout her elementary school years in a midsize urban school in central New York state. Although Ro is non-vocal, her communicative intent is evident. Her intense gaze allows her to eyepoint so that her friends may interpret her needs, usually better than her family and teachers can. Ro has used a wide variety of communication devices, ranging from technical equipment such as the DynaVox, Cheaptalk, Computer Touchwindow, and Big Mack to less technical but still effective methods such as preset quick boards, dry erase boards, and sticky notes.

Ro's peers have always been intrigued by her multiple communication systems. Over the years, they have been active participants in supporting Ro to communicate by programming these devices for her, including the use of their familiar language patterns (e.g., "Do you feel 'dissed'?") (Beukelman & Mirenda, 1998). Ro relies mainly on the use of sticky notes and an inquiring partner. If we wanted to know, for example, with whom she was hanging at lunch, we would use three sticky notes. Two notes would be the name of a friend, and the third note would say "more possibilities." Ro would look over the choices presented and choose her answer by gazing intently at just one note. Through nonvocal means, Ro reveals herself as a sensitive young woman, exhibiting many deep thoughts and emotions. Adults and peers also have used American Sign Language to help Ro focus receptively. One can tell that she wants to communicate when she gets close physically and puts her face close to the other person's. At times, she actually has tapped her classmates on the shoulder to get their attention.

Music is an important part of Ro's life. She prefers Carly Simon and Mariah Carey. After school, she listens to her compact discs. She often likes to "chill" and watch the soap operas on television. Sometimes her friends came over just to sit, have quiet time together, sleep, and eat. Her leisure time also is spent happily with someone reading to her. Her favorites are diaries or books about the Civil War era and slavery. Friends enjoy reading *TEEN* magazine with her during homeroom period. Ro is an outgoing and social teenager. She loves being around kids, is motivated by them, and thrives on their attention and interaction with them.

Adults need to help Ro with all daily living skills, such as toileting, eating, and climbing stairs. Ro's safety has always been a concern for us. Although Ro's friends and classmates are aware of her need for adult support, they also have articulated how intrusive adult support is in terms of their ongoing relationship with Ro (cf. Giangreco, Edelman, Luiselli, & McFarland, 1997; Grenot-Scheyer & Leonard-Giesen, 1997).

Ro has a supportive extended family. She has two younger sisters—Josie, age 14, and Mary, age 11. Her sisters have been gifts to Ro and to us. Their most notable contribution is in keeping life going as usual. Their busy social lives have been in small part Ro's social life. Ro is present at many of her sisters' activities, such as baseball and basketball games and cheerleading competitions. In her faith community, she is involved in a 2-year preparation program to receive the Sacrament of Confirmation. Many of the young adults in this church program are school and neighborhood kids, and some are friends of our family. Ro's neighbors have come to know her through our family's annual holiday open house, Halloween excursions, and everyday activities.

Our Wishes for Ro

From our perspective as Ro's parents, we have talked to, debated with, cajoled, and pleaded with educators about the value of Ro's inclusion in school and its benefits to many different people because we believe in it. It is the way we live as a family, and it is how we experience our faith community and our neighborhood. Inclusion is not just an education environment. For us, inclusion extends far beyond the walls of the school: It is a recipe for living.

An inclusive lifestyle for Ro has always been a priority for us, and that means in school as well as in the community. After Ro's successful inclusion in preschool and elementary school, we were ready to work with the school district to include Ro in the neighborhood middle school. As a result, a full middle school program and academic schedule was sought, planned for, and initiated. Our district heard our perspective and responded to our preferences as required by the Individuals with Disabilities Education Act (IDEA) Amendments of 1997 (PL 105-17; cf. Turnbull, Turnbull, Shank, & Leal, 1999).

A great deal of time and effort was devoted to preparing the middle school environment for Ro prior to her first day at school there. Although the administration at Kennedy Middle School was open minded, it took a full year of planning with the administration, faculty, and other students' parents to redefine the middle school structure to accommodate a quality inclusive education program. This transition planning was critical (Erwin & Soodak, 1995).

Dovetailing with the Consortium

Ironically, during the summer prior to her middle school inclusion, we received a telephone call from Luanna H. Meyer, who is also the foreword author of this book, inviting Ro and our family to be part of a 5-year university grant. Her research group, the Consortium for Collaborative Research on Social Relationships of Children and Youth with Diverse Abilities, was studying the social relationships of children and youth with disabilities (see also Chapter 5). With the message "Middle school kids . . . don't even like themselves. Why would they like your child?" still in the backs of our minds, and the friendships that we knew Ro had experienced in elementary school in the forefront of our minds, we gratefully and enthusiastically accepted Dr. Meyer's invitation. It was a chance to set the record straight, to demonstrate through observations, interviews, and case histories what we already had learned. During the next 4 years, consortium staff documented the relationships that Ro developed in school. These social relationships spanned the spectrum from passing acquaintances to close friendships (Meyer, Minondo, et al., 1998). Regarding social interaction, Ro was her own best ambassador. The friendships and relationships that she made are not only a testimony to inclusive education but also a reinforcement of the greater human factor that we all need friends. We found it was possible not only for Ro to need friends but also that Ro's friends would come to need her!

RO'S FIRST YEAR IN MIDDLE SCHOOL

In her first year at Kennedy Middle School, we initiated and supported much of what happened socially for Ro. There were times when we believed that we needed to facilitate social relationships for Ro. There were just as many times, however, that we knew that adults should just stay out of the planning. I (Ro's mom) remember driving Ro and her friend Nancy home from an outing. The girls seemed quiet. Because the silence was uncomfortable for me, I talked incessantly to both girls. When I took a breath, however, I glanced in the rearview mirror and saw that Ro and Nancy were not even listening to my nervous conversation. Nancy was whispering something into Ro's ear. Then they both started to laugh and giggle. They were obviously involved in their own discussion, in their own way. I decided to stay out of it.

Much of what we learned about Ro and her relationships with friends came to us directly from those friends. In 1992, we participated in a conference workshop entitled "Building Friendships: Students, Parents, Teachers, and Friends Talk." Ro was in sixth grade at the time. Ms. W, her teacher, and Ro's two friends since preschool, Susan and Teresa, also were on the panel. The audience posed tough questions that day; in particular, they asked about the difficulties of friendship. Susan was asked, "What is the hardest thing about being Ro's friend?" I (Ro's mom) held my breath. I thought Susan's answer might be that Ro drools, is a messy eater, or has temper tantrums. Susan hesitated, then bit her lower lip and said, "The hardest thing about being Ro's friend is that she always has a parent or an adult with her." I was relieved and once more was amazed by the perceptive and straightforward response of Ro's classmate.

People rated the session as excellent, with participants' comments including "powerful," "inspiring," "touching," and "moving." Every person in that room was noticeably moved by the discussion with the young people that day. We have never forgotten that lesson. Although Ro needs significant support, parents and teachers can be an obstacle indeed when it comes to other young people's making and remaining friends with Ro. Our role as adults, therefore, is setting up the social environment and putting Ro there with her peers. The wonderful interactions and relationships that we had witnessed in preschool and elementary school and had only dreamed of happening for her in middle school were beginning to unfold.

By the end of her first year of middle school, Ro had shown her new teachers and her parents again that there were some students who definitely wanted to be friends with her and others who were intrigued by her. We planned an end-of-the-year party at our house. Everyone in Ro's homeroom was invited. By opening our house, Ro's middle school classmates saw that she lived in a typical house and that she had a bedroom and a dog. This event seemed to overcome any fears or misgivings that they may have had. In retrospect, this may have been the single most important invitation that Ro extended to her classmates. Many conversations and friendships developed because of this experience. It somehow solidified for them that they and Ro had some common and shared life experiences.

Shared school activities continued, with Ro attending her first dance in middle school. Teachers who were acting as chaperones at the dance monitored Ro's activities, but we wanted to give her some space. She would stand and sway to the music. Students did approach her and ask her to dance in groups. A boy even asked her to dance! She needed no other support except to be placed in the environment with natural supports for safety purposes. That school year Ro also indicated an interest in the school play. The play director viewed Ro's participation in the school play as a safety concern. As a compromise, Ro gladly agreed to sell and take tickets at the door with a friend.

Melina

Some of Ro's close friends made the transition to high school at the end of Ro's first year at middle school. Thus, we thought those relationships were over. We were pleasantly surprised, however, when on the first day of school there was a knock on our door. It was Melina. She said, "Where's Ro? I need to tell her about high school." She said to Ro, "I couldn't find my locker. You have only half an hour for lunch. The line was so long, I never got to eat!" She also had some advice for Ro. Melina told her, "Stay in middle school as long as you can!"

When Ro first saw Melina that afternoon, her response was distant. Given her past fondness for Melina, this reservation was curious. Why was she acting this way? Then we understood that she might have been upset for having been left behind in middle school. We talked about that after Melina left. The next day, Melina brought Joy to our house after school. They stopped for sodas and had come over just to hang with Ro after school. Ro's responses to her friends this time suggested the old familiarity.

As Ro's parents, we continued to work hard at fostering Ro's social environment but tried not to interfere with it. Our job was to let it happen. During Melina's drop-by visits, when I would hear nothing from the living room, I'd slip back occasionally and peek in just to see them watching television side by side. Sometimes Ro would fall asleep, leaning on Melina. Those were the times when I would remind myself that Ro was her own best ambassador. She didn't need me to make friends for her. Her friends liked her for who she was.

Melina had been described by one of the Consortium's participant observers as the friend who had broken the social barrier for Ro in middle school. Melina often told her teachers that Ro would cheer her up on the bad days and that at times she could cheer up Ro in return. A reporter doing a documentary on Rett syndrome was filming at the school one day, and the reporter asked Melina to tell the story about how she and Ro had first met. She said, "Well, on the first day, we just saw each other, and we've been friends ever since. There was a bond, I guess." In a physical sense, Melina was quite an intimidating student in middle school. She was a tough-talking and tough-acting kid but also was kind at heart. Ro, in some ways, could not have picked a better first friend in middle school. Melina told us, "Sometimes teachers think I hang with Ro because of all the attention I get, but the truth is, I need Ro more than she needs me!" This was the type of information that we had known when Ro was in preschool and elementary school. The reciprocal nature of these friendships, though hard for us and other adults to understand, was clear to Melina.

RO'S SECOND YEAR IN MIDDLE SCHOOL

Ro continued to make new friends the second year, and Melina and her old friends, who were in high school, still stayed in touch. The seeds of friendship had been planted, and Ro was starting to reap the benefits. The same was true for Melina, Joy, and others.

Along with us, her teachers looked at providing additional supports for these friendships during Ro's second year in middle school. Having seen the impact on Ro and the community and how Ro's peers in fact were attracted to her as a peer and friend, we all became interested in facilitating Ro's friendships. A lunchroom chat group was initiated in which students could talk about school and other topics. Teachers helped set up peer tutoring during academic classes and homeroom period for Ro. Finding ways for Ro to let people know who she was became a priority. Peers saw her in school. Many classmates recognized her at dances, but they didn't know much about her. She was nonverbal, and only those who were confident enough to ask her questions or to experiment with her somewhat complex and unpredictable communication systems knew anything about her.

Because October was Rett Syndrome Awareness Month, Ro agreed to provide one fact about Rett syndrome to the school community each day of the month. She shared the mayoral and gubernatorial proclamations that her family had secured to create awareness of the syndrome. The kids were fascinated, especially with regard to receiving the information in this manner. On one occasion, Ro told them that Rett syndrome occurs in 1 of every 15,000 live female births. After class, a young male student left class shaking his head and smiling. The teacher asked, "What are you smiling at?" He responded, "I can't believe how lucky we are! Imagine Ro is 1 in 15,000!" At the end of the month, the class decided to choose Rett syndrome as their yearly community project and made its theme "Friends Helping Friends."

Teachers and students outside the inclusive education team were beginning to take notice as well. Although they were somewhat apprehensive of why a kid such as Ro was attending their school, they too began to develop relationships with Ro. In many ways, it was the students who made the inclusive education team see Ro for who she was and taught them how to be friends with her.

Ro's interactions with a gym teacher are a perfect illustration. The gym teacher had been working in the school district for 30 years. Upon seeing Ro, he said to Ro's teacher and to Ro, "I don't have those kids in my class." We could have insisted that Ro had rights and that this teacher could not keep Ro out of the class, but we didn't. Over the years, we have learned that these situations, though they may appear to be obstacles to our dreams, are really opportunities. Gently, we told the principal that Ro would be in the general gym class and that the school needed to find out which supports the gym teacher needed to make it happen. He needed to know that Ro was going to be a part of that middle school gym class!

While eating at a local restaurant during the winter holidays, we ran into the gym teacher. He at least acknowledged us and then spoke loudly to Ro, as if she had a hearing problem. Joe and I smiled and said, "Well, at least he's talking to her." In January, Ro's teacher told us that Ro had become disruptive during gym. Apparently, Ro had been going to gym with her class for 4 months and doing similar but parallel activities. She had been restricted to one of the corners of the gym with her assistant for safety purposes. Every day, a couple of classmates retreated from the general gym class and joined Ro. Over time, almost half the gym class was in the corner. The gym teacher was finding it disruptive to have to spend time redirecting the other kids.

While walking at the mall in April, we heard someone whistle twice. Down a few stores, we saw a man with a baseball hat on. He was the whistler. He came walking up to us and, though I (Ro's mom) didn't know who he was, Ro recognized him. She stood there smiling up at him. He said, "Hello, Miss Vargo. How's your vacation going?" A few seconds later, the man looked at me and said nonchalantly, "Oh, hi. You probably don't recognize me. I'm Ro's gym teacher." The story gets better. In June, after bringing Ro in from the bus in the afternoon, I opened her backpack. In it, I found a whistle. I was confused until I read the enclosed note from a teacher. The teacher had written, "Today the gym teacher retired. He wanted Ro to have the whistle he has worn around his neck for 30 years!" At that moment, I realized many things about Ro's relationships. She didn't need her parents' facilitation. Rather, our role was to insist on her being included and to secure the support systems. Most important, kids are the best at showing us how it is possible (Giangreco et al., 1997).

RO'S LAST YEAR IN MIDDLE SCHOOL

During Ro's last year in middle school, we recognized that her social relationships needed an after-school outlet and that this was not happening (Rynders et al., 1993). Other students who were Ro's age were seeing each other outside school. Through head-nod gestures to indicate yes and no, Ro generated a list of six girls whom she wanted to invite to be a part of an after-school girls group. Each of the six girls was asked whether she would like to participate in an outing with Ro once a month, and each agreed. A supper club was born. The girls as a group chose places to go and activities to do over supper. The expenses for teacher assistant support and the cost of the activity (e.g., movie, miniature golf, snacks) were absorbed by a special school district fund. Thus, one typical obstacle to most teenagers' going out was eliminated—money. The girls were given a budget of about $7.00 per outing per girl and were good about staying within it.

How to get where they wanted to go was the next obstacle. Although the funds could have paid for a bus and a driver, we said that this was not a usual mode of transportation for teens. As Ro's mother, I was used to providing transportation to the other two girls in the house, so wouldn't it be okay if I drove? Because there usually were six or seven girls going each time, we needed another driver. In a natural way, another mom volunteered to drive as well. This seemed more typical than using a school district bus, and it overcame any hesitancy from the other parents. Ro's teaching assistant from school agreed to be the support person. The other girls knew the teaching assistant from school and were comfortable with having her along. The excursions were fun. Ro would look forward to them and would be sad when they were postponed. The supper club members went to the movies, played putt-putt, attended a makeup party, went to a local amusement park, shopped at the mall, and went out to supper. The best outing was Ro's 16th birthday party, for which we hired a limousine to take her and her friends around town for the evening!

Joan was an eager and regular member of the supper club. Each of the girls had a relationship with Ro, but Joan and Ro's friendship was a bit closer than the others'. At times, there was some infighting about how the others would walk ahead of Ro instead of with her. I once overheard in the car that Joan was not going out with the supper club that week because she was mad. When I asked what Joan was mad about, there was lots of eye shifting and no real answers were given. Ro was obviously upset about Joan's not going, and she began to hit her head and cry. When the supper club event was over, I asked Ro privately whether she knew why Joan had not come. She nodded "yes." I remember her being more angry than sad. The next day, the teaching assistant casually asked Joan why she hadn't joined the supper club the previous night. The reason came in rants and rages about the other girls in the group. They were not staying with

Ro. They would either be walking ahead or not waiting for Ro. Joan said it just wasn't right. Ro responded with rants and rages of her own to this excuse from Joan. Using her sticky note response strategy, she wrote, "Knock it off." Joan returned to the group for all other monthly excursions. It became clear that though all of the girls were friends, friendship meant different things to each member. From our perspective, it appeared that Ro enjoyed all types of friendships.

The success of the supper club was highly dependent on the manner of the adult support that Ro's teaching assistant provided. She was in the background. She never spoke for Ro but rather encouraged the girls to talk to Ro. She was there primarily for safety reasons and to support Ro's personal care needs.

At the end of the school year, the girls in the supper club were asked to respond to a number of questions that Consortium personnel posed to them. The most telling feedback for us was that Ro in particular would have preferred to go on the girls' outings without an adult present. This surprised us because all of the girls and Ro really liked Ro's teaching assistant. From our perspective, Ro's teaching assistant had done an exceptional job in supporting Ro without being intrusive. Caroline, Ro's teaching assistant, had a natural, instinctive way of knowing when to back off and when to step in—a skill that we, as Ro's parents, have not yet mastered. The following brief interview excerpt captured things from the girls' perspectives:

Interviewer: What was it like to have somebody like Ms. Matthias hanging out with some teenagers?

H: It was cool because she knew what we like and everything.

O: She was fun about everything.

H: She never got mad, either.

O: Well, maybe once or twice, but you couldn't tell. You can never tell when she's mad or not. Sometimes she has these mean looks on her face, but sometimes she doesn't.

L: [Placed LIKED IT and DIDN'T LIKE IT and NEED MORE OPTIONS on Ro's communication board, and then asked her the following question.] Ro, did you like it that I hung around with you guys, or didn't you like it?

Ro: [Ro shakes her head "no."]

Interviewer: Oh, you didn't like it, Ro.

H: She just wanted to be by herself, I guess.

O: Yeah, but you know how Ms. Matthias is.

> *L:* Would you rather have been alone?
>
> *Ro:* [Ro does not look back at board. She just shakes her head "no" again.]
>
> *L:* Okay, you didn't like it, okay.

"But how could we have done it otherwise?" was the interviewer's next question. Two of the girls said they would have been comfortable with helping Ro with eating, cutting her food, and reminding her to eat only small bites of food. Support with toileting was an issue with regard to which Ro herself was uncomfortable with peer support. Ro apparently did not want her friends to take on this role.

Although the supper club carried its own merit of providing ongoing social engagements for Ro, it solidified some of her friendships so that her participation in school events also was enhanced by these friendships. For example, the girls would hang together at basketball games and dances.

THINKING BACK OVER
RO'S MIDDLE SCHOOL EXPERIENCE

Many people were skeptical about including Ro in the academic and social life of her neighborhood middle school. The teachers and staff had little or no experience with inclusive education. Although they struggled to find the planning time and curriculum modifications to support an inclusive education environment for Ro, Ro's participation left little doubt about the social benefits for all students. These benefits were apparent to everyone involved with Ro. It was obvious that students at Kennedy Middle School were making gains in tolerance, acceptance, friendship, and learning about themselves.

> *Interviewer:* Did you learn anything special about your friends?
>
> *H:* That they're always there for me when I need them.
>
> *T:* You have fun with them.
>
> *O:* Like, from Joan or so forth, I learned that I could sort of trust her, in a way—same with Joan and Lee, everyone in the group.
>
> *Interviewer:* So, Ro, do you agree with these guys?
>
> *Ro:* [Ro nods "yes."]
>
> *Interviewer:* Ro, do you feel like you learned more things about these guys since the first supper club? Yes? No?
>
> *Ro:* [Ro nods "yes."]

It didn't hurt that the middle school principal was motivated to bring her middle school forward and thought that inclusion should be a part of school reform and academic excellence. Block scheduling and thematic instruction were being initiated at the same time. These initiatives created the flexibility to facilitate Ro's participation in general education classrooms (Downing, 1996).

Parents also played a key role. In fact, we initiated Ro's participation and helped to make it work. We take no credit for Ro's achievements. Her social strides and relationships have been her own. There is much to lose and everything to gain for parents in pursuing friendships for kids with special needs. It can mean finding acceptance and security. It can mean discovering the one thing or the one person who motivates them beyond their seemingly limited capabilities, and it can mean building a better world for all kids to live in. Creating and maintaining friendships means taking even more difficult risks, such as knowing as a parent when to back off and trust others. This, for us, has been very difficult—the letting go—but is worth the risk. Ro's friends have said quite plainly, year after year, that sometimes it's either us as Ro's parents or another supervising adult who makes being friends with Ro difficult. We know also that we need to let go a bit and trust that Ro's friends can and will take care of Ro when we are not there and that everything will be okay.

Together, administrators, teachers, and parents were committed to making Ro's inclusive education experience work. They shared time and information. They remained flexible. The result was that instruction at Kennedy Middle School got better. Modeling for a better world of problem solvers and getting along despite our differences set a new standard. Middle schools are ripe for inclusive education. At a time when at least one teacher believed middle school kids "don't even like themselves," these kids found themselves! Ro had struggled all her life to fit in, to be accepted for who she is, to find real friends, to find ways to cope with her limitations, and to acknowledge her strengths—but so does every other middle school kid. For the first time in Ro's life, she shared her struggle with her peers. There seems to have been no better place than middle school for the seeds of friendship to be planted and to grow.

RO'S STORY CONTINUES TO UNFOLD

Susan, participating in an open forum on inclusion 10 years after she first met Ro, challenged the Director of Special Education publicly about why there were no kids like Ro in her middle school and why they had become invisible after being present in elementary school.

Joan moved away to another state with her mother after middle school graduation. Ro and Joan did not see each other for 3 years. In

1998, Joan and Ro were reunited in their health careers class as juniors in high school. They still say hi to each other but are not as close as they were in middle school.

In December 1998, some 6 years after first meeting Ro, Melina sent Ro a Christmas card. It began, "Dear Ro and Family: How is everything? It's been such a long time. You might have forgotten me, but I have never forgotten you. I have been good. I graduated from high school. I am now a home health aide, helping others, and I will also be taking a sign language class in January. Love ya, Melina." In the envelope, along with the letter, was a picture of Melina and her date at the high school prom.

In June 1999, Suneeta invited Ro to her graduation party upon her graduation from Nottingham High School. She had not seen Ro in 7 years!

In June 2000, Ro herself graduated from Martin Luther King Jr. High School and assumed her rightful place in our community with her friends.

DISCUSSION QUESTIONS

1. How can educators and families who are strong, assertive advocates for inclusion encourage less-assertive families to join in sharing knowledge about their children with disabilities?

2. Ro's teaching assistant is skilled in facilitating and then stepping back from peer interactions. Which skills has she probably acquired that should become part of preparation for teacher's aides in your district?

3. In your local school district, how might a teaching assistant share knowledge and expertise with colleagues and family members?

4. Think about Ro's preference to hang with her friends without adult supervision. As Ro's advocate, what steps could you take to support her in meeting her goal?

5. Would you have recommended that the special education staff act earlier in the school year to encourage the physical education teacher to change his attitude toward including Ro in his general physical education class?

6. Why do you or don't you see Ro's parents' holding an open house for Ro's peers as a critical step in facilitating Ro's friendships at school?

7. What would it take for parents in your inclusive education program to use this strategy or a "sharing ourselves and others" type of activity?

9

Ted's Story

Looking Back and Beyond

Hyun-Sook Park, Stacey Hoffman,
Susan Whaley, and Jean Gonsier-Gerdin

The formation of social relationships between youth with disabilities and those without disabilities has been considered both a rationale for and an anticipated outcome of inclusive education (Perske, 1993; Strully & Strully, 1989). Understanding the social relationships of students as they exit the school system, then, is particularly important. One criterion by which the effectiveness of inclusive schooling can be evaluated is the degree to which students, upon graduation, are prepared to develop the networks of social relationships and support that they will need in order to cope with the changes necessitated by life in the general community (Halpern, 1985, 1993; Tappe & Gaylord-Ross, 1990). In the 1990s, we were involved in studies that explored this outcome, investigating what was happening both in the social lives of students in transition and, later, with regard to interventions to facilitate social relationships. Our studies of students in transition from school to community life were part of a larger collaborative project, the Consortium for Collaborative Research on Social Relationships of Children and Youth with Diverse Abilities, that examined the social relationships of children and youth with diverse abilities from early childhood, through transition, and into adulthood (Meyer, Grenot-Scheyer, et al., 1992a).

The information reported in this chapter is based on a 2-year study that involved participant observations and interviews with 21 students ages

16–22 who had moderate to severe cognitive delays. We observed students in a variety of settings, including worksites, community college classes, and other community locations. We conducted a series of individual and focus group interviews with the students as well as with their families, co-workers, and significant others in order to obtain more information and gain a better understanding of the contexts in which their social lives occurred. (For more detail on the methodology used, see Park, Chadsey-Rusch, & Storey, 1998.)

SOCIAL OPPORTUNITIES
OR ACQUAINTANCES, MEMBERSHIPS,
AND FRIENDSHIPS AND COMPANIONSHIPS

We categorized observed relationships as one of three types of social relationships: social opportunities or acquaintances, memberships, and friendships and companionships. *Social opportunities* or *acquaintances* refers to social contacts that may potentially lead to social exchanges. *Memberships* refers to the status of belonging to or being part of a social group such as college or high school students, employees, a faith congregation, or workout club members. *Friendships* and *companionships* refer to relationships that involve more than just social acquaintance and are characterized by intimacy, reciprocity, and affection (Berndt, 1982; Bukowski, Newcomb, & Hartup, 1996; Kennedy & Itkonen, 1996). Whereas social opportunities and/or memberships are prerequisites for friendships and other close social relationships, the former do not necessarily result in the latter (Haring, 1991). Even if a person attains membership in a social group, he or she does not necessarily form close social relationships or friendships with others in that group.

The findings of this 2-year study were discouraging. Students with disabilities had expanded social opportunities, but did not succeed in developing and maintaining close friendships or companionships that could be maintained after graduation. Some students developed social acquaintances and attained memberships at worksites and in classrooms; most of the students, however, did not develop close social relationships with others without disabilities that were maintained over any significant period of time. Our focus group interviews indicated that the majority of these students feared that they would not be able to stay in contact with their peers after graduation and would be left alone in the community (Park, Hoffman, & Whaley, 1999). Their families expressed similar concerns, citing a lack of safety of people with disabilities in the community, inadequate companionship, and the lack of places where people with disabilities could go for social activities in the community. These findings are parallel to the findings of Walker's (1999) study, in which she reported that many people with disabilities still were isolated and had limited friendships and companionships in the community. The following story about Ted describes social relationships that appeared to be typical of the majority of the students of transition age in this study.

TED'S STORY

Background

Ted was 18 years old when we first met. He is Chinese American. At the time of the study, he was enrolled in an inclusive transition program for students with severe disabilities, in which he was learning independent living and vocational skills. He also attended community college classes. Since age 9, Ted had attended school in a medium-size urban school district in California, where he was enrolled in special day classes with some integration with general education peers for a portion of the school day (e.g., recess, lunch, buddy activities with students without disabilities). He was reported to have moderate cognitive delays.

Ted's background was interesting. His grandparents and parents had emigrated from China to Venezuela, where he was born and resided until he was 8 years old. In Venezuela, Ted received his schooling in a general education public school program. His family then immigrated to the United States. Ted's family spoke both Chinese and Spanish at home. Because his parents spoke Chinese, Ted and his siblings communicated with their parents in Chinese. When Ted and his siblings spoke among themselves, they used Spanish. Ted enjoyed conversing in Spanish and often watched Spanish-language channels on television.

Although somewhat shy and quiet, once Ted made an initial contact, he could become friendly (even overly friendly, according to some people). When speaking English but not when speaking Spanish, Ted repeated statements continually, which seemed to drive people away. Ted did not have friends inside or outside school at the time of our research. He had held a variety of jobs, including busing tables in a medium-size café and at a restaurant, being part of a group of students who made packets for children staying at a large hospital, and doing maintenance work at a flower shop. He also had done maintenance work at a city park, raking and pitching leaves into a bin. When he was not working or receiving community-based instruction (e.g., learning how to ride a bus), he attended weightlifting or music classes at a community college.

Social Opportunities at Work

Ted's inclusive transition program provided more potential social opportunities for him to interact with young people without disabilities
than the special day classes he had attended earlier in his school career had. These social opportunities occurred mainly at worksites.
Our interview and observation data indicated that Ted's primary motivating factor for work was the opportunity to be with people without disabilities. For at least two reasons, however, these potential social contacts did not necessarily result in social interactions with
others. First, Ted's work hours and the nature of his job meant that he
worked alone at many worksites. For example, he did most of his
work at the restaurant before it was open to customers and most of
his ground maintenance work alone at the park. Second, Ted's co-
workers preferred interacting with Ted's job coaches, when the job
coaches were present, to interacting with Ted. The mere presence of
the job coach who accompanied Ted to supervise his work and teach
him the job often prevented Ted from interacting with others. The following is one example from our observation data.

Ted finishes cutting the first column of the article, but his job coach finds
it is too long for the page. She explains to Ted, "We are going to have to
cut it. We need a scissors." They cannot find the scissors in the material
box. The job coach asks Ted to ask the receptionist for the scissors. When
Ted asks the receptionist, she says "Okay" and leaves her seat. Ted stands
there for a few minutes and comes back to the work table. Then the receptionist comes back with the scissors and tells the job coach that someone
must have used the scissors and then returned them to the wrong place.

> Observer's comment: The receptionist could have conveyed the
> same message and given the scissors to Ted. Instead, she came all the
> way to the job coach and handed her the scissors, not Ted. This was
> definitely differential treatment. The unintended function of the job
> coach as "barrier to social interaction" rather than "facilitator of social
> interaction" was consistent across workers and jobsites in our data.

Because of Ted's interests in food, travel, and speaking Spanish,
his transition teachers attempted to find a Mexican restaurant in
which both workers and customers spoke Spanish where Ted could
work. None of the restaurants that they contacted, however, was willing to employ students with disabilities. A search for a travel agency
as a potential worksite was unsuccessful as well.

Membership in Community College Classes

There was virtually no interaction between Ted and students without disabilities in his initial classes at the community college (i.e., weight-lifting, music). This relationship was something similar to that of being a *ghost,* the word Black (1996) used to describe the invisible status of a student with disabilities in general education classrooms. After realizing that Ted had a talent in and a preference for speaking Spanish, Ted's teachers helped him register for a Spanish class. In this beginner-level conversation class, he started gaining a high social status because he was ahead of his classmates in speaking Spanish. He was even able to answer some of the instructor's questions when other students could not. His classmates began interacting with him spontaneously, and he accordingly gained membership (a feeling of being accepted as a peer) in the class. However, he did not form close friendships with any of his classmates.

Social Opportunities with Peers with Disabilities

Ted's quest to develop areas of social interaction and to belong to a group held true with his peers with disabilities when they had a chance to hang out or work together on the same projects at worksites. Ted usually initiated the interactions with his peers with disabilities. Frequently, he was ignored by the student to whom he was talking. The following excerpt describes this relationship.

Observer's comment: One day Ted says to Sam as they are stuffing envelopes, "I ran out of these, Sam. Give me some more." Sam does not answer Ted, and the envelopes are over by Sam and Rose. So then Ted says to Rose, "Rose, can you get me some, please?" She gives him more envelopes, and Ted thanks her twice, but she does not answer him either time.

One of the reasons that Ted was left out by his peers was because he repeated statements frequently, especially when the topic related to places. Ted would ask repeatedly, "Where do you live? Have you been to Venezuela?"

Social Opportunities Outside School and Work

At the beginning of his participation in the Consortium, Ted's social life after school was one of isolation most of the time. Then he began participating in a new after-school leisure program called Young Life Club. Coordinated by a college student without disabilities, this club brought students from the transition program together with college students without disabilities for leisure activities. They met once a week to play cards or video games and ended each get-together with a pizza. This social activity instantly became Ted's favorite, an observation he expressed in several interviews. Even though our observations indicated that he was still left out by his peers with disabilities in the club, Ted received sufficient attention by talking to college students without disabilities. He was not participating in playing games most of the time, probably because he lacked both skills and interest. Instead, he preferred talking to people, which sometimes became a bit overwhelming for the other people to whom he spoke. He regarded the coordinator as a role model and began combing his hair in the same way as the coordinator did. Unfortunately, the Young Life Club had to disband when the coordinator found that changes in his personal life made it impossible for him to devote sufficient time to the club and because he was not able to find someone to replace himself. Without a doubt, the discontinuation of the club deeply disappointed Ted. He hoped for a long time that someone would revive the club. He said he was sad "because we not start Young Life; we wait for somebody to come back and start Young Life."

Ted did not have any social activities for a while after the Young Life Club was discontinued. After a time, he participated in other after-school leisure and sports programs that served only students with disabilities. When asked which type of club he preferred, Ted immediately picked the Young Life Club, saying, "It's not the same," without being able to describe the reason more elaborately. Other than his occasional participation in the leisure program with people with disabilities, Ted went directly home most of the time. At home, he did not have much socialization except talking occasionally to his parents in Chinese and to his oldest sister, who acted as his advocate, in Spanish. He did not have much in the way of interactions with his other siblings (two older sisters and one older brother). He did not have any friends to call on the telephone, so he often called the teachers and staff, which eventually became a problem. On the weekends, his oldest sister sometimes took him to the mall to eat out or to go window shopping.

Family Expectations/Support

Because they thought that he did not have the ability to hold a job, Ted's family had relatively low expectations for him. They did not expect too much from Ted. As his sister put it, "If he can learn it, okay, fine. Otherwise, just leave [him alone]." These low expectations did not help Ted to learn the important functional skills that could help him develop and sustain social activities with other people. His parents feared that people without disabilities were likely to take advantage of Ted. Their concerns prevented him from learning necessary community-life skills such as riding a bus, which could help him with his transportation needs. After his teachers continued to communicate with Ted's parents through his sister, Ted finally obtained permission from his parents to learn to take the bus from school to home. This was a development he liked a lot. His parents did not support the idea of allowing him to learn how to ride a bus from home to other places in the community, however, because they were concerned for his safety. His limited transportation skills restricted his participation in some social activities in the community. Because he always had to rely on someone else for a ride, he often missed social activities. This is consistent with our findings in another study that students who have transportation skills are more active socially than those who do not have such skills (see Harry, Park, & Day, 1998).

Ted's family also had different expectations for his residential options. They did not think he was capable of living in his own apartment, even with support. Indeed, members of Ted's family had agreed that his siblings, especially his oldest sister, would take care of him throughout his adulthood. He did not seem to have much preference regarding where he would like to live.

Ted's Hopes and Wishes

Even though he was not able to express them specifically when asked, Ted revealed certain hopes and wishes during our interviews. He was deeply fond of Venezuela and wanted to return there. He said he still remembered names of his friends from the school that he attended while living in Venezuela. He often talked about the people he would like to take along with him. Ted was interested in the opposite sex, an observation that his sister also made. When asked about his Christmas wish, he replied that he wanted to have "a date [with a girl]." He would say that he liked the flower shop he worked at the best because the lady in the shop was pretty and nice. Ted was concerned about finding himself alone at home and away from his peers with and without disabilities. When he was about to graduate from the transition program, he became extremely motivated to perform his job better, knowing that worksites could serve as a good social opportunity to be with others without disabilities.

DISCUSSION

As we have analyzed and interpreted Ted's story along with those of other participants in our study, we have identified several contextual variables that are important to consider in thinking about access to the three levels of social relationships that we identify at the outset of this chapter. These include both setting variables and people variables. These variables have led us as educators to questions that might inform or guide our next steps in thinking about support for our youngest through our oldest students with disabilities.

Settings for Social Opportunities

Ted, like the majority of students in our study, had limited social relationships at work. Several variables seemed to affect his socialization at work. The nature of the job itself could provide few or no social opportunities (e.g., a maintenance job at the park). Certain ecological variables within a worksite, such as his schedule, could also reduce social opportunities (see Park et al., 1998, for more information on ecological variables). In addition, we found that worksites had work cultures that might facilitate or hinder socialization among workers. Some worksites were more flexible than others in allowing socialization among workers as long as the workers' jobs were getting done. Some worksites provided more social get-togethers among workers. We found, too, that individual co-workers' social expectations and social goals affected the individual's degree of socialization with workers with or without disabilities. It was not uncommon for co-workers to separate their personal lives from their work lives and be uninterested in developing close relationships with other co-workers, regardless of whether they had disabilities.

Ted also had limited social relationships in community classes just as he did at worksites. Perhaps work settings and community college campuses are not the best social opportunity settings. This led us to ask whether we needed to expand social opportunities beyond worksites and community college classes to include less-structured settings (e.g., hobby clubs, community classes offered by parks and recreation departments).

We found that the community lacked leisure and recreation programs that served students with and without disabilities. For Ted, the Young Life Club was it. When that club was discontinued, no other integrated social options were available. How can we increase leisure and recreation options for Ted to participate in activities with young people without disabilities? How can we work with existing community recreation programs to include individuals like Ted rather than create separate programs for people with and without disabilities?

People in the Settings

Job Coaches   Throughout the data, we observed that Ted's job coaches clearly represented barriers to potential social opportunities for him because co-workers tended to communicate with the job coaches rather than with Ted regarding both job-related and non–job-related matters (see also Park et al., 1998). The receptionist at Ted's jobsite could have communicated with Ted directly regarding the material needed rather than locating the job coach to communicate with. How can support personnel such as job coaches observe a delicate balance in their roles so that they serve as facilitators, not as barriers, in supporting appropriate social interactions with others at work while trying to teach necessary skills to workers with disabilities? How can job coaches recruit and use natural support from co-workers in both job-related and non–job-related matters?

Parents   Ted's parents feared letting go and allowing their son to take reasonable risks. They seemed unaware of his deep and intense need to have significant and long-lasting social relationships. Despite good intentions, their low expectations had a negative, inhibiting impact on Ted's social relationships. How can we better support parents in observing the delicate balance between their role as protectors and their role as risk facilitators? What is the culturally appropriate and inclusive approach to this collaborative effort with Ted's family?

Co-workers and Classmates   Because potential employers could not see Ted's potential as an employee, his teachers did not succeed in getting Ted a job at a Mexican restaurant or at a travel agency, either of which might have provided Ted with different social experiences. We found that Ted's co-workers and his classmates in his Spanish class often treated him as a child rather than as a young adult peer. Different (often low) expectations and the lack of information about Ted prevented them from seeing Ted as an individual who could perform a job and who was an equal to any of his classmates. What are the strategies for changing the perceptions and attitudes of people without disabilities toward Ted? What would be the most effective way of sharing information about Ted with classmates and with other employees at worksites?

Ted   Discovering and using Ted's talent to speak multiple languages and his preference for speaking Spanish was a great breakthrough in placing him in a better-matched class at the community college and in changing his social status among his peers. At the same time, we also noted that Ted had few experiences or interests in common with the people he did meet. For example, Ted (not unlike most students in our study) lacked age-appropriate leisure skills and hobbies, and this limited the range of topics available for conversation and the range of activities in which to engage outside school or work. Ted did not participate in any of the same games as other college students without disabilities in the Young Life Club. Learning not to repeat questions might have helped Ted in making and maintaining friendships. Learning to speak up for himself at home and certain skills such as riding a bus or calling a cab could have better assisted him in facilitating his social relationships with others. Personal safety skills could have helped him protect himself in the community and would have alleviated his parents' concerns about his safety so that he could have attended more social outings with his peers.

One important notion to keep in mind is that what Ted learns (i.e., his new skills) cannot be exercised maximally without consideration of the settings to which he has access and the roles and expectations of the people he meets. This notion prompts us to reflect on what could have been done differently at various stages of Ted's schooling regarding settings and people. How could Ted have been provided with more social opportunities? How had the roles of adults as facilitators been played out in his classrooms, during recess, at lunch, and in other school environments? How were the expectations of Ted's peers shaped? How could they have been helped to have a clearer, more fair understanding of Ted?

These reflections might help us devise more effective ways to support the social relationships of school-age individuals with disabilities. With regard to Ted, the larger task at hand is to find an effective way using a life-span approach to assist Ted in developing and maintaining close social relationships with others throughout the remainder of his adult life.

CONCLUSIONS

We have discussed several contextual variables that we believe should be considered throughout schooling and adulthood in supporting the social relationships of people with disabilities. This life-span approach requires collaborative participation from various people who can influence these contextual variables. A participatory action research approach is one process that can ensure this kind of collaboration. In participatory action research, all of the community stakeholders participate actively in the decision-making processes and become empowered to support the development and maintenance of the social relationships and friendships of people with disabilities (see, e.g., Park, Gonsier-Gerdin, Hoffman, Whaley, & Yount, 1998).

We should be ever mindful that supporting the social relationships of people with disabilities requires us to recognize that all people need various kinds of relationships with others. These include close or intimate friendships, companionships, acquaintanceships, mentorships, same-age friendships, cross-age friendships, and family relationships. All people, including people with disabilities, may also need social relationships and friendships with people with disabilities as much as they need the same kinds of social connections with people without disabilities (Harry et al., 1998). Ted definitely showed an interest in having a sense of belonging with his peers with disabilities as well as his peers without disabilities. When people with disabilities have rich, ample opportunities to develop and maintain a wide range of social relationships, including friendships with others who may or may not have disabilities, they will have the kinds of social support networks required to fulfill the different support functions that are needed to ensure every person's quality of life.

10

At the End of the Day

What Do We Know?
What's for Tomorrow?

Marquita Grenot-Scheyer,
Debbie Staub, and Mary Fisher

Our work with the Consortium for Collaborative Research on Social Relationships of Children and Youth with Diverse Abilities and other research projects, opportunities to practice our craft in schools and universities, and our own experiences as mothers support a long-held belief that there is an intricate and important relationship among how students learn, how teachers teach, and the community in which they experience their school lives. The set of case studies presented in this book has both reinforced our beliefs about the positive outcomes for some students in inclusive schools and highlighted the difficulties that some children and their families face in their attempts to obtain an education (for the child) in what they consider to be the least restrictive environment (LRE). We are reminded of how current service delivery models affect children's lives and the lives of their families and teachers in complicated and profound ways. This chapter presents some final thoughts about what we have learned and what we can anticipate for the future.

Our Consortium colleagues (Meyer, Grenot-Scheyer, Harry, Park, & Schwartz, 1992) proposed a model of social relationships that has implications beyond the relationships and friendships of children and youth with and without disabilities. This model informs us with regard to how children learn and relate to one another, how teachers teach and interact with one another and their students and their families, and ultimately how classrooms and schools are structured. There are four components, or "legs," of the model:

1. Child repertoire
2. Peer skills, support, and expectations
3. Adult mediation
4. Social-ecology

Our research has supported our conviction that each of these components must be addressed in order that the child may have successful social and academic outcomes.

CHILD REPERTOIRE

The case studies in this book as well as our experiences and research in schools support a belief long held by educational theorists: Social context affects all learning. We have long understood that cognitive and communicative skills develop out of social interaction and that a child's development cannot be understood apart from the social world of the child (Vygotsky, 1978). A child's repertoire and his or her ability to learn and interact with a number of individuals in his or her school and community do matter greatly. This is not to suggest that certain child-specific criteria (e.g., a prescribed developmental level, positive interactive behaviors, a reliable communication system) must be demonstrated by the child prior to his or her being educated in an inclusive setting. We absolutely do not support a prerequisite model that was evident in our field decades ago. Rather, teachers, parents, and others must identify areas of need and provide opportunities for children to learn the skills necessary to gain access to the core curriculum in authentic and meaningful ways. The story of Charlotte in Chapter 4 is a good example of a child who is at risk for being assigned to a more restrictive setting and the response of the education team (including her parents), which developed a positive behavioral support plan. Implementation of the plan allowed Charlotte the opportunity and instruction necessary to learn new and more appropriate ways to communicate and interact.

PEER SKILLS, EXPECTATIONS, AND SUPPORT

Our understanding of the contributions and impact that children without disabilities have on their peers with disabilities and the concomitant impact on their skills, expectations, and support continues to deepen as children with and without disabilities increasingly attend school together. Although the case studies in this book focus primarily on children and youth with disabilities, other researchers have looked closely at the outcomes of school inclusion for children without disabilities (Grenot-Scheyer, Staub, Peck, & Schwartz, 1998; Helmstetter, Peck, & Giangreco, 1994; Peck, Donaldson, & Pezzoli, 1990; Staub, 1998; Staub & Peck, 1994/1995). We have identified three main effects for children with and without disabilities identified as friends (Grenot-Scheyer et al., 1998). These include warm and caring companionships, growth in social cognition and self-concept, and development of personal principles.

From our Consortium study, we have come to understand the importance of the skill repertoire and expectations that a child without disabilities has as he or she relates to her peers with disabilities. We have identified several key areas of importance, including the ability to empathize and take the perspective of others, engage in a positive interaction style, provide creative solutions and ideas, and demonstrate a commitment to principles of social justice and the inclusion of all.

ALYSSA AND JIMMY

Alyssa is a child without disabilities whom we know and who embodies the preceding principles in her daily life. She attended kindergarten and first grade with a young boy named Jimmy, who demonstrated developmental delays in a number of areas. She and Jimmy quickly developed a relationship based on a shared sense of humor. She seemed to empathize with Jimmy and often questioned the teacher and her own mother about how it must feel to have a disability. She was often the one to find creative solutions with regard to how to better include Jimmy in all facets of the school day. It was Alyssa who raised questions about the future of Jimmy's education. She wondered whether he would continue to be included or whether there would be a time when he would be relegated to the special education bungalows that she became aware of when she moved to her new school in second grade. Prior to this experience, Alyssa had assumed that Jimmy and other children with disabilities would continue in general classrooms with support. Her realization that there was a separate place for Jimmy and other children with disabilities aroused great concern in her and violated her sense of what was right and just.

As important as the contributions of children without disabilities are, so too are the supports that teachers, parents, and others provide to children without disabilities who interact with and learn alongside children with disabilities. Our work indicates that children and youth without disabilities do interact with their peers with disabilities but often with limited knowledge about how to socialize and communicate with them. Without direct guidance and assistance, they may withdraw from interactions with their peers with disabilities. Specific structures, such as the student aide program described in Chapter 7, may be necessary to ensure successful interaction and learning opportunities.

ADULT MEDIATION

As can be seen in the stories in this book and in the work of others (Cole & Meyer, 1991), adult mediation can have a profound impact on the social interactions of children and the learning that occurs as a result of such interactions. We view adult mediation as any behavior by an adult that facilitates or interferes with the interaction and learning of students.

In our work (Grenot-Scheyer & Leonard-Giesen, 1997), we have been mindful of two key questions:

1. What is the nature of support and instruction that paraprofessionals, teachers, and other specialized personnel provide?
2. What is the influence and impact of adult mediation?

We have identified three levels of adult mediation that are described briefly in the subsections that follow: facilitated, blocked, and missed.

Facilitated

Our data revealed many examples of an adult's (e.g., instruction assistant, teacher) facilitating or helping an interaction or learning opportunity along. Within this category, adult behavior can be either proactive or responsive. That is, there were many instances when a peer without disabilities asked an adult whether he or she could assist or play with a student with disabilities, and other times the adult initiated such facilitation in a more proactive manner. When the adult gets it just right, the learning opportunity or social interaction appears to unfold naturally, with the adult knowing when and just how much to intervene.

Blocked

Unfortunately, too many times, an adult comes to the rescue of a student with disabilities, interrupting the social interaction and learning that is occurring. Our data revealed many times when an adult became a barrier between the child with disabilities and his or her peers without disabilities and between the child and his or her general education teacher. Adults often lack the skills necessary to mediate social interactions and naturalistic learning opportunities except within a helping frame. Such help often results in more isolation and separation of the student with disabilities.

Missed

The third category of adult mediation that we have learned about is that of missed opportunities. Our data revealed numerous examples of missed opportunities for social interaction and learning. Adults often did not notice when a peer without disabilities was watching nearby or in some way was showing interest in a student with disabilities. The adult did not invite the peer without disabilities into the interaction and thus did not capture and use the teachable moment.

The phenomenon of adult mediation is pervasive, and the social and learning consequences thereof for children with disabilities are profound. Teachers and other service providers must carefully select, structure, and monitor the type of adult mediation provided to students when considering supports for students with disabilities in inclusive classrooms and other environments.

SOCIAL-ECOLOGY

Various dimensions of the environment can be characterized as the social-ecology of that context. Our research revealed patterns of social interaction and learning as functions of different features of the environment (Grenot-Scheyer, Park, & Meyer, 1993). That is, certain features or characteristics of inclusive classrooms and schools either support or inhibit learning across a variety of dimensions as well as have a strong impact on the development and maintenance of a student's social relationships. We have developed and validated a measure of *accommodating diversity in the classroom* (Grenot-Scheyer, Leonard-Giesen, Fisher, & Meyer, 1997) that is designed to identify exemplars of positive classroom structures and characteristics that teachers might use to promote acceptance and inclusion in their classrooms and schools. The measure indicates a number of features that are evident in programs reflecting a variety of teaching styles and practices, thus demonstrating maximum generalizability across teachers in different schools.

As indicated previously, we believe that all four "legs" of the model must be addressed, evaluated, and emphasized by all members of education teams, including parents. Such an orientation may move us from pockets of excellence to more sustained high-quality education for all students in inclusive settings.

Systemic Change and Sustainability of Recommended Practices

Many of the case studies in this book offer cause for hope and indeed are inspiring with regard to the potential of some schools to truly include each and every learner. These cases are representative of a beginning. They are stories about the process of initial change and about bringing inclusive schooling into being. In that sense, they are a start; however, we are not finished yet. It is critical that we embrace the notion of newness at this point and emphasize the need to nurture our endeavor. Its growth requires careful attention. This is a nascent and, as such, critical period. Implementation can no longer be left to individual teachers, families, and schools. We have begun to move beyond and step out of the tradition that "persists in disproportionate representation of students of color and low socioeconomic status . . . fails to show positive results from pull-out services . . . and neglects to consult students [and their families] about their feelings and preference" (Brantlinger, 1997, p. 428). We know that inclusion can work. We are learning every day how to do it better. We are learning every day which outcomes and factors must be addressed. We are sharing our stories with our community, acknowledging problems, and celebrating successes.

It is imperative that efforts to align the initiatives of special education with those in general education be accomplished so that such efforts may be sustained. Services and resources cannot be fragmented, constituents must not be pitted against each other in the struggle for resources, and ultimately a seamless education for all children must result. As McLaughlin as well as others have suggested, inclusive schooling cannot be sustained outside general education and school reform efforts:

> Educational restructuring initiatives are most effective for students with disabilities when they are directed toward the creation of inclusive schools or unified schools or school systems. These schools and school systems are collaborative, problem-solving entities in which staff share a common vision and a sense of purpose of educating all students to the highest possible standards. (McLaughlin, 1996, p. 641)

Policy Implications

The policy implications for the type of school renewal that we envision for all children are clear. Regardless of whether these efforts are termed *restructuring*, *reform*, or *reinvention*, their primary purpose should be to develop and support schools that have the capacity to accept, educate, and care about each member of the school community. Too many classrooms, schools, and communities remain in which participation in general education settings for more than 60% of a school day alongside age peers is "for everyone except [a student or students with disabilities]." A report (U.S. Department of Education, 1998) to Congress indicated that 20% of children and youth ages 6–11 who are identified for special education supports and services and 30% who are ages 12–17 receive special education supports and services in separate classes or facilities. Although 95% attend school with their peers without disabilities, for children ages 6–21,

Approximately 46% were removed from their regular classes for less than 21% of the day; about 29% received special education and related services outside regular classes for 21%–60% of the day, and 22% were served outside the regular classroom for more than 60% of the day. (U.S. Department of Education, 1998, p. vii)

Certain policies clearly inhibit educational renewal efforts. Grimes and Tilly (1996) described several fundamental errors in the service delivery system that also are evident in the case studies presented in this book. These errors include the following:

- Special education continues to be separate from general education in the delivery of services to students.

- The primary method of service delivery places a heavy reliance on pull-out programs.

- Specialized programs and services available through special education are available only to those who qualify, even though there are children at risk and in need of such services.

- Overreferral and overrepresentation of students of differing ethnicities in special education persists.

How do we move from the fragmented system to ensure an appropriate education for all students in inclusive settings? Meyer (1997) suggested that we stop tinkering around the edges and develop education systems that integrate resources, personnel, and systems of general and special education and recognize and use the expertise of special and general education personnel to address the needs of all children. In Meyer's view, outcomes for all students, especially those requiring specialized supports, would not be compromised but rather would be improved. We agree that meaningful change in the fabric of schools must come from within schools rather than as a response to external pressures. Successful reform must be created, implemented, evaluated, and owned by those who will benefit from it.

What's for Tomorrow?

Although there is much to celebrate, the all-too-many struggles that we face at the end of this day are evident. Tomorrow is a new day, however— an opportunity to affirm our beliefs and put our values to the test. As we look toward this new day, we return to the seven values fundamental to inclusion that were presented in Chapter 1, and we take what we have learned from the case studies presented in this book to identify our expectations of an inclusive tomorrow for children, teachers, families, schools, and communities.

Inclusion and School Renewal Are Linked

Schools of tomorrow will integrate all key players in discussions of school reform. Consequently, including students with disabilities will not be a peripheral issue to be handled only within the special education structures of the school. Rather, special educators, general educators, and communities will work together to identify common ground and develop shared agendas for creating school communities that meet everyone's needs. The interests and concerns of those who advocate for inclusion will be aligned with those of general education reformers who work to develop more responsive school communities. Educators will seek to create schools that are both "challenging and caring for the full range of students they serve" (Schaps, 1997, p. 20).

Teachers, families, and students will identify practices that lead to the creation of supportive education communities designed to meet the individualized needs of *all* students. Support and acceptance of students' diversity will be a common goal: "An essential component of wide-ranging school reform is a shared agenda; the understanding that fixing the school for some children must mean fixing the school for all children" (Sapon-Shevin, 1994/1995, p. 70).

School renewal will be supported with the necessary resources needed to gain the full commitment of all team players. Furthermore, parents of both general and special education students will be involved in discussions and planning about inclusion to create a common understanding that addresses concerns from the outset. Finally, the pace of change will fit the setting. Collaborative planning will result in an appropriate plan of action and a pace that matches the needs of individual schools.

Inclusion Presents a Strong Moral Imperative

For the last 25 years of the 20th century, parents and families went to amazing lengths to secure inclusive school placements for their children. Their motivation was driven by two common themes: 1) a desire for their children to belong and 2) their view that inclusion is a basic right (Erwin & Soodak, 1995). In 21st-century schools, parents of children with disabilities no longer have to fight for their child's right to be educated alongside their peers without disabilities with appropriate supports and outcomes. The inclusion of children with disabilities in general education settings is supported by legislation (i.e., the Individuals with Disabilities Education Act [IDEA] Amendments of 1997 [PL 105-17]) and backed by a large body of research that points to the efficacy of inclusive placement. Just as the majority of Americans no longer question the rights of children of differing ethnicities to attend public schools, educators and community members in tomorrow's schools will no longer question why children of all ability levels should have the right to attend their neighborhood school or their school of choice. On the contrary, educators, community members, and families finally will ask not why but *how* schools can be improved for *all* children, because improving schools is a moral imperative.

Learning and Belonging Happen Together

In tomorrow's schools and classrooms, communities of learning in which children are encouraged to care about each other as well as their learning will be a reality for all students. Appreciation of differences will be encouraged and fostered through a curriculum that emphasizes friendship, caring, and respect for diversity. Teachers will create classroom activities that are centered on cooperation, not on competition. Students will actively participate in developing rules and discussions regarding diversity, and fairness will be commonplace. Classroom practices that teach self-control, problem solving, and helping one another will reinforce a sense of community at all grade levels.

Although we can create classroom contexts that enhance the development of positive relationships and thus caring school communities, we can do so only when such schools are inclusive of all learners not only rhetorically but also in practice. In tomorrow's schools, students, families, and educators will 1) recognize and value the importance of social context for learning for all learners, 2) structure learning environments that not only teach values but also allow students to experience such values in everyday routines, and 3) implement classroom and instruction strategies that foster peer relationships in caring community schools (Grenot-Scheyer, Harry, et al., 1998).

Equity, Access, and Support Are Critical

In tomorrow's classrooms, the standard curriculum will become a thing of the past. Instead, it will be replaced with a curriculum that is fluid and flexible and adapted to fit the needs of individual students. Activities in the general classroom will be used as vehicles to teach students goals that are important to them. Furthermore, educators will capitalize on individual differences as opportunities for discussion and problem solving, not as a basis for separation.

The wide variety of learning strategies that have been developed and proved effective for meeting the diverse needs of all students will be implemented by trained and knowledgeable teachers. General and special educators will come together at initial planning stages and use their expertise to make the curriculum accessible to all learners. Furthermore, in collaboration with special education staff, general education teachers will adjust their instruction to support the needs of individual students.

Students Learn in Different Ways

Providing equitable and accessible education to all learners requires the acknowledgment that students of all ability levels learn in different ways. Although there has been a long history of promoting this belief (i.e., Gardner, 1993), educators seldom use approaches beyond those that support visual and/or auditory ways of learning. Research has revealed that students learn and perform better when they are taught in ways that at least partially match their learning strengths (Sternberg, 1997). The educators of tomorrow will deliver instruction in a way that capitalizes on different ways of learning.

Schools of tomorrow will embrace and practice approaches to teaching that are embedded in the theories of major contributors to the field of education, including Bruner, Dewey, Greene, Noddings, Paley, Piaget, and Vygotsky. These education greats share the belief that teaching for thinking, problem solving, and understanding has positive effects on student achievement. Tomorrow's educators will use approaches that 1) emphasize development through doing, 2) extend student knowledge by building on what they already know, and 3) increase students' involvement in and responsibility for what they learn (McGregor & Vogelsberg, 1999). By continuing our tradition of meeting the individual needs of students, we will implement practices and teaching strategies that acknowledge the many and varied ways in which students learn.

Inclusive Education Has Benefits for All Involved

As several of the case studies in this book reveal, outcomes of inclusive schooling practices have been identified not only for students with disabilities but also for parents, teachers, and students without disabilities. Researchers have established a considerable body of evidence that points to the mutual rewards of inclusive schooling. When children with disabilities have repeated opportunities to interact with peers without disabilities, they have demonstrated improvements in their communication skills, social skills, and functional skills and even improved chances to live more full, normalized lives as adults (Staub, 1998). Children and teenagers who tutor or help children with disabilities have been found to have better attitudes toward human differences, to show greater patience with and tolerance for other people in general, to feel better about themselves, and to be more likely to engage in relationships with people with disabilities in their adult lives (Staub & Peck, 1994/1995; Staub, Spaulding, Peck, Gallucci, & Schwartz, 1996).

How will the school of tomorrow ensure that these mutual rewards continue and grow for all inclusive schools and communities? First, tomorrow's schools will implement democratic classroom practices that give students a voice in how the classroom is run and how decisions are made. Teachers will promote problem-solving and critical thinking skills in their students, and they will expect their students to seek out each other for help and support rather than rely on adults. Time to value and acknowledge the diverse gifts and contributions that each child brings to a classroom setting will be an integral part of each school day. Students without disabilities will be taught effective ways to communicate and interact with their peers with disabilities and be given plenty of opportunities to practice their skills. Working together, special and general education teachers will make accommodations in classroom routines and activities so that all students can actively participate. Curricula will be designed to give students ample opportunities to work together to achieve common goals and reveal their strengths through their personal learning styles.

Administrators will provide time for faculty to visit and revisit the value of inclusion at their schools and in their classrooms. They will ensure that teachers have the training, assistance, and guidance that they need to teach children with a wide range of abilities. Administrators will publicly ensure that families and community members are aware of the benefits of inclusion and will take the necessary steps to educate people who are not.

Parents and students will work with teachers and administrators to make their classrooms and schools safe and welcoming. Parents of children with disabilities will be involved actively as members of their children's schools, and parents of children without disabilities will make every effort to invite children with disabilities to schoolwide functions and activities and include them in these functions and activities.

Collaboration Is Essential

Collaboration occurs when all members of a school community work together and support each other in an effort to provide the highest-quality curriculum and instruction for the diverse population of students whom they serve (Pugach & Johnson, 1995a). Although collaboration historically has not been part of the job of teaching, in tomorrow's schools, collaboration will be the foundation upon which high-quality education is provided to *all* students.

Collaboration that involves families, students, administrators, general educators, and special educators will be recognized as not only a necessary component of inclusion but also the cornerstone on which inclusive practices are delivered. Furthermore, administrators will recognize the power of team collaboration and use collaborative structures to guide and evaluate inclusive schooling practices.

Effective collaboration requires time for teaming, reflection, and commitment on the part of all team members. Collaborative teams of tomorrow will capitalize on the best thinking of all while respecting the diverse contributions that team members make. Members of collaborative teams will celebrate the creativity generated by working together with others. Finally, collaborators of tomorrow will recognize that collaboration is complex and requires the acknowledgment that many of the problems in schools are either blatant or subtle inequities in the way schools treat students with differences. By working together, the educators, administrators, families, and students of tomorrow will ensure that school communities are challenging, motivating, and safe places to learn for *all* children and adults alike.

What's for the Next Year and Beyond: The Next Decade, the Next Generation?

At this juncture, then, we must focus our attention on the problematic issues of the generalization and sustainability of inclusive school interventions. It has worked in Brooklyn, New York. It has worked in Long Beach, California, and Redmond, Washington. It has worked in Syracuse, New York. Believing that our intervention is right and good and having evidence that it can work for some, how can we make it work for all? As we focus, we recognize that to effect long-term change, our attention must be directed at more than one audience. Several years ago, Baer (1993) delineated the interrelationship between policy and procedure, observing that one class of policy decisions requires two types of procedures: 1) those teaching students the particular policy-related skills and 2) those teaching society how to implement that policy. Baer stated,

> Whether policy expands or constricts will depend less on the new procedures for teaching target skills than on the procedures for teaching a society whether or not to espouse, fund and implement a new policy. Thus, policy and procedure should never be discussed separately—except, of course, by those who have no intention of improving either of them. (Baer, 1993, pp. 270–271)

In this section, we address newly effective procedures for teaching society to expand the policy of inclusion so that by 2020, inclusive schooling will be simply the typical way of schooling in the United States. The seven values identified in Chapter 1 will be business as usual. As we imagine education across the United States moving toward second-generation inclusion, we ask ourselves the following: What has to happen to create this change? Which procedures can teach society about inclusive schools? Which procedures will be most efficient? Belonging and membership are seemingly simplistic concepts to grasp and support, but even some special educators have yet to embrace these as priorities for children and youth who receive special education supports and services. Even special educators have yet to reach consensus regarding the need for a unified system of education versus maintaining a dual system of general and special education.

Ideas for Procedures to Teach Society

Recommendations by Grimes and Tilly (1996) regarding lasting educational change in conjunction with Schnorr's (1997) analysis of successful interventions present an appropriate starting point to guide the development of procedures to teach communities about inclusion. We have grouped their respective recommendations together in the next subsections for purposes of discussion.

Identify Essential Components

As we share and compare stories, we must identify and emphasize only what is essential about inclusive schooling. With the essential components identified, we must be careful to acknowledge and emphasize that each incarnation of inclusive schooling has been and will continue to be unique, with each reflecting a particular community. Building on social-ecological approaches and given the literature base, the four components that emerged from our Consortium research may capture the essential features of inclusive schooling. It may be that the list of variables associated with each leg of the table that appear to be critical to the success of an inclusive school community are instead unique to the schools in which we have worked. Time and additional research will tell. We do know that one overarching intervention is not the single answer, as exemplified by the stories in this book alone. Instead, we must understand the commonality in our purpose and realize that our goal can be approached from both the top and the bottom. As schools adopt an inclusive philosophy, they may need initial support from the *outside* to create the version that can work *inside* their particular communities.

Clarify Multiple Outcomes with Participants

We must increase our efforts to share and celebrate our successes and problems with our neighbors. Beyond efforts to communicate with educators, we must engage community leaders, neighboring districts, neighboring schools, and building colleagues. We must work with bureaucracies and all those groups and individuals with vested interests in our efforts to identify the multiple outcomes that are indicators of meaningful change. Everyone must agree on valued outcomes and understand how the fundamental values that characterize inclusive schooling relate to program success. Then, when community members and families (i.e., noneducators) judge our schools, it will be from an informed perspective. They will understand the significance of the benefits outlined in Chapter 1.

Be prepared to wait for results. Mostly, educators must realize that change does not happen overnight. In order to sustain change, we must take the long view. We must anticipate that the changes we initiate may not be successful for a decade or two. In fact, we may never reach our utopian vision. As Brantlinger pointed out, "Utopia is a vision, perhaps remote but one that inspires, provides direction for action, and suggests forms for mundane practice" (1997, p. 449).

Develop a Critical Mass

Meanwhile, we have to avoid discouragement and maintain our confidence. We have to stay hard at work. Collaboration with community agencies, families, colleagues, and students must be a first step in creating the intensity and critical mass that both Grimes and Tilley (1996) and Schorr (1997) found in initiatives that survived or showed promise for survival. Local, regional, statewide, and national networks can operationalize this strategy.

Procedures to Teach Society

Our procedures for teaching society include the following elements:

- Identify and articulate the essential characteristics of inclusive education policy.
- Make the rationale for inclusion explicit, and clarify its basis in both moral beliefs and empirical evidence compiled to date.
- With constituent groups, identify and describe the desired outcomes of inclusive education.
- Make sure that all educators, families, and youth who participate in inclusive schools agree on these valued outcomes.
- Help community members understand how inclusive schools are related to these outcomes so that the results can be used to judge the success of the program.
- Network and collaborate with other programs to gain critical mass.

We can look toward and build on existing models in pursuing sustained, lasting change. These include recent research-based consortiums that rely on participatory and collaborative research models (e.g., Consortium for Collaborative Research on Social Relationships of Children and Youth with Diverse Abilities, Consortium on Inclusive Schooling, National Institute for Urban School Improvement), professional development school models (e.g., Coalition for Essential Schools, Holmes partnerships) as well as community agency wraparound service models (e.g., LaGrange, Illinois, public schools; Casey Family Programs). As we note throughout this chapter, in order to continue our move toward a unified system of education, collaboration is critical.

Collaboration must occur at the school level, the community level, and the university level. Both in-service and preservice teacher preparation must support and reflect fundamental change. Griffin and Pugach (1997) suggested that now is the time to initiate conversations about hard questions such as "What is special education?" "What do we understand by the term *all children*?" "How will we share responsibility for seeing that students such as Cecilia (see Chapter 5) and Andre (see Chapter 6) have the opportunity to participate in science as the national science standards require?" "What does it mean when Jamal (see Chapter 3) cannot attend his neighborhood school?" We must remain confident in our capacity to change through collaboration. We have good evidence for being sure and will collect more evidence over time. Researchers will continue to examine the theory supporting practice. Educators will continue to engage in practice supporting theory. Families will participate in theory building and practice. Communities will be informed about multiple outcomes and how these outcomes dovetail with community interests.

What We're Looking for at the End of the Day: Moving on Toward Tomorrow

So, if we were to view the long term from the perspective of a teacher's life, what changes might we see in the next 5, 10, or 20 years? This book tells the story of teachers only tangentially to that of their students. In this chapter, we change perspectives and address our target audience directly, imagining a week in the life of a support teacher (previously known during the 1990s as a *special educator*) in the 2020s. We borrow the five themes of the reflective practitioner articulated by Grenot-Scheyer, Coots, and Bishop-Smith (1999). Reflective practitioners

- Care about the whole kid
- Know the content well
- Teach well
- Collaborate with others
- Are lifelong learners

We have interwoven these themes throughout an imagined day for a teacher named Anna. This is our attempt to portray what teachers think about on a daily basis. How might a day in the life of Anna, the lead support person for the K–1 team at Barbara Jordan Elementary School, look in 5–10 years or so? How might what she knows and does be reflected in her practice?

CARE ABOUT THE WHOLE KID

It is Monday morning at 7:15, and Anna has arrived early to attend the leadership team's weekly update from the wraparound service providers for Ginny, José, and Sam—all 7-year-olds in the primary multi-age program. Today there are good reports all around—foster parents, counselors, and recreation staff report that each child had a positive weekend. No big incidents. Anna is relieved—it's likely the kids will be off to a good start. She walks the nonschool team members to the parking lot door along with the principal and schmoozes for just a minute. There is a feeling of mutual support and pride in the mutual accomplishment. The first buses are rolling into the driveway. Anna checks her watch and heads back to the conference room in need of her calendar plan book. "Fun kid things" on tap for the day are a snack date with John-David, Joseph, Ann, and Kate from Room 7 (they invited her yesterday at recess—ostensibly to share their newly published books, but maybe they just miss her company), her reminder note to check in with Ginny personally about her weekend as soon as she gets in from the bus, and the lunch bunch from Room 9 in their room at 12:00 P.M. These little social interludes always make her day—hanging with friends, and her age does not exclude her. The tough time will be chatting with Joey before going home. Despite their regular noncontingent-type chats, Anna does not feel Joey connects with school much at all. Maybe she should "sub" for Tamra, Joey's classroom teacher, so that Tamra can spend this additional, regular time with Joey.

Other events for the day include introducing Jon (Room 8) to the new paraprofessional, Mr. Minondo, and together demonstrating read-only memory (ROM) for him. Anna sensed in their first meeting that Mr. Minondo might be inclined to talk about, but not to, Jon, so this collaborative demonstration by student and teacher must carefully and obviously convey how respect for children is operationalized at Barbara Jordan Elementary School. Finally, there is Sam's child study team meeting. His dad plans to come because he's been invited to share his photography interest with Sam's class during art today, which is great from Anna's perspective. This will present a challenge, however, to the new presenting teacher, whose preservice preparation program was focused more on children's impairments than on their strengths.

Know the Content Well

Anna next previews the day's individual accommodations and supports. These include snack check-in with Lauren about her new adapted utensil, support for Jon's group during K–1 team time, when children are regrouped for sound unit exploration, music with Room 7 (the music teacher is looking for ideas to include all students in the spring program and has asked Anna to come check things out and later brainstorm with her), Room 9 for science and night unit pre-assessment (i.e., "What makes day and night?"; prepare text in large 16-point font using picture-word symbols for Lucy, print out directions in braille for Kevin), and collect probe data on the playground with regard to social interactions for Joey. Definitely enough to do today, and if the vision specialist brings in a replacement braille typewriter, it may be a pretty smooth day! Anna is making a note to check in with Sam, Ginny, and Joey about school–home notebooks. She forgot to check on Friday, and Sam's foster mom had to make two telephone calls because Sam arrived home somewhat agitated, so she wrote, "Make sure classroom teachers saw notes from this morning and/or responded."

Teach Well

Anna thinks, "So far, so good for individual children. Now what about classroom teacher support?" She'll have to remember to hide each morning in the conference room. No one has found her to ask those innumerable "just a quick second before the bell" questions. It's great that the classroom paraprofessionals are feeling clear about their assignments. . . . As Anna reviews this section in her plan book, she's feeling confident about her small-group reading workshop time in Room 7. She's already well versed in implementing the two activities that Tamra's asked her to lead: a small-group lesson regarding characters and another small-group lesson on "word families." Read-alouds during Room 6 time with Ginny and Sam will be routine. Today she should audiotape-record for their Students Share Their Learning (SSTL) program for families next Thursday night. She'll have to get the time for Paula's minilesson in Room 6. Anna wants to observe this minilesson about sensory and feeling vocabulary words—something she's read about but never has seen demonstrated with a large group. The afternoon will be a continuation of the sound unit—Anna takes the lead in explaining the various sound stations to the team and hanging with Jon's group during these firsthand experiences. The Professional Development School (PDS) Initiative around science has been a huge advantage for the children in terms of shared expertise between Barbara Jordan Elementary School and the university.

Collaborate with Others

This 10-minute preview feels like a stolen but well-spent moment. Anna collects her book and heads down the hall to greet Mr. Minondo and welcome him to his first full day at Barbara Jordan Elementary School. Anna introduces him to the team. He tags along with her to the buses, where they greet arriving students. The children look curious and excited about the prospect of a new adult in their lives, and Anna is thinking, "How nice to have another man on the team!" The next 50 minutes are set aside to provide a program overview for Mr. Minondo. Then he will shadow her all day through Monday's long lunch with other support people from primary and intermediate grades. Arranged by the building principal, this scheduled time has made a significant difference in keeping support people informed about building-level issues. Everyone is hoping that the parent–teacher organization will continue to provide parent volunteers for this endeavor so that this meeting time can become part of regular collaborative efforts in the building. In fact, this hour block might be the perfect time frame for community businesspeople who are interested in volunteering a lunch hour each week. During the meeting, Anna explains the new arrangement with the "science problem solvers teacher inquiry group" and the university's engineering students and preservice inclusive educators that starts on Tuesday mornings. Anna conveys her enthusiasm for the project, asking, "How can we not be excited about college students' interviewing kids about their classroom environment needs and designing adaptations or equipment that they imagine together?" She notes that it will be important to help the university students anticipate the importance of community to each class at Barbara Jordan Elementary School and the welcome that the children will offer and suggests how the university students might respond.

Be a Lifelong Learner

As they leave the support meeting, Mr. Minondo indicates to Anna his interest in pursuing a special education certificate and asks her directly how she obtained her teacher certification. It's his impression that her program was comprehensive based on this first day following her schedule. Anna thinks back to her preservice program, remembering its behavioral bent and categorical focus. She tells Mr. Minondo she learned important content and skills that she continues to practice, then she talks with Mr. Minondo as they walk back to her office about the myriad things she continues to learn every week from school-based colleagues, students, families, and—now—community agency people. She describes the local university's collaborative program as a great starting place but shares her perspective that teaching and learning about teaching is a continuing, lifelong process. From Anna's perspective, it is a career and a vocation. For example, to make things work for her students, she must stay on top of new initiatives growing out of collaborative research between the university, K–12 school, family, and community. It's almost sounding like her new schpiel; she and her team just shared this idea in their panel for preservice teachers last month. But she does hold it dear and hopes her sincerity carries it off for her new colleague. She's glad Mr. Minondo asked. It's encouraging to know that certification is on his mind—perhaps another convert for the children. And now it's time to collect some favorite assessments to share with her university-based elementary science methods course tonight. Oh yes, and it's her night for snacks for the group. Micheala brought pizza last week—guess it's nice to be an administrator on leave. Anna's thinking: cheese, health food chips, and diet soda. . . . Her watch says 1:30, and that means a very fast walk (don't get caught running by any children) to make it on time for team time.

CONCLUSIONS

At the end of the day, we have ourselves and our relationships. These relationships are defined by each of us and the world around us. As individuals, depending on our worldviews, we may believe that we have more or less to say about the definition. As educators, we must set the stage for critical reflection by those in and intersecting with our learning communities. "Empowerment is not something I can give to someone: It is a potential within all of us and developed during our life's journey. We are empowered when we achieve control over our lives" (Delgado-Gaitan, 1998, p. xiv). We share these stories as one opportunity to clarify our needs as individuals and members of school communities to better grasp the social context within which empowerment can take place and better define our roles in that development, mindful that in this endeavor (building confidence for inclusion) we are limited only by the reach of our collective imagination (Pugach, 1995).

References

Affleck, J., Madge, S., Adams, A., & Lowenbraun, S. (1988). Integrated classroom versus resource model: Academic viability and effectiveness. *Exceptional Children, 54,* 339–348.

Armstrong, T. (1994). *Multiple intelligences in the classroom.* Alexandria, VA: Association for Supervision and Curriculum Development.

Asher, S.R., Parker, J.G., & Walker, D.L. (1996). Distinguishing friendship from acceptance: Implications for intervention and assessment. In W.M. Bukowski, A.F. Newcomb, & W.W. Hartup (Eds.), *The company they keep: Friendships in childhood and adolescence* (pp. 366–405). Cambridge, England: Cambridge University Press.

Ayres, B.J., & Hedeen, D.L. (1997). Quick-guide #5: Creating positive behavioral supports. In M.F. Giangreco (Ed.), *Quick-guides to inclusion: Ideas for educating students with disabilities* (pp. 113–139). Baltimore: Paul H. Brookes Publishing Co.

Ayres, B.J., Meyer, L.H., Ervelles, N., & Park-Lee, S. (1994). Easy for you to say: Teacher perspectives on implementing most promising practices. *Journal of The Association for Persons with Severe Handicaps, 19,* 84–93.

Baer, D.M. (1993). Policy and procedure, as always. In R.A. Gable & S.F. Warren (Eds.), *Strategies for teaching students with mild to severe mental retardation* (pp. 269–277). Baltimore: Paul H. Brookes Publishing Co.

Barron, J., & Barron, S. (1992). *There's a boy in here.* New York: Simon & Schuster.

Belle, D. (Ed.). (1989). *Children's social networks and social supports.* New York: John Wiley & Sons.

Bennet, T., DeLuca, D., & Bruns, D. (1997). Putting inclusion into practice: Perspectives of teachers and parents. *Exceptional Children, 64*(1), 115–131.

Berk, L.E. (1999). *Infants, children, and adolescents* (3rd ed.). Needham Heights, MA: Allyn & Bacon.

Berndt, T.J. (1982). The features and effects of friendship in early adolescence. *Child Development, 53,* 1447–1460.

Beukelman, D.R., & Mirenda, P. (1998). *Augmentative and alternative communication: Management of severe communication disorders in children and adults* (2nd ed.). Baltimore: Paul H. Brookes Publishing Co.

Biklen, D. (1989). Redefining schools. In D. Biklen, D. Ferguson, & A. Ford (Eds.), *Schooling and disability: 88th Yearbook of the National Society for the Study of Education, Part II* (pp. 1–24). Chicago: University of Chicago Press.

Biklen, S.K., & Larson, M.J. (1998). The academy and the street: Using community fieldworkers to study children's social relations in school. In L.H. Meyer, H.-S. Park, M. Grenot-Scheyer, I.S. Schwartz, & B. Harry (Eds.), *Making friends:*

The influences of culture and development (pp. 31–45). Baltimore: Paul H. Brookes Publishing Co.

Billingsley, F., Gallucci, C., Peck, C.A., Schwartz, I.S., & Staub, D. (1996). "But those kids can't even do math": An alternative conceptualization of outcomes for inclusive education. *Special Education Leadership Review, 3*(1), 43–56.

Black, J.W. (1996). *Ghost, guest, and classmate: Student membership and teacher decision-making in the design of curricular and instructional adaptations for students with severe disabilities in inclusive classrooms.* Unpublished doctoral dissertation, Syracuse University, Syracuse, NY.

Bondy, A., & Frost, L. (1994). The Picture Exchange Communication System. *Focus on Autistic Behavior, 9,* 1–19.

Brantlinger, E. (1997). Using ideology: Cases of nonrecognition of the politics of research and practice in special education. *Review of Educational Research, 67*(4), 425–459.

Bricker, D.D. (1995). The challenge of inclusion. *Journal of Early Intervention, 19,* 179–194.

Brinker, R.P., & Thorpe, M.E. (1984). Integration of severely handicapped students and the proportion of IEP objectives achieved. *Exceptional Children, 51,* 168–175.

Bromley, D.B. (1977). *Personality description in ordinary language.* New York: John Wiley & Sons.

Bronfenbrenner, U. (1979). *The ecology of human development: Experiments by nature and design.* Cambridge, MA: Harvard University Press.

Bruner, J.S. (1990). *Acts of meaning.* Cambridge, MA: Harvard University Press.

Bukowski, W.M., Newcomb, A.F., & Hartup, W.W. (Eds.). (1996). *The company they keep: Friendship in childhood and adolescence.* New York: Cambridge University Press.

California Department of Education. (1997). *Guidelines for language, academic, and special education services required for limited-English-proficient students in California public schools, K–12.* Sacramento: Author.

Carr, W., & Kemmis, S. (1986). *Becoming critical: Education, knowledge, and action research.* Philadelphia: Falmer Press.

Cole, D.A., & Meyer, L. (1991). Social integration and severe disabilities: A longitudinal analysis of child outcomes. *Journal of Special Education, 25,* 340–351.

Comer, J.P. (Ed.). (1996). *Rallying the whole village: The Comer process for reforming education.* New York: Teachers College Press.

Coots, J.J., Bishop, K.D., Grenot-Scheyer, M., & Falvey, M.A. (1995). Practices in general education: Past and present. In M.A. Falvey (Ed.), *Inclusive and heterogeneous schooling: Assessment, curriculum, and instruction* (pp. 7–22). Baltimore: Paul H. Brookes Publishing Co.

Cronin, S. (1998). Culturally relevant antibias learning communities: Teaching Umoja. In L.H. Meyer, H.-S. Park, M. Grenot-Scheyer, I.S. Schwartz, & B. Harry (Eds.), *Making friends: The influences of culture and development* (pp. 341–351). Baltimore: Paul H. Brookes Publishing Co.

Delgado-Gaitan, C. (1998). Foreword. In L.H. Meyer, H.-S. Park, M. Grenot-Scheyer, I.S. Schwartz, & B. Harry (Eds.), *Making friends: The influences of culture and development* (xiii–xv). Baltimore: Paul H. Brookes Publishing Co.

Diamond, K.E., & LeFurgy, W.G. (1994). Attitudes of parents of preschool children toward integration. *Early Education and Development, 5*(1), 69–77.

Donnellan, A.M., Mirenda, P.L., Mesaros, R.A., & Fassbender, L.L. (1984). Analyzing the communicative functions of aberrant behavior. *Journal of The Association for Persons with Severe Handicaps, 9,* 201–212.

Downing, J.E. (1996). *Including students with severe and multiple disabilities in typical classrooms: Practical strategies for teachers.* Baltimore: Paul H. Brookes Publishing Co.

Education for All Handicapped Children Act of 1975, PL 94-142, 20 U.S.C. §§ 1400 *et seq.*

Eichinger, J., & Downing, J.E. (1996). Instruction in the general education environment. In J.E. Downing, *Including students with severe and multiple disabilities in typical classrooms: Practical strategies for teachers* (pp. 15–34). Baltimore: Paul H. Brookes Publishing Co.

Erwin, E.J., & Soodak, L.C. (1995). I never knew I could stand up to the system: Families' perspectives on pursuing inclusive education. *Journal of The Association for Persons with Severe Handicaps, 20*(2), 136–146.

Evans, I.M., Goldberg-Arnold, J.S., & Dickson, J.K. (1998). Children's perceptions of equity in peer interactions. In L.H. Meyer, H.-S. Park, M. Grenot-Scheyer, I.S. Schwartz, & B. Harry (Eds.), *Making friends: The influences of culture and development* (pp. 133–147). Baltimore: Paul H. Brookes Publishing Co.

Evans, I.M., & Meyer, L.H. (1985). *An educative approach to behavior problems: A practical decision model for interventions with severely handicapped learners.* Baltimore: Paul H. Brookes Publishing Co.

Falvey, M.A., Grenot-Scheyer, M., Coots, J.J., & Bishop, K.D. (1995). Services for students with disabilities: Past and present. In M.A. Falvey (Ed.), *Inclusive and heterogeneous schooling: Assessment, curriculum, and instruction* (pp. 23–39). Baltimore: Paul H. Brookes Publishing Co.

Ferguson, D.L. (1994). Is communication really the point? Some thoughts on interventions and membership. *Mental Retardation, 32*(1), 7–18.

Ferguson, D.L. (1995). The real challenge of inclusion: Confessions of a "rabid inclusionist." *Phi Delta Kappan, 77,* 281–287.

Fiering, C., & Lewis, M. (1989). The social networks of boys and girls from early through middle childhood. In D. Belle (Ed.), *Children's social networks and social supports* (pp. 119–150). New York: John Wiley & Sons.

Finn-Stevenson, M., & Zigler, E. (1999). *Schools of the 21st century: Linking child care and education.* Boulder, CO: Westview Press.

Fisher, D., Sax, C., & Pumpian, I. (1999). *Inclusive high schools: Learning from contemporary classrooms.* Baltimore: Paul H. Brookes Publishing Co.

Fisher, M. (1996). *Friends make a difference.* Unpublished doctoral dissertation, University of Virginia, Charlottesville.

Fisher, M., Bernazzani, J.P., & Meyer, L.H. (1998). Participatory action research: Supporting social relationships in the cooperative classroom. In J.W. Putnam (Ed.), *Cooperative learning and strategies for inclusion: Celebrating diversity in the classroom* (2nd ed., pp. 137–165). Baltimore: Paul H. Brookes Publishing Co.

Fiske, A.P. (1992). The four elementary forms of sociality: Framework for a unified theory of social relations. *Psychological Review, 99,* 689–723.

Forest, M. (1991). It's about relationships. In L.H. Meyer, C.A. Peck, & L. Brown (Eds.), *Critical issues in the lives of people with severe disabilities* (pp. 399–407). Baltimore: Paul H. Brookes Publishing Co.

Forest, M., & Lusthaus, E. (1989). Promoting educational equality for all students: Circles and maps. In S. Stainback, W. Stainback, & M. Forest (Eds.), *Educating all students in the mainstream of regular education* (pp. 43–57). Baltimore: Paul H. Brookes Publishing Co.

Freire, P. (1985). *The politics of education: Culture, power, and liberation* (D. Macedo, trans.). Westport, CT: Bergin & Garvey.

Fried, R.L., & Jorgensen, C.M. (1998). Equity and excellence: Finding common ground between inclusive education and school reform. In C.M. Jorgensen, *Restructuring high schools for all students: Taking inclusion to the next level* (pp. 15–28). Baltimore: Paul H. Brookes Publishing Co.

Friend, M.P., & Cook, L. (1999). *Interactions: Collaboration skills for school professionals* (3rd ed.). New York: Longman.

Fryxell, D., & Kennedy, C.H. (1995). Placement along the continuum of services and its impact on students' social relationships. *Journal of The Association for Persons with Severe Handicaps, 20,* 259–269.

Fuchs, D., & Fuchs, L.S. (1994). Inclusive schools movement and the radicalization of special education reform. *Exceptional Children, 60,* 294–309.

Fulk, B.M., Brigham, F.J., & Lohman, D.A. (1998). Motivation and self-regulation: A comparison of students with learning and behavior problems. *Remedial and Special Education, 19*(5), 300–309.

Furman, W., & Buhrmeister, D. (1987). Children's perceptions of the personal relationships in their social networks. *Developmental Psychology, 21*(6), 1016–1024.

Gardner, H. (1993). *Frames of mind: The theory of multiple intelligences.* New York: Basic Books.

Gaylord-Ross, R., & Peck, C.A. (1985). Integration efforts for students with severe mental retardation. In D.D. Bricker & J. Filler (Eds.), *Serving students with severe mental retardation: From research to practice* (pp. 185–207). Reston, VA: Council for Exceptional Children.

Geertz, C. (1973). *Interpretation of cultures: Selected essays.* New York: Basic Books.

Giangreco, M.F., Edelman, S.W., Luiselli, T.E., & McFarland, S.Z. (1997). Helping or hovering? Effects of instructional assistant proximity on students with disabilities. *Exceptional Children, 64*(1), 7–18.

Goals 2000: Educate America Act of 1994, PL 103-227, 20 U.S.C. §§ 5801 *et seq.*

Grandin, T. (1995). *Thinking in pictures: And other reports from my life with autism.* New York: Doubleday.

Grandin, T., & Scariano, M.M. (1996). *Emergence: Labeled autistic.* New York: Warner Books.

Gray, C. (1995). Teaching children with autism to "read" social situations. In K.A. Quill (Ed.), *Teaching children with autism: Strategies to enhance communication and socialization* (pp. 219–241). Albany, NY: Delmar Publishers.

Grenot-Scheyer, M. (1999). Curricular adaptations to support elementary age students with disabilities in inclusive settings. In T.J. Hassold & D. Patterson (Eds.), *Down syndrome: A promising future, together* (pp. 189–195). Philadelphia: Lippincott Williams & Wilkins.

Grenot-Scheyer, M., Coots, J.J., & Bishop-Smith, K. (1999). *What teachers need to know, do, and be: Reflections from the field.* Unpublished manuscript, California State University, Long Beach.

Grenot-Scheyer, M., Harry, B., Park, H.-S., Schwartz, I.S., & Meyer, L.H. (1998). Directions and recommendations for future research: Integrating the academic and social lives of America's children and youth. In L.H. Meyer, H.-S. Park, M. Grenot-Scheyer, I.S. Schwartz, & B. Harry (Eds.), *Making friends: The influences of culture and development* (pp. 403–411). Baltimore: Paul H. Brookes Publishing Co.

Grenot-Scheyer, M., Jubala, K.A., Bishop, K.D., & Coots, J.J. (1996). *The inclusive classroom.* Westminster, CA: Teacher Created Materials.

Grenot-Scheyer, M., & Leonard-Giesen, S. (1997). *Adult mediation: Syracuse Working Conference.* Unpublished manuscript, California State University, Long Beach.

Grenot-Scheyer, M., Leonard-Giesen, S., Fisher, M., & Meyer, L.H. (1997). *Accommodating diversity in the classroom: What do teachers think of best practice?* Unpublished research report.

Grenot-Scheyer, M., Park, H.-S., & Meyer, L.H. (1993). And what about schools and classrooms? The impact of classroom organization on sociality. *TASH Newsletter, 19*(9), 6–7.

Grenot-Scheyer, M., Schwartz, I.S., & Meyer, L. (1997). Blending best practices for young children: Inclusive early childhood programs. *TASH Newsletter, 4,* 8–10.

Grenot-Scheyer, M., Staub, D., Peck, C.A., & Schwartz, I.S. (1998). Reciprocity and friendships: Listening to the voices of children and youth with and without disabilities. In L.H. Meyer, H.-S. Park, M. Grenot-Scheyer, I.S. Schwartz, & B. Harry (Eds.), *Making friends: The influences of culture and development* (pp. 149–167). Baltimore: Paul H. Brookes Publishing Co.

Gresham, F.M., & MacMillan, D.L. (1997). Social competence and affective characteristics of students with mild disabilities. *Review of Educational Research, 67*(4), 377–415.

Griffin, C.C., & Pugach, M.C. (1997). Framing the progress of collaborative teacher education. In L.P. Blanton, C.C. Griffin, J.A. Winn, & M.C. Pugach (Eds.), *Teacher education in transition: Collaborative programs to prepare general and special educators* (pp. 249–270). Denver: Love Publishing Co.

Grimes, J., & Tilly, W.D. (1996). Policy and process: Means to lasting educational change. *School Psychology Review, 25*(4), 465–476.

Hallahan, D.P. (1998). Perspective: Sound bytes [sic] from special education reform rhetoric. *Remedial and Special Education, 19*(2), 67–69.

Halpern, A.S. (1985). Transition: A look at the foundations. *Exceptional Children, 51,* 479–486.

Halpern, A.S. (1993). Quality of life as a conceptual framework for evaluating transition outcomes. *Exceptional Children, 59,* 486–498.

Haring, T.G. (1991). Social relationships. In L.H. Meyer, C.A. Peck, & L. Brown (Eds.), *Critical issues in the lives of people with severe disabilities* (pp. 195–217). Baltimore: Paul H. Brookes Publishing Co.

Haring, T.G. (1993). Research basis of instructional procedures to promote social interaction and integration. In R.A. Gable & S.F. Warren (Eds.), *Strategies for teaching students with mild to severe mental retardation* (pp. 129–164). Baltimore: Paul H. Brookes Publishing Co.

Haring, T.G., & Breen, C.G. (1992). A peer-mediated social network intervention to enhance the social integration of persons with moderate and severe disabilities. *Journal of Applied Behavior Analysis, 25*(2), 319–333.

Harry, B., Grenot-Scheyer, M., Smith-Lewis, M., Park, H., Xin, F., & Schwartz, I.S. (1995). Developing culturally inclusive services for individuals with severe disabilities. *Journal of The Association for Persons with Severe Handicaps, 20,* 99–109.

Harry, B., Kalyanpur, M., & Day, M. (1999). *Building cultural reciprocity with families: Case studies in special education.* Baltimore: Paul H. Brookes Publishing Co.

Harry, B., Park, H.-S., & Day, M. (1998). Friendships of many kinds: Valuing the choices of children and youth with disabilities. In L.H. Meyer, H.-S. Park, M. Grenot-Scheyer, I.S. Schwartz, & B. Harry (Eds.), *Making friends: The influences of culture and development* (pp. 393–402). Baltimore: Paul H. Brookes Publishing Co.

Hartup, W.W. (1996). The company they keep: Friendships and their developmental significance. *Child Development, 67,* 1–13.

Hedeen, D.L., Ayres, B.J., Meyer, L.H., & Waite, J. (1996). Quality inclusive schooling for students with severe behavioral challenges. In D.H. Lehr & F. Brown (Eds.), *People with disabilities who challenge the system* (pp. 127–171). Baltimore: Paul H. Brookes Publishing Co.

Helmstetter, E., Peck, C.A., & Giangreco, M.F. (1994). Outcomes of interactions with peers with moderate or severe disabilities: A statewide survey of high school students. *Journal of The Association for Persons with Severe Handicaps, 19*(4), 263–276.

Hodgdon, L.A. (1996). *Visual strategies for improving communication: Vol. 1. Practical supports for school and home.* Troy, MI: QuirkRoberts Publishing Co.

Hunt, P., Alwell, M., & Goetz, L. (1988). Acquisition of conversation skills and the reduction of inappropriate social interaction behaviors. *Journal of The Association for Persons with Severe Handicaps, 13,* 20–27.

Hunt, P., & Farron-Davis, F. (1992). A preliminary investigation of IEP quality and content associated with placement in general education versus special education classes. *Journal of The Association for Persons with Severe Handicaps, 17,* 241–253.

Hunt, P., Farron-Davis, F., Beckstead, S., Curtis, D., & Goetz, L. (1994). Evaluating the effects of placement of students with severe disabilities in general education versus special classes. *Journal of The Association for Persons with Severe Handicaps, 19*(3), 200–214.

Hunt, P., & Goetz, L. (1997). Research on inclusive educational programs, practices, and outcomes for students with severe disabilities. *Journal of Special Education, 31*(1), 3–29.

Hunt, P., Goetz, L., & Anderson, J. (1986). The quality of IEP objectives associated with placement on integrated vs. segregated school sites. *Journal of The Association for Persons with Severe Handicaps, 11,* 125–130.

Hunt, P., Staub, D., Alwell, M., & Goetz, L. (1994). Achievement by all students within the context of cooperative learning groups. *Journal of The Association for Persons with Severe Handicaps, 19*(4), 290–301.

Hurley-Geffner, C.M. (1995). Friendships between children with and without developmental disabilities. In R.L. Koegel & L. K. Koegel (Eds.), *Teaching children with autism: Strategies for initiating positive interactions and improving learning opportunities* (pp. 105–125). Baltimore: Paul H. Brookes Publishing Co.

Individuals with Disabilities Education Act (IDEA) Amendments of 1991, PL 102-119, 20 U.S.C. §§ 1400 *et seq.*

Individuals with Disabilities Education Act (IDEA) Amendments of 1997, PL 105-17, 20 U.S.C. §§ 1400 *et seq.*

Individuals with Disabilities Education Act (IDEA) of 1990, PL 101-476, 20 U.S.C. §§ 1400 *et seq.*

Janney, R., Black, J., & Ferlo, M. (1989). *A problem-solving approach to challenging behaviors.* Syracuse, NY: Syracuse University, Special Projects.

Janney, R., & Snell, M. (1996). How teachers use peer interactions to include students with moderate and severe disabilities in elementary general education classes. *Journal of The Association for Persons with Severe Handicaps, 21,* 72–80.

Jorgensen, C.M. (1998). *Restructuring high schools for all students: Taking inclusion to the next level.* Baltimore: Paul H. Brookes Publishing Co.

Jorgensen, C.M., Fisher, D., Sax, C., & Skoglund, K.L. (1998). Innovative scheduling, new roles for teachers, and heterogeneous grouping: The organizational factors related to student success in inclusive, restructuring schools. In C.M. Jorgensen, *Restructuring high schools for all students: Taking inclusion to the next level* (pp. 49–70). Baltimore: Paul H. Brookes Publishing Co.

Kauffman, J.M., & Hallahan, D.P. (Eds.). (1995). *The illusion of full inclusion: A comprehensive critique of a current special education bandwagon.* Austin, TX: PRO-ED.

Kaye, K. (1982). *The mental and social life of babies: How parents create persons.* Chicago: University of Chicago Press.

Kennedy, C.H., & Itkonen, T. (1994). Some effects of regular class participation on the social contacts and social networks of high school students with severe disabilities. *Journal of The Association for Persons with Severe Handicaps, 19,* 1–10.

Kennedy, C.H., & Itkonen, T. (1996). Social relationships, influential variables, and change across the life span. In L.K. Koegel, R.L. Koegel, & G. Dunlap (Eds.), *Positive behavioral support: Including people with difficult behavior in the community* (pp. 287–304). Baltimore: Paul H. Brookes Publishing Co.

Kishi, G.S., & Meyer, L.H. (1994). What children report and remember: A six-year follow-up of the effects of social contact between peers with and without severe disabilities. *Journal of The Association for Persons with Severe Handicaps, 19*(4), 277–289.

Kohn, A. (1991). Caring kids: The role of the school. *Phi Delta Kappan, 72,* 496–506.

Lancy, D.F. (1993). The case study. In D.F. Lancy, *Qualitative research in education: An introduction to the major traditions* (pp. 137–167). New York: Longman.

Larson, M., Minondo, S., & Vargo, R. (1995, December/January). Turning point: Friendships in middle school years. *TASH Newsletter, 21,* 17–19.

Lave, J., & Wenger, E. (1991). *Situated learning: Legitimate peripheral participation.* New York: Cambridge University Press.

Lawrence-Lightfoot, S. (1983). *The good high school: Portraits of character and culture.* New York: Basic Books.

Levin, H.M. (1997). Doing what comes naturally: Full inclusion in accelerated schools. In D.K. Lipsky & A. Gartner, *Inclusion and school reform: Transforming America's classrooms* (pp. 389–400). Baltimore: Paul H. Brookes Publishing Co.

Lincoln, Y.S., & Guba, E.G. (1985). *Naturalistic inquiry.* Thousand Oaks, CA: Sage Publications.

Lipsky, D.K., & Gartner, A. (1997). *Inclusion and school reform: Transforming America's classrooms.* Baltimore: Paul H. Brookes Publishing Co.

Logan, K.R., Bakeman, R., & Keefe, E.B. (1997). Effects of instructional variables on engaged behavior of students with disabilities in general education classrooms. *Exceptional Children, 63*(4), 481–497.

Lusthaus, E., & Forest, M. (1987). The kaleidoscope: A challenge to the cascade. In M. Forest (Ed.), *More education integration* (pp. 1–17). Downsview, Ontario, Canada: G. Allan Roeher Institute.

Mayer-Johnson, R. (1981). *The Picture Communication Symbols book.* Solana Beach, CA: Mayer-Johnson Co.

McClannahan, L.E., & Krantz, P.J. (1999). *Activity schedules for children with autism: teaching independent behavior.* Bethesda, MD: Woodbine House.

McDonnell, J., Thorson, N., McQuivey, C., & Kiefer-O'Donnell, R. (1997). Academic engaged time of students with low-incidence disabilities in general education classes. *Mental Retardation, 35*(1), 18–26.

McGee, J., Menousek, P., & Hobbs, D. (1987). Gentle teaching: An alternative to punishment for people with challenging behaviors. In S.J. Taylor, D. Biklen, & J. Knoll (Eds.), *Community integration for people with severe disabilities* (pp. 147–183). New York: Teachers College Press.

McGregor, G., & Vogelsberg, R.T. (1999). *Inclusive schooling practices: Pedagogical and research foundations. A synthesis of the literature that informs best practices about inclusive schooling.* Baltimore: Paul H. Brookes Publishing Co.

McKean, T.A. (1996). *Soon will come the light*. Arlington, TX: Future Horizons.

McLaughlin, M. (1996). School restructuring. In *Improving the implementation of the Individuals with Disabilities Education Act: Making schools work for all of America's children* (pp. 635–659). Washington, DC: National Council on Disability.

Meyer, L.H. (1997). Tinkering around the edges? *Journal of The Association for Persons with Severe Handicaps*, *22*(2), 80–82.

Meyer, L.H., Grenot-Scheyer, M., Harry, B., Park, H.-S., Peck, C.A., & Schwartz, I.S. (1992). *Consortium for collaborative research on social relationships: Inclusive schools and communities for children and youth with diverse abilities* (U.S. Department of Education, Cooperative Agreement No. H086A20003). Syracuse, NY: Syracuse University.

Meyer, L.H., Grenot-Scheyer, M., Harry, B., Park, H.-S., & Schwartz, I.S. (1997, September). *The Consortium for Collaborative Research on Social Relationships: Working Conference on Naturalistic Interventions to Support the Social Lives of Children and Youth with Diverse Abilities*. Syracuse, NY: Syracuse University.

Meyer, L.H., Minondo, S., Fisher, M., Larson, M.J., Dunmore, S., Black, J.W., & D'Aquanni, M. (1998). Frames of friendship: Social relationships among adolescents with diverse abilities. In L.H. Meyer, H.-S. Park, M. Grenot-Scheyer, I.S. Schwartz, & B. Harry (Eds.), *Making friends: The influences of culture and development* (pp. 189–221). Baltimore: Paul H. Brookes Publishing Co.

Meyer, L.H., Park, H.-S., Grenot-Scheyer, M., Schwartz, I.S., & Harry, B. (1998a). Participatory research approaches for the study of the social relationships of children and youth. In L.H. Meyer, H.-S. Park, M. Grenot-Scheyer, I.S. Schwartz, & B. Harry (Eds.), *Making friends: The influences of culture and development* (pp. 3–29). Baltimore: Paul H. Brookes Publishing Co.

Meyer, L.H., Park, H.-S., Grenot-Scheyer, M., Schwartz, I.S., & Harry, B. (Eds.). (1998b). *Making friends: The influences of culture and development*. Baltimore: Paul H. Brookes Publishing Co.

Meyer, L.H., Park, H.-S., Grenot-Scheyer, M., Schwartz, I.S., & Harry, B. (1998c). Participatory research: New approaches to the research to practice dilemma. *Journal of The Association for Persons with Severe Handicaps*, *23*(3), 165–177.

Miles, M.B., & Huberman, A.M. (1994). *Qualitative data analysis: An expanded sourcebook* (2nd ed.). Thousand Oaks, CA: Sage Publications.

Miller, A., & Eller-Miller, E. (1989). *From ritual to repertoire: A cognitive-developmental systems approach with behavior-disordered children*. New York: John Wiley & Sons.

Moos, R.H. (1979). *Evaluating educational environments*. San Francisco: Jossey-Bass.

Murray-Seegert, C. (1989). *Nasty girls, thugs, and humans like us: Social relations between severely disabled and nondisabled students in high school*. Baltimore: Paul H. Brookes Publishing Co.

National Center on Educational Restructuring and Inclusion (NCERI). (1994). *National Study of Inclusive Education*. New York: City University of New York, National Center on Educational Restructuring and Inclusion.

National Center on Educational Restructuring and Inclusion (NCERI). (1995). *National Study of Inclusive Education*. New York: City University of New York, National Center on Educational Restructuring and Inclusion.

Newcomb, A.F., & Bagwell, C.L. (1996). The developmental significance of children's friendship relations. In W.M. Bukowski, A.F. Newcomb, & W.W. Hartup (Eds.), *The company they keep: Friendship in childhood and adolescence* (pp. 289–321). New York: Cambridge University Press.

Nisbet, J. (1996). The interrelationship of education and self-esteem. In L.E. Powers, G.H.S. Singer, & J. Sowers (Eds.), *On the road to autonomy: Promoting self-competence in children and youth with disabilities* (pp. 155–170). Baltimore: Paul H. Brookes Publishing Co.

Noddings, N. (1992). *The challenge to care in schools: An alternative approach to education.* New York: Teachers College Press.

O'Connor, R.E., & Jenkins, J.R. (1996). Cooperative learning as an inclusion strategy: A closer look. *Exceptionality, 6*(1), 29–51.

Odom, S.L., Horn, E.M., Marquart, J.M., Hanson, M.J., Wolfberg, P., Beckman, P.J., Lieber, J., Li, S., Schwartz, I.S., Janko, S., & Sandall, S. (1999). On the forms of inclusion: Organizational context and individualized service models. *Journal of Early Intervention, 22*(3), 185–199.

Odom, S.L., Peck, C.A., Hanson, M., Beckman, P.J., Kaiser, A., Lieber, J., Brown, W.H., Horn, E.M., & Schwartz, I.S. (1996). Inclusion at the preschool level: An ecological systems analysis. *SRCD Social Policy Report, 10,* 18–30.

Olson, M.R., Chalmers, L., & Hoover, J.H. (1997). Attitudes and attributes of general education teachers identified as effective inclusionists. *Remedial and Special Education, 18*(1), 28–35.

Orelove, F.P., & Sobsey, D. (1996). *Educating children with multiple disabilities: A transdisciplinary approach* (3rd ed.). Baltimore: Paul H. Brookes Publishing Co.

Park, H.-S., Chadsey-Rusch, J., & Storey, K. (1998). Social relationships or no social relationships: Social experiences at worksites. In L.H. Meyer, H.-S. Park, M. Grenot-Scheyer, I.S. Schwartz, & B. Harry (Eds.), *Making friends: The influences of culture and development* (pp. 317–337). Baltimore: Paul H. Brookes Publishing Co.

Park, H.-S., Gonsier-Gerdin, J., Hoffman, S., Whaley, S., & Yount, M. (1998). Applying the participatory action research model to the study of social inclusion at worksites. *Journal of The Association for Persons with Severe Handicaps, 23*(3), 189–202.

Park, H.-S., Hoffman, S., & Whaley, S. (1999). *Social relationships and personal safety training in transition programs.* Unpublished raw data.

Peck, C.A., Donaldson, J., & Pezzoli, M. (1990). Some benefits nonhandicapped adolescents perceive for themselves from their social relationships with peers who have severe handicaps. *Journal of The Association for Persons with Severe Handicaps, 15*(4), 241–249.

Peck, C.A., White, O., Billingsley, F., & Schwartz, I.S. (1992). *The Inclusive Education Research Project.* Proposal submitted to the U.S. Department of Education. Washington State University, Bellingham.

Perske, R. (1993). Introduction. In A.N. Amado (Ed.), *Friendships and community connections between people with and without developmental disabilities* (pp. 1–6). Baltimore: Paul H. Brookes Publishing Co.

Petty, K., & Firmin, C. (1991). *Feeling left out.* New York: Barron's.

Pugach, M.C. (1995). On the failure of imagination in inclusive schooling. *Journal of Special Education, 29,* 212–223.

Pugach, M.C., & Johnson, L.J. (1995a). *Collaborative practitioners, collaborative schools.* Denver: Love Publishing Co.

Pugach, M.C., & Johnson, L.J. (1995b). Unlocking expertise among classroom teachers through structured dialogue: Extending research on peer collaboration. *Exceptional Children, 62*(2), 101–110.

Pugach, M.C., & Wesson, C.L. (1995). Teachers' and students' views of team teaching of general education and learning-disabled students in two fifth-grade classes. *Elementary School Journal, 95,* 279–295.

Putnam, J.W. (Ed.). (1998). *Cooperative learning and strategies for inclusion: Celebrating diversity in the classroom* (2nd ed.). Baltimore: Paul H. Brookes Publishing Co.

Rainforth, B., & York-Barr, J. (1997). *Collaborative teams for students with severe disabilities: Integrating therapy and educational services* (2nd ed.). Baltimore: Paul H. Brookes Publishing Co.

Richardson, P., & Schwartz, I.S. (1998). Making friends in preschool: Friendship patterns of young children with disabilities. In L.H. Meyer, H.-S. Park, M. Grenot-Scheyer, I.S. Schwartz, & B. Harry (Eds.), *Making friends: The influences of culture and development* (pp. 65–80). Baltimore: Paul H. Brookes Publishing Co.

Rimland, B., & Edelson, S.M. (1995). A pilot study of auditory integration training in autism. *Journal of Autism and Developmental Disorders, 25*, 61–70.

Roach, V. (1998). Foreword. In C.M. Jorgensen, *Restructuring high schools for all students: Taking inclusion to the next level* (pp. xv–xx). Baltimore: Paul H. Brookes Publishing Co.

Roach, V., Ascroft, J., Stamp, A., & Kysilko, D. (1995). *Winning ways: Creating inclusive schools, classrooms, and communities.* Alexandria, VA: National Association of State Boards of Education.

Rynders, J.E., Schleien, S.J., Meyer, L.H., Vandercook, T.L., Mustonene, T., Colond, J.S., & Olson, K. (1993). Improving integration outcomes for children with and without disabilities through cooperatively structured recreation activities: A synthesis of research. *Journal of Special Education, 26*, 386–407.

Salend, S.J., Johansen, M., Mumper, J., Chase, A.S., Pike, K.M., & Dorney, J.A. (1997). Cooperative teaching: The voices of two teachers. *Remedial and Special Education, 18*(1), 3–11.

Salisbury, C.L., Evans, I.M., & Palombaro, M.M. (1997). Collaborative problem-solving to promote the inclusion of young children with significant disabilities in primary grades. *Exceptional Children, 63*(2), 195–209.

Salisbury, C.L., Palombaro, M.M., & Hollowood, T.M. (1993). On the nature of change of an inclusive elementary school. *Journal of The Association for Persons with Severe Handicaps, 18*(2), 75–84.

Sapon-Shevin, M. (1994/1995). Why gifted students belong in inclusive schools. *Educational Leadership, 52*(4), 64–70.

Sapon-Shevin, M. (1999). *Because we can change the world: A practical guide to building cooperative, inclusive classroom communities.* Needham Heights, MA: Allyn & Bacon.

Schaps, E. (1997, January). Pushing back for the center. *Education Week, 16*(17), 20.

Schaps, E., & Solomon, D. (1990). Schools and classrooms as caring communities. *Educational Leadership, 48*(3), 38–42.

Schnorr, R.F. (1990). "Peter? He comes and he goes . . .": First graders' perspectives on a part-time mainstreamed student. *Journal of The Association for Persons with Severe Handicaps, 15*(4), 231–240.

Schnorr, R.F. (1997). From enrollment to membership: Belonging in middle and high school classes. *Journal of The Association for Persons with Severe Handicaps, 22*(1), 1–15.

Schorr, L.B. (1989). *Within our reach: Breaking the cycle of disadvantage.* New York: Anchor/Doubleday.

Schorr, L.B. (1997). *Common purpose: Strengthening families and neighborhoods to rebuild America.* New York: Anchor/Doubleday.

Schwartz, I.S., Staub, D., Gallucci, C., & Peck, C.A. (1995). Blending qualitative and behavior analytic research methods to evaluate outcomes in inclusive schools. *Journal of Behavioral Education, 5*, 93–106.

Sizer, T.R. (1992). *Horace's compromise: The dilemma of the American high school.* Boston: Houghton Mifflin Co.

Slavin, R.E., Dolan, L.J., & Madden, N.A. (1994, December). *Scaling up: Lessons learned in the dissemination of Success for All.* Baltimore: Johns Hopkins University, Center for Research and Education of Students Placed at Risk.

Stainback, W., & Stainback, S. (Eds.). (1990). *Support networks for inclusive schooling: Interdependent integrated education.* Baltimore: Paul H. Brookes Publishing Co.

Stanovich, P.J., Jordan, A., & Perot, J. (1998). Relative differences in academic self-concept and peer acceptance among students in inclusive classrooms. *Remedial and Special Education, 19*(2), 120–126.

Staub, D. (1996, September/October). Inclusion and the other kids. *Learning Magazine,* 76–78.

Staub, D. (1998). *Delicate threads: Friendships between children with and without special needs in inclusive settings.* Bethesda, MD: Woodbine House.

Staub, D., & Hunt, P. (1993). The effects of social interaction training on high school peer tutors of schoolmates with severe disabilities. *Exceptional Children, 60*(1), 41–57.

Staub, D., & Peck, C.A. (1994/1995). What are the outcomes for nondisabled children in inclusive settings? *Educational Leadership, 52,* 36–41.

Staub, D., Spaulding, M., Peck, C.A., Gallucci, C., & Schwartz, I.S. (1996). Using nondisabled peers to support the inclusion of students with disabilities at the junior high school level. *Journal of The Association for Persons with Severe Handicaps, 21*(4), 194–205.

Sternberg, R.J. (1997). What does it mean to be smart? *Educational Leadership, 54*(6), 20–24.

Strauss, A.L. (1987). *Qualitative analysis for social scientists.* New York: Cambridge University Press.

Strully, J., & Strully, C. (1985). Friendship and our children. *Journal of The Association for Persons with Severe Handicaps, 10*(4), 224–227.

Strully, J.L., & Strully, C.F. (1989). Friendships as an educational goal. In S. Stainback, W. Stainback, & M. Forest (Eds.), *Educating all students in the mainstream of regular education* (pp. 59–68). Baltimore: Paul H. Brookes Publishing Co.

Tappe, P., & Gaylord-Ross, R. (1990). Social support and transition coping. In R. Gaylord-Ross, S. Siegel, H.-S. Park, S. Sacks, & L. Goetz (Eds.), *Readings in ecosocial development.* San Francisco: San Francisco State University.

Tharp, R.G., & Gallimore, R. (1988). *Rousing minds to life: Teaching, learning, and schooling in social context.* New York: Cambridge University Press.

Thompson, B., Wickham, D., Wegner, J., & Ault, M. (1996). All children should know joy: Inclusive, family-centered services for young children with significant disabilities. In D.H. Lehr & F. Brown (Eds.), *People with disabilities who challenge the system* (pp. 23–56). Baltimore: Paul H. Brookes Publishing Co.

Thousand, J.S., & Villa, R.A. (2000). Collaborative teams: A powerful tool in school restructuring. In R.A. Villa & J.S. Thousand (Eds.), *Restructuring for caring and effective education: Piecing the puzzle together* (2nd ed., pp. 254–291). Baltimore: Paul H. Brookes Publishing Co.

Topper, K., Williams, W., Leo, K., Hamilton, R., & Fox, T. (1994). *A positive approach to understanding and addressing challenging behaviors.* Burlington: University of Vermont, Center for Developmental Disabilities.

Torres, C.A. (1995). Participatory action research and popular education in Latin America. In P.L. McLaren & J.M. Giarelli (Eds.), *Critical theory and educational research* (pp. 237–255). Albany: State University of New York Press.

Turnbull, A.P., Turnbull, H.R., Shank, M., & Leal, D. (1999). *Exceptional lives: Special education in today's schools* (2nd ed.). Upper Saddle River, NJ: Merrill.

Turnbull, H.R., & Turnbull, A.P. (1998). Getting an enviable life. *MRDD Express, 9*(2), 1.

U.S. Department of Education. (1995). *17th annual report to Congress on the implementation of the Individuals with Disabilities Education Act.* Washington, DC: Author.

U.S. Department of Education. (1998). *To assure the free, appropriate education of all children with disabilities: 20th annual report to Congress on the implementation of the Individuals with Disabilities Education Act.* Washington, DC: Author.

Udvari-Solner, A. (1995). A process for adapting curriculum in inclusive classrooms. In R.A. Villa & J.S. Thousand (Eds.), *Creating an inclusive school* (pp. 110–124). Alexandria, VA: Association for Supervision and Curriculum Development.

Van der Klift , E., & Kunc, N. (1994). Epilogue: Beyond benevolence: Friendship and the politics of help. In J.S. Thousand, R.A. Villa, & A.I. Nevin (Eds.), *Creativity and collaborative learning: A practical guide to empowering students and teachers* (pp. 391–401). Baltimore: Paul H. Brookes Publishing Co.

Vaughn, S., & Klingner, J.K. (1998). Students' perceptions of inclusion and resource room settings. *Journal of Special Education, 32*(2), 79–88.

Villa, R.A., & Thousand, J.S. (1995). *Creating an inclusive school.* Alexandria, VA: Association for Supervision and Curriculum Development.

Vittimberga, G.L., Scotti, J.R., & Weigle, K.L. (1999). Standards of practice and critical elements in an educative approach to behavioral intervention. In J.R. Scotti & L.H. Meyer (Eds.), *Behavioral intervention: Principles, models, and practices* (pp. 47–69). Baltimore: Paul H. Brookes Publishing Co.

Vygotsky, L.S. (1978). *Mind in society: The development of higher psychological processes* (M. Cole, V. John-Steiner, S. Scribner, & E. Souberman, Eds. & Trans.). Cambridge, MA: Harvard University Press.

Walker, P. (1999). From community presence to sense of place: Community experiences of adults with developmental disabilities. *Journal of The Association for Persons with Severe Handicaps, 24*(1), 23–32.

Wang, M.C., & Birch, J.W. (1984). Comparison of a full-time mainstreaming program and a resource room approach. *Exceptional Children, 51*(1), 33–40.

Westling, D.L., & Fox, L. (1995). *Teaching students with severe disabilities.* Upper Saddle River, NJ: Merrill.

Williams, D. (1992). *Nobody nowhere: The extraordinary autobiography of an autistic.* New York: Times Books.

Wolery, M., & Bredekamp, S. (1994). Developmentally appropriate practices and young children with disabilities: Contextual issues in the discussion. *Journal of Early Intervention, 18,* 331–341.

Wolery, M., Martin, C.G., Schroeder, C., Huffman, K., Venn, M.L., Holcombe, A., Brookfield, J., & Fleming, L.A. (1994). Employment of educators in preschool mainstreaming: A survey of general early educators. *Journal of Early Intervention, 18,* 64–77.

Yin, R.K. (1984). The case study as serious research strategy. *Knowledge, 3,* 97–114.

Zigmond, N. (1995). An exploration of the meaning and practice of special education in the context of full inclusion of students with learning disabilities. *Journal of Special Education, 29*(2), 109–115.

Zigmond, N., & Baker, J.M. (1990). Mainstreaming experiences for learning disabled students (Project MELD): Preliminary report. *Exceptional Children, 57,* 176–185.

Index

Page numbers followed by *f* denote figures; those followed by *t* denote tables.

child care versus therapeutic versus
     preacademic programs, 45
child with autism, 49
community child care center, 23–24
inclusive elementary school-based
     preschool, 31–32
itinerant service delivery, 22, 24
legislative mandate for, 5, 19, 41
organizational structures of inclusive
     programs, 42–43
peer relationships in, 35–41
rationale for, 41
self-contained infant-toddler
     program, 114
teachers' preparation, certification,
     and salaries in, 43–44
understanding inclusion at preschool
     level, 41–46
university-based, 28–29, 43
Educate America Act of 1994, 5
Education for All Handicapped
     Children Act of 1975
     (PL 94-142), 75
Educational research on importance of
     listening to children and youth,
     17–18
Eligibility for inclusive school
     placement, 75, 76
English language development class,
     76–77, 82–83, 86
Equity, 6, 8, 171–172
Ethnicity, 75

Families, *see* Parents/families
Family child care setting, 22, 28
Family resource services, 28
FAPE, *see* Free appropriate public
     education
Federal legislation, 5, 19, 41, 75, 139,
     171
Frames that children without
     disabilities have regarding peers
     with disabilities, 95–96, 96t
Ghost/Guest, 98–100, 155
"I'll Help _____", 103–104
Inclusion Kid/Different Friend,
     101–103
interventions for social remediation,
     108–109
Just Another Kid, 104–105
others' views of, 107–109

Regular Friend/Friend Forever,
     105–106
Free appropriate public education
     (FAPE), 1, 41, 42
Friendship surveys, 97–98
Friendships, 13–14, 55–56, 91–92, 94,
     118
     see also Peer relationships
Functional skills, 132
Future of inclusive education, 170,
     174–175

Goals 2000 Act, 5
Gym class, 144

Head Start, 23, 42, 43
Health problems, 114–116, 119–120,
     127
Hearing impairment, 76, 82
Helpee relationships, 38–39, 109–110,
     118, 122–123
     student aide program, 126–127,
     129–130
Helper relationships, 39–40, 96t,
     103–104, 118

IDEA, *see* Individuals with Disabilities
     Education Act
IEP, *see* Individualized education
     program
IFSP, *see* Individualized family service
     plan
Improving America's Schools Act of
     1994 (PL 103-227), 5
Inclusive education
     attributes of successful programs, 9t
     benefits of, 6–7, 172–173
     case studies of, 15–17
     collaboration for, 7, 11, 173–174,
     180
     critical values of, 5–7
     definition of, 2, 42, 114
     disagreements about practical
     implications of, 7–8
     eligibility for, 75, 76
     equity, access, and support for, 6, 42,
     171–172
     future of, 170, 174–175